Contents

Index to tables

viii

Index to figures

Acknowledgements

The author wishes to thank the following who collaborated in the research:

Ernst and Young Management Consultants who was responsible for the survey of the stock of specialised housing for elderly people; the costings exercises for specialised housing, maintaining an elderly person at home, comparative costs of housing and housing with care options and the benchmark study of the costs of aids and adaptations; the allocation model and estimates of needs; and, a study of allocation policies and practices to specialised housing. The principal staff who worked on the project were Michael Gardiner, who had overall responsibility for the Ernst and Young input, Michael Doel-Carter, Dr Helen Van Horick, Julie Schwarz, Mark Sadler, Jonathan Isherwood and Michael Everett.

MORI who undertook the national and regional surveys of elderly people in the community, residents of specialised housing, informal carers and non-elderly disabled adults. Some sections of chapters describing the findings from these surveys are based on MORI preliminary reports of the results and methodologies used. The main staff who worked on the project were Toby Taper, who had overall responsibility for the MORI input, Anna Treseder, Angela Miles and Nick Coleman.

Robert Wann who worked as a sub-contractor to Ernst and Young on the costs of aids and adaptations, Dr Alan O'Dell (Building Research Establishment), who supplied secondary data from the English House Condition Survey on repairs costs and, Professor Anthea Tinker, Director, Age Concern Institute of Gerontology, who provided helpful comments on key methodological documents of the study.

In the Department, Dr David Riley who gave advice and management support throughout the project and provided extremely helpful comments on early drafts of this report; Marian Biskupski, who produced detailed tables for secondary analysis of the datasets collected by Ernst and Young and MORI and further developed the allocation model syntax; and all other colleagues in DoE who gave advice and commented on drafts.

In the Department of Health, Raphael Wittenberg for advice and information on the unit costs of health and social care services and, through DH contacts, Dr Ann Netten, Personal Social Services Research Unit, University of Kent.

The Steering Group for the study: Judith Littlewood (DoE), Dr David Riley (DoE), Steve Ongeri (Housing Corporation), Mirisa Micallef, Tracey Roose and Charlie Legg (NFHA), Arthur Hunt (ADSS), Matthew Warburton (AMA), Ross Fraser (ADC), Will Tuckley (ALA), Edna Collinson (LBA) and Jason MacGilp (Institute of Housing).

Those who participated in the needs assessment seminar held in July 1992: Dr I Carpenter (Consultant, Geriatric Medicine), Mrs Sue Wardman (The Guinness Trust), Mr J Head (Housing, LB Merton), Mr Harris (Housing, Dudley MDC), Mrs Spafford (Dudley Social Services), Mr Young (Lancashire Social Services), Mrs Pailing (Hampshire Social Services), Ms Paterson (Housing, LB Bexley), Mr Robertson (Springboard Housing Association), Mrs McNee (Scottish Office), Mr Selwyn Goldsmith (DoE), Ms Shawcross (Social Services Inspectorate), Dr Griffiths (Department of Health) and Mr Hoddinott (Abbeyfield Society).

The officials of housing departments, housing associations, social services authorities, Abbeyfield and Almshouse societies who responded to the four national postal surveys conducted as part of the study.

The elderly people, informal carers and non-elderly disabled adults who gave details about their homes and lives and their opinions about their needs in such a helpful way.

Summary of findings and conclusions

Introduction

1.   This report sets out the main findings of a programme of research commissioned by the Department of the Environment on the housing needs of elderly[1] and disabled people in England. This summary presents an overview of the main results of the research and is intended to be read in conjunction with relevant sections of chapters in the full report. These chapters describe the detailed findings from the research and provide the necessary context for interpreting the results presented below.

Objectives

2.   The overall objectives of the programme of research were to:

i. provide reliable regional estimates of the housing needs of elderly people requiring subsidised[2] provision by local authorities and housing associations and national estimates for disabled people;

ii. identify more accurate indicators of need for subsidised housing provision for elderly and disabled people for use in informing the allocation of capital resources to local authorities and, through the Housing Corporation, to housing associations; and,

iii. examine the extent to which the unmet need for subsidised provision by elderly people can be most cost-effectively met through housing options.

Methods

3.   The research used a wide variety of methods including group discussions, postal surveys, costings analyses, large-scale interview surveys, case conferences and data modelling. There were *ten* main elements to the study as follows:[3]

i. A national survey of the provision of subsidised specialised housing for elderly and disabled people;

ii. A national survey of the costs of specialised housing for elderly people;

---

[1]   All those aged 65 or over.

[2]   'Subsidised' refers to all forms of public or charitable subsidy towards the capital or revenue costs of providing or improving the accessibility and repair of accommodation occupied by elderly people. This includes sheltered housing for rent, disabled facilities grants towards housing adaptations and specially-designed accommodation for those in wheelchairs.

[3]   Individual reports on all of these main elements were produced plus two further reports on minor surveys of the cost of aids and adaptations and allocations policies and practices for specialised housing for elderly people. Details of the reports are given in Appendix 1.

iii. A national survey of the costs of maintaining an elderly person at home;

iv. A study of the comparative costs of housing and housing with care options for elderly people;

v. A national and regional survey of elderly people in the community (sample size: 8,901 households);

vi. A national survey of elderly residents of specialised housing (sample size: 3,569 households);

vii. A national survey of informal carers to elderly people (sample size: 832 carers);

viii. A national survey of non-elderly disabled adults (sample size: 850 households);

ix. An allocation model and estimates of need for subsidised housing provision; and,

x. An investigation of potential indicators of need for subsidised housing provision.

Key questions
4.   In order to address the objectives set out above, the study sought answers to four key questions:

A. What is the current provision of subsidised specialised housing for elderly and disabled people?;

B. What are the most cost-effective forms of subsidised housing and housing with care provision for elderly people?;

C. What are the current housing and care characteristics and circumstances of elderly and disabled people at both national and regional levels?; and,

D. What are the best estimates and indicators of need by elderly and disabled people for subsidised housing and housing with care provision for planning local housing strategies?

A.   CURRENT PROVISION OF SUBSIDISED SPECIALISED HOUSING FOR ELDERLY AND DISABLED PEOPLE

5.   There are five basic housing options for elderly and disabled people living in private households in the community:

● staying put with no additional support;

- staying put with necessary house repairs only;

- staying put with repairs and aids and adaptations only or with health and social care support as well;

- a move to smaller, ordinary or mainstream housing; or,

- a move to specialised housing, such as sheltered or wheelchair housing.

The last of these options is the only one where there is a fixed stock of provision specifically designated for elderly people as opposed to provision that is also regularly used for other client groups. A study was, therefore, conducted of the supply of subsidised specialised housing for elderly and disabled people to contrast with estimates of need.

A national study of the provision of subsidised specialised housing for elderly and disabled people (Chapter 2)

Elderly people

6.   Grossed-up figures (based on the survey data) suggest that in 1990 there was approximately 16% more subsidised sheltered housing provision for elderly people in England than was previously estimated to exist (**Paragraph 2.9**);

7.   On a national and regional scale, there is evidence of a significant over-provision of traditional or ordinary sheltered housing with a resident or non-resident warden and communal facilities and an under-provision of very sheltered housing with extra-care support. The scale of over- or under-provision, however, does vary by region with, for example, Southern regions generally having lower levels of under-provision of very sheltered housing than Northern regions This study did not specifically look at the balance of supply and assessed need for specialised housing at the local level. (**Paragraphs 2.52-2.53**);

8.   Very sheltered housing still accounts for only a small amount of all specialised housing for elderly people in England (2% – grossed-up figure for provision). It is, nevertheless, growing at a proportionately much faster rate than any other form of provision (**Paragraphs 2.8 and 2.43**);

9.   Ordinary sheltered housing with resident or non-residential warden support and at least one communal facility is still the main form of subsidised specialised housing provision for elderly people in England. It accounts for just over a half (51% – of the grossed-up figure for provision) of the total stock (**Paragraph 2.8**);

10.   There is a North/South split in the nature of subsidised specialised housing provision for elderly people. DoE regions in the north of the country tend to place greater reliance on sheltered housing without communal facilities and very sheltered housing for frail elderly people is more scarce. In contrast, DoE regions in the south of the country have a greater proportion of traditional sheltered housing with communal facilities within their stock and more

provision of extra-care sheltered accommodation (**Paragraph 2.11**);

11.   Based on planned provision, housing associations are increasing in importance as providers of specialised accommodation for elderly people – the share of the total stock in England owned and managed by housing associations appears to be growing (**Paragraph 2.46**);

12.   There is a trend towards providing more self-contained as opposed to non self-contained accommodation in specialised housing schemes for elderly people (**Paragraph 2.50**).

Non-elderly disabled adults

13.   Mobility housing/housing adapted for disabled people is the dominant form of specialised housing provision for non-elderly disabled adults, outnumbering wheelchair units by roughly two to one (**Paragraph 2.7**);

14.   There is, however, extreme regional variability in the dominance of mobility/adapted units with provision in some regions outnumbering wheelchairs units by up to seven to one (**Paragraph 2.12**);

15.   Housing associations are more likely to provide wheelchair units than mobility housing/housing adapted for disabled people and the opposite is true for local authorities. Some caution should be exercised with this finding, however, which is based on Housing Investment Programme (HIP) data. All new build housing association units are generally developed to mobility standards and there has been a considerable house adaptations programme for housing association tenants over the last decade. The regional variability described above, moreover, can be partly explained by the presence of housing association provision in regions. The proportion of the stock owned and managed by housing associations varies from 4% in Northern region to 31% in London (**Paragraphs 2.17-2.18**);

16.   On a national scale, there appears to be some shortfall in the numbers of subsidised wheelchair units for non-elderly disabled adults (**Paragraph 2.56**).

B.   THE COST-EFFECTIVENESS OF HOUSING AND HOUSING WITH CARE OPTIONS FOR ELDERLY PEOPLE

17.   It is important to consider the cost-effectiveness of different options in order to ensure that limited capital and revenue resources are used to the best effect in meeting the requirements of the maximum number of households in need. It is useful to establish the broad range of costs of housing and housing with care options for elderly people at the same level of physical or mental frailty, so that expensive solutions are not automatically provided without looking at equally effective and cheaper alternatives.

18.   The annual gross cost of providing a place in specialised housing for elderly people increases significantly from low- to high-dependency schemes. For example, the annual gross cost of a place in very sheltered accommodation is, on average, over 75% greater than the cost of a place in ordinary sheltered housing (**Paragraph 3.46**);

19.   As far as it is practicable to make a like-for-like comparison, local authority provision is consistently cheaper across all specialised housing options for elderly people. The difference between the major providers – local authorities and housing associations – is approximately £500 per person per annum at the highest levels of dependency amongst elderly residents (**Paragraphs 3.47-3.48**);

20.   For the most part, local authorities appear to have built specialised accommodation for elderly people at a lower unit capital cost than other providers. Whereas the annualised capital cost of a place in local authority specially-designed accommodation is approximately £3,720, the equivalent figures for housing associations and Almshouses are £4,540 and £4,790 respectively. This overall finding does vary, to some extent, depending upon the type and age of accommodation being considered. For example, the annualised capital cost of a place in housing association very sheltered housing is approximately £4,529 compared with £5,041 for a place in local authority frail elderly accommodation. Local authorities also have an older profile to their stock with a higher proportion of schemes built between 1961 and 1970. Whilst all costs were up-rated to present day prices, older schemes were built to lower space standards and this could have the effect of slightly reducing overall capital costs (**Paragraphs 3.13-3.17**);

21.   Local authorities also appear to have lower unit revenue or running costs for their specialised accommodation than other providers. For instance, the revenue cost of a place in local authority ordinary sheltered housing is roughly £840 per person per annum compared with £1,130 for housing associations and £3,570 for Abbeyfields. There is an even greater difference for very sheltered housing with local authority schemes being run at approximately £2,500 per person per annum compared with £7,280 for housing associations and £9,930 for Abbeyfields. This figure and the housing association figure includes schemes registered as residential care homes and this accounts for a large part of the difference with local authorities, as high staffing ratios are imposed on housing associations by registration. From the limited data available, however, the figure for housing associations without registered homes – £3,026 – is still approximately £500 more expensive per person per annum (**Paragraphs 3.18-3.23**);

22.   One explanation (which is borne out by the data) – for ordinary sheltered housing, in particular – is that local authorities are making greater use of visiting social and health care services to provide support to their residents, which enables them to have lower revenue costs than housing association providers who tend to rely on permanent care staff. As a result, and this applies to very sheltered housing as well, housing associations tend to have higher staff-

to-resident ratios than local authorities. The research found that, whereas local authority sheltered housing schemes had an average of 7.0 full-time equivalent staff to 100 residents, housing association sheltered housing schemes had 10.4 staff to 100 residents. For very sheltered housing, the ratios rise to 17.8 for local authorities and 45.0 for housing associations (**Paragraphs 3.24-3.26**).

The costs of maintaining an elderly person at home (Chapter 3)

23.   The annual gross cost of maintaining an elderly person at home is mainly determined by the capital cost of the accommodation they occupy and the size of their household. The average gross cost of maintaining a single elderly person at home is approximately £5,130 per annum compared with £3,350 for an elderly couple and the average gross cost of enabling elderly people in detached houses to remain at home is £7,470 per annum compared with £3,660 for those in flats/maisonettes (**Paragraph 3.49**);

24.   Taking into account informal care costs and state benefit payments, the cost of enabling an elderly person to remain at home also varies by the level of dependency or frailty of an individual. The addition of these costs results in the annual gross cost of maintaining a single elderly person at home rising from £4,340 to roughly £7,320 per annum for someone with no dependency and from £4,430 to £13,780 for a highly dependent elderly person (**Paragraph 3.45**);

25.   The annual estimated gross cost of informal care received by an elderly person ranges from an average of approximately £2,800 for a medium-dependency person to £5,500 for a high-dependency person. These figures should, however, be treated with extreme caution as carers' estimates of the time spent in providing support (on which these costs are partly based) in comparison with elderly dependants' estimates of the amount of care provided often vary significantly (**Paragraph 3.40**);

26.   The annual gross cost can also vary by the type of carer with non-resident carers costing, on average, roughly £2,800 per person per annum and resident carers costing £7,220. This is not, moreover, because resident carers are dealing with more dependent elderly people than non-resident carers. It is principally because resident carers seem, overall, to be offering more hours care to their dependents than non- resident carers (**Paragraphs 3.40-3.41**).

A comparison of the costs of housing and housing with care options for elderly people (Chapter 3)

27.   At all levels of dependency and assessed need, staying at home options for elderly people are considerably cheaper than a move to specialised accommodation. For low dependency elderly people the specialised housing option available to them – specially-designed accommodation without warden support – is approximately £1,100 more expensive per person per annum than staying at home. For medium- and high- dependency people, the costs of some specialised housing options e.g. very sheltered housing, can be as much as roughly £7,500 per person per annum more expensive than the costs of staying at home options (**Paragraph 3.44**);

28.   This finding is very different, however, for medium- and high-dependency elderly people when informal carers costs and state benefits are

included. Staying at home options then become more expensive than many specialised housing options, although very sheltered housing is still the most costly form of provision. This finding should be treated with extreme caution, however, as the data on informal care may not be reliable **(Paragraph 3.45)**;

29.   At the same levels of dependency, residents of specialised housing are receiving twice as much and, for some forms of provision, three times as much health and social care support than elderly people in ordinary, mainstream housing in the community **(Paragraph 3.46)**.

C. NATIONAL AND REGIONAL HOUSING AND CARE CHARACTERISTICS AND CIRCUMSTANCES OF ELDERLY AND DISABLED PEOPLE

30.   Data collected in the national surveys of elderly people, residents, informal carers and non-elderly disabled adults on the housing, social and financial circumstances, level of health and dependency and housing aspirations of elderly and disabled people, was used in this study to produce estimates of need for subsidised housing provision.

A national survey of elderly people (Chapter 4)

31.   Elderly people are much more likely than non-elderly people to live alone and almost twice as many of those aged 85 and over live alone than those aged 65-74. Elderly people living alone, moreover, are less likely to be owner-occupiers than elderly couples and more likely to rent, in particular from local authorities **(Paragraphs 4.7 and 4.28)**;

32.   Very elderly people aged 85 and over are less likely to own the property they live in than the rest of the population (with the exception of those under 25) and, along with those aged 75-84, are more likely to rent their accommodation than younger elderly people, although not from any particular type of landlord **(Paragraph 4.27)**;

33.   The level of dependency of elderly people varies noticeably by tenure, with those classified as `fully independent' more likely to be owner-occupiers and those with higher dependency scores more likely to rent, particularly from local authorities **(Paragraph 4.28)**;

34.   Among elderly people, owner-occupation is highest in the South East (64%), South West (62%) and Eastern (61%) regions, local authority renting is highest in the Northern (45%), London and East Midlands regions (both 35%) and private sector renting is highest in the London region (8%) **(Paragraph 4.30)**;

35.   A high proportion of elderly households, whether renting or owner-occupying, under-occupy their accommodation[4]. Elderly couples within all tenures are particularly likely to under-occupy their accommodation **(Paragraph 4.41)**;

---

[4]   The term 'under'occupation' as used here, refers to the number of bedrooms in a property occupied by a household in excess of the Bedroom Standard. A full definition of the Bedroom Standard is given in Appendix 5.

36. Almost two-fifths of elderly households have had adaptations made to their homes. The most frequently fitted including additional handrails (both inside and outside) and a warden/emergency alarm system. Adaptations are well targeted – the presence of adaptations is strongly related to the age, household type and level of dependency of an elderly person -single elderly people and elderly couples aged 75 or over and those in medium to high dependency groupings are more likely to have obtained adaptations than elderly couples aged 65-74 and those in low dependency groupings (**Paragraph 4.46**);

37. Only 3 in 10 elderly people say they require any or additional aids and adaptations. As might be expected, the more dependent elderly people are the more likely they are to state they needed adaptations. The most frequently requested adaptation is a converted bathroom /shower, particularly by dependent elderly people (**Paragraph 4.47**);

38. When asked about the most suitable accommodation for them, over four-fifths of elderly people wish to remain in their present homes. 69% of the sample opt for their home exactly as it is without any repairs or adaptations to make it easier to live in and 15% think they need some physical changes to their housing. Only 15% wish to move to other accommodation. Council tenants, private renters and respondents with a high dependency score are more likely than average to opt for staying put with repairs and adaptations to their present homes (**Paragraph 4.50**);

39. Two-thirds of those who indicated a wish to live in alternative accommodation would prefer a bungalow and approximately one-sixth would like to live in a flat or maisonette. A flat or maisonette is more popular with private renters, single elderly people and those already in flats or maisonettes. A bungalow is more likely to be sought by two- person elderly households, those in semi-detached houses and owner- occupiers (**Paragraph 4.52**);

40. Care and support services are well-targeted – respondents with higher dependency scores and those living alone and aged 75 or over are generally the most likely to receive visits from health and social care services (**Paragraph 4.59**);

41. Demand for additional care and support services amongst elderly people appears to be extremely low. Only 3% of respondents would like to have a home help and 2% said they needed visits from the doctor or social worker. Those already in receipt of some services, the very elderly (those aged 85 or over) and the highly dependent are most likely to request any or additional visits (**Paragraph 4.61**);

42. Over half the elderly households in the survey contained someone receiving a pension from a former employer (51%). There is quite low receipt of certain types of allowances and benefits amongst the elderly population, for example, only 6% receive any form of attendance allowance. Some caution, however, should be exercised here as some elderly respondents may not have

been fully aware of the types and names of allowances they received **(Paragraphs 4.11-4.13)**.

<table>
<tr><td>**A national survey of residents of specialised housing for elderly people (Chapter 5)**</td><td>

43.   Compared to earlier studies, recent entrants to specialised housing for elderly people are more likely to come from a residential care or nursing home, whether run by a local authority, private or voluntary organisation. For very sheltered housing, there has been a four-fold increase over the last 5 years **(Paragraph 5.30)**;

</td></tr>
</table>

44.   The proportion of recent entrants to specialised housing for elderly people from the private rented sector is approximately four times greater than the proportion of elderly people in this tenure within the community as a whole **(Paragraph 5.28)**;

45.   Housing association tenants appear to have slightly lower levels of satisfaction with their present accommodation in specialised housing schemes (68% are very satisfied, although 94% are satisfied overall, ie very and fairly satisfied) than Abbeyfield/Almshouse tenants (78% are very satisfied and 96% are satisfied overall) or local authority tenants (73% are very satisfied and 94% are satisfied overall) **(Paragraph 5.39)**;

46.   A high proportion of **recent entrants** to both ordinary sheltered (two-fifths) and very sheltered (one-fifth) housing appear to have no physical or mental frailty, despite the fact that the former was designed for less active elderly people and the latter is provided specifically for frail older people. Housing association schemes have higher numbers of elderly people with no dependency than local authority or Abbeyfield/ Almshouse schemes, particularly amongst new entrants. It should be pointed out, however, that local housing authorities have the potential to significantly influence the selection of new tenants in housing association schemes through nomination agreements and this may partly account for this finding. **(Paragraph 5.18)**;

47.   Compared to earlier studies, the proportion of **all** residents in ordinary and very sheltered housing schemes with no dependency appears to be increasing as does the proportion of residents with a high level of dependency. This polarisation in the profile of dependency amongst residents is more pronounced for local authorities and Abbeyfield/Almshouse tenants than it is for housing association tenants, and for recent entrants than for the sample as a whole. This conflicts with the widely-held belief that ordinary sheltered housing tenants, as a whole, are becoming more dependent and placing an increasing burden upon wardens **(Paragraph 5.23)**;

48.   One in six recent entrants to specialised housing schemes would have preferred to have stayed in their previous homes **(Paragraph 5.31)**;

49.   Receipt of social and health care services by residents is well-targeted: the very elderly aged 85 or over, those with high levels of dependency and those

in very sheltered housing schemes are more likely to receive visits than other residents. Residents of specialised housing appear to be more likely to be in receipt of services at all levels of dependency than elderly people in the community. For those in receipt of health and social care services, however, there is no difference in the frequency with which these services are delivered to elderly people in either setting **(Paragraphs 5.42-5.44)**;

50.	At all levels of dependency, a higher proportion of residents of specialised housing receive attendance allowance than elderly people in the community as a whole **(Paragraph 5.12)**.

A national survey of informal carers of elderly people (Chapter 6)

51.	Three-quarters of informal carers for elderly people are women. Women are more likely than average to be non-resident carers and men to be resident carers. Resident carers are, on average, older than non- resident carers. In fact, non-resident carers are particularly likely to be aged 45-64. Men who are carers are also almost twice as likely to be aged 65 or over (63%) than women carers (36%) **(Paragraph 6.5)**;

52.	Two in five carers have been looking after their dependant for up to 5 years, three in ten for between 5 and 10 years and a similar proportion for 10 years or more. There is little difference in this profile according to whether the carer is resident or non-resident **(Paragraph 6.8)**;

53.	Elderly people looked after by resident carers are no more dependent than those looked after by non-resident carers. More or less the same proportion of non-resident carers are looking after elderly people at each level of dependency as resident carers **(Paragraph 6.9)**;

54.	Resident carers are much more likely to have helped their elderly dependents' with domestic, personal care and key practical tasks such as nursing help in times of sickness and gardening than non-resident carers **(Paragraphs 6.10 and 6.21)**;

55.	Resident carers are providing, on average, twice as much time in care support to their elderly dependants than non-resident carers. 86% of resident carers spend 10 or more hours each week in providing support to their dependent, with half of them (51%) spending 30 hours or more. This compares with 38% of non-resident carers providing 10 or more hours care per week, and 7% of them spending 30 hours or more **(Paragraph 6.22)**;

56.	This finding, moreover does not vary even for the most frail elderly dependants. Almost all resident carers looking after high dependency elderly people (94%) spend 10 or more hours each week in providing support compared with 45% of non-resident carers looking after frail elderly people. This extra time input is also not simply spent in performing domestic and practical tasks, but applies to personal care and mobility tasks for dependants as well **(Paragraph 6.22)**;

57.   Men carers are more likely to be providing 10 or more hours care to their dependants (73%) than women carers (58%). This is probably due to the fact that men are more likely to be resident carers than women and resident carers provided more time in care support (**Paragraphs 6.22 and 6.5**);

58.   The majority of informal carers think they are helping as much as they can. Just over one in ten say they would like to help more and only 2% think they do too much. Resident carers are more likely to say they that they are helping as much as they can and non-resident carers to say they would like to help more. There is no difference by type of carer or by the level of frailty of the dependent elderly person in the numbers of carers who think they do too much. Carers with highly dependent elderly people are, however, more likely to say they are helping as much as they can and less likely to state they would like to do more (**Paragraphs 6.23-6.24**);

59.   For almost all of the 16 health and social care services covered by the survey, a significantly higher proportion of non-resident carers say their dependants receive visits than resident carers (**Paragraph 6.33**);

60.   Approximately one in ten non-resident informal carers contribute towards the costs of repairs and maintenance or re-decoration of their dependant's home. Contributions tend to fall into two main groupings: 46% of non-resident carers had contributed up to £100 and 19% had paid £300 or more (**Paragraph 6.27**);

A national survey of non-elderly disabled adults (Chapter 7)

61.   Non-elderly disabled adults are less likely to owner-occupy than the population as a whole and more likely to rent from a local authority or live with relatives/friends. In fact, almost a half of younger disabled adults aged 16-29 live with relatives/friends as part of their household. Single disabled adults aged 16-59 are also significantly less likely to be owner-occupiers than the single adult population aged 16-59 and much more likely to rent from a local authority or housing association (**Paragraphs 7.29-7.30**);

62.   Just over a third of non-elderly disabled adults have adaptations in their home, a slightly lower figure to that among elderly disabled people. The most frequently fitted adaptations are additional hand rails (both inside and outside) and a specially-designed or adapted bath or shower (**Paragraph 7.35**);

63.   Adaptations appear to be targeted upon the most severely disabled and dependent. Least likely to have adaptations and improvements to their home are non-elderly disabled people with children, private renters and those living with relatives or friends. Local authority and housing association tenants are no more likely to have had adaptations than owner-occupiers (**Paragraph 7.35**);

64.   Not surprisingly, the more severely disabled respondents are the more likely they are to state they need any or additional adaptations. The most frequently requested adaptation is a specially designed or adapted bath or shower, especially by highly dependent disabled people (**Paragraph 7.36**);

65.   When asked about the most suitable type of accommodation for them, fewer non-elderly disabled adults wish to remain at home (with or without adaptations) than elderly people – seven out of ten compared with approximately eight out of ten elderly people. Amongst those who do wish to remain at home, however, a higher proportion want aids and adaptations (23%) than elderly people (15%) **(Paragraph 7.39)**;

66.   Twice as many non-elderly disabled adults think that they need alternative accommodation than elderly people. Respondents aged 16- 29, not surprisingly, are particularly keen on other accommodation – only approximately one in two wish to remain in their current homes. Of all those who say they need other accommodation, just over a half would prefer to live in a bungalow and 29% would prefer to live in a house. Only a third want to live in housing specifically designed for easy access, and over two-fifths say they would not want to live in this type of accommodation **(Paragraphs 7.40-7.41)**;

67.   18% of non-elderly disabled adults considered themselves likely to move within 12 months of the survey. Younger respondents aged 16-29 were most likely to expect to move (38%, including 28% who said they were very likely to move within 12 months of the survey) **(Paragraph 7.48)**;

68.   Care and support services from statutory agencies for non-elderly disabled adults seem to be well targeted – respondents with higher dependency scores are more likely to receive home visits than those with low or medium levels of dependency. For any given level of dependency, however, non-elderly disabled adults are generally less likely to receive visits from health and social care services than elderly people. This is despite the finding that a greater proportion of non-elderly disabled adults are classified as being dependent at all levels of dependency than elderly people **(Paragraph 7.49)**;

69.   Latent demand for care and support services amongst the non- elderly disabled population is quite low. The most frequently requested services, amongst those not currently receiving them, were a physiotherapist (5%), a doctor (4%), a chiropodist (6%) and a social worker (5%) **(Paragraph 7.50)**;

70.   37% of non-elderly disabled adults receive an invalidity pension. This is a higher proportion of the non-elderly disabled adult population than found in previous studies. 23% of non-elderly disabled adults receive a mobility allowance. This is also a higher proportion than found in previous studies **(Paragraphs 7.13 and 7.15)**.

D. ESTIMATES AND INDICATORS OF NEED BY ELDERLY AND DISABLED PEOPLE FOR SUBSIDISED HOUSING AND HOUSING WITH CARE PROVISION

The allocation model and estimates of need (Chapter 8)

Elderly people

71.   The model assessed that the majority of elderly households have no need or desire for any form of subsidised specialised housing or change in their housing circumstances or care support to enable them to remain at home. Some two-thirds of the national sample of elderly households are allocated to the same form of housing as they occupy at the moment, with no subsidised provision of aids and adaptations or social and health care services (**Paragraph 8.23**);

72.   The main reasons for this are that a large proportion of the total sample (45%) do not wish to move and are not physically or mentally dependent and, therefore, do not justify the need for aids and adaptations to remain at home. Roughly one in eight elderly households, moreover, who are physically or mentally dependent, do not want to move and state that they currently have sufficient formal and/or informal care and support and sufficient aids and/or adaptations. On average, however, this group receives significantly fewer aids and adaptations and less health and care support than the full sample of households participating in the national survey of elderly people in the community. Lastly, approximately one in eleven of the sample are allocated to the group with no assessed need for subsidised housing provision because they fail the means test for home improvement grants (**Paragraphs 8.24, 8.38 and 8.39**);

73.   Only a small proportion of the total sample (6%) is allocated to staying at home options with house adaptations and repairs. This is probably due to a number of factors, including relatively low levels of expressed desire for aids and adaptations, the application of means-testing to the provision of grants for adaptations and repairs and anxieties about the upheaval created by the building process associated with repairs and adaptations work (**Paragraph 8.25**);

74.   One in seven elderly households are allocated to staying at home options which only involve the input of additional health and social care services (**Paragraph 8.26**);

75.   Approximately one in twelve elderly households are assessed as needing a move to alternative accommodation covering a range of options. The majority of households would either move to smaller or the same size ordinary/mainstream housing (2.5%) or specialised housing (4%). Twice as many elderly households are allocated to ordinary or traditional sheltered housing as are allocated to very sheltered or extra-care housing (**Paragraphs 8.27-8.30**);

76.   Eventual outcomes for elderly households vary significantly by the age of household members, the household type, level of dependency and tenure. For example, those aged 75 and over are up to four and a half times more likely to be assessed as having a need for staying at home options involving adaptations, repairs and domiciliary care support than elderly people aged 65 – 74 **(Paragraphs 8.32-8.37)**;

Non-elderly disabled adults

77.   For the restricted range of housing options examined in relation to this group, the allocation model would suggest that 2% nationally have a need for wheelchair housing and 3% a need for mobility housing/housing adapted for disabled people **(Paragraph 8.31)**.

Indicators of need for subsidised housing and housing with care provision for elderly people (Chapter 8)

78.   In addition to estimates of need the study was also designed to examine whether there are clear proxy indicators of need for subsidised housing provision for elderly people.

79.   Two methods were carefully examined for producing proxy measures of need. The first of these, which is essentially an attempt to produce a shortened version of the allocation model using data from regular surveys, such as the General Household Survey, proved to be unsuccessful because of the complexity of even an abbreviated version of the model **(Paragraphs 8.41-8.42)**;

80.   The second approach, which looks at the characteristics (some included in the model, most not included) of households allocated to options, did not find sufficient clustering of factors relating to housing, social and financial circumstances to enable target populations to be consistently identified for different forms of subsidised housing provision **(Paragraphs 8.43-8.44)**;

81.   Thus, the estimates of need or prevalence rates produced by the allocation model are the simplest practicable method of quantifying demand for subsidised housing provision for elderly and disabled people **(Paragraph 8.45)**.

Conclusions (Chapter 9)

82.   The findings from this study confirm several of the key findings from previous studies of elderly peoples' housing needs. The desire of most elderly people to remain in their current homes is not a new finding. It has, however, now been confirmed by an up-to-date large-scale regionally representative study **(Paragraphs 9.3-9.6)**;

83.   The findings from this study, however, also run counter to some previous findings. For example, the study would suggest that wardens of specialised housing schemes are still coping with the demands of a balanced 'fit' and 'frail' community as opposed to an increasingly uniform high dependency resident population **(Paragraphs 9.7-9.9)**;

84.   The study provides several pointers to future housing needs analysis amongst the elderly and disabled populations including:

- the importance of looking separately at the needs of the over 75 year olds;

- the significance of peoples' aspirations as well as their objective needs;

- the recognition that some people will not want provision despite their objective circumstances;

- the particular preferences of young disabled adults aged 16 – 29; and,

- the importance of assessing need for a combined package of housing and care inputs to enable an elderly or disabled person to remain at home (**Paragraphs 9.10-9.15**);

85.   The profile of housing and housing with care needs amongst the elderly population seems to be changing:

- the range of options available to elderly people is increasing with the growing significance of staying at home options and the development of different types of specialised housing, such as Category 1.5 and Category 2.5 accommodation;

- the range of characteristics and circumstances of elderly people and their households that need to be taken into account in assessments of housing needs for planning purposes is also expanding; and,

- there seems to be some shift in emphasis towards higher care solutions and away from lower care housing solutions to elderly peoples' needs (**Paragraphs 9.17-9.21**);

86.   The general conclusion of the study is that the majority of elderly and disabled people have no assessed need for any form of subsidised housing or housing with care provision. Of those that do, most can be enabled to remain at home with adaptations and health and social care support but some require a move to alternative accommodation. Current specialised housing provision meets almost all of this demand and, in fact, there is evidence of over-provision of ordinary sheltered housing. There is, however, some shortfall in units for those with high levels of dependency and disability and extra-care requirements (**Paragraph 9.26**).

1 Introduction and background

1.1   This Chapter sets out the policy background to the study and the aims of the research. It then briefly describes the range of housing and housing with care options for elderly and disabled people, the different elements of the study and the main aspects of the research design. Finally, the chapter outlines the structure of the report.

Policy background

1.2   Meeting the housing needs of elderly and disabled people has been a relatively active area of policy interest for government, both central and local, and housing providers for most of the second half of this century. Amongst the major landmarks have been the issuing of several influential Circulars in the 1950s and 60s on different aspects of the design of dwellings for older people (Circular 32/56: Housing of Old People and Circular 82/69: Housing Standards and Costs – Accommodation Specially Designed for Old People). In the 1970s, the Department of the Environment published design guidance for mobility and wheelchair housing and issued further Circulars on housing and adaptations for people with physical disabilities (HDD 2/74 and 2/75 and Circulars 74/74 and 59/78). The 1980s saw the publication of research recognising the importance of policies and initiatives aimed at enabling elderly people where possible to remain in their own homes (Tinker, 1984). This coincided with a major review of `care in the community' policies leading to new arrangements for the delivery of community care services, in which housing provision for elderly and disabled people, amongst others, has a significant role to play (Caring For People: Community Care in the next decade and beyond, Cmnd 849, 1989, National Health Service and Community Care Act 1990 and Circular 10/92: Housing and Community Care). Lastly, the Department of the Environment introduced the Disabled Facilities Grant in the late 1980s, for use by elderly and disabled people to pay for adaptations to their houses to make it easier for them to remain in their own homes (Local Government and Housing Act 1989).

1.3   This active policy interest has continued into the 1990s for a number of reasons:

i. *changes in the demographic profile of the elderly population.* There has been a general growth in the last two decades in the proportion of the population in England aged 65 and over. The most significant increases have been amongst those aged 75 and over and particularly people 85 and over (Table 1.1). In fact, towards the end of this century the numbers of those aged under 75 will steadily fall and the numbers of those aged 85 and over will increase dramatically. The decline in numbers in the 65-

Table 1.1 Population of England aged 65 and over, and proportions of the total population of England aged 65 and over, 1971-2021

	1971		1981		1991	
	Pop 000s	% tot pop	Pop 000s	% tot pop	Pop 000s	% tot pop
65-74	3,928	8.5	4,224	9.2	4,231	8.8
75-84	1,785	3.9	2,148	4.7	2,622	5.5
85+	404	0.9	480	1.0	765	1.6
Tot pop	46,018	13.3	45,772	14.9	48,068	15.9
	2001		**2011**		**2021**	
	Pop 000s	% tot pop	Pop 000s	% tot pop	Pop 000s	% tot pop
65-74	4,039	8.1	4,511	8.8	5,369	10.3
75-84	2,736	5.5	2,748	5.4	3,275	6.3
85+	1,022	2.0	1,220	2.4	1,366	2.6
Tot pop	49,921	15.6	51,289	16.6	52,124	19.2

Sources:
1971: OPCS, Census 1971: age, marital condition and general tables, Great Britain, HMSO, 1974. Note: figures for England in the published tables are not separated from figures for Wales. Numbers here are for England and Wales (table 9, p.28), less the numbers for Wales only (table 10, p. 51).
1981: OPCS, Census 1981: sex, age and marital status, Great Britain, HMSO, 1983. Table 3 (England), p7.
1991-2021: OPCS, 1991-based population projection, national projections, series PP2 no. 18, September 1993 (microfiche).

74 age group, however, will be halted at the end of the century and numbers will grow again to their 1970s levels by the first decade of the 21st century. This growth in the numbers of older elderly people, who are more likely to be frail than those aged under 75, has implications for the provision of housing, health and social care support. Higher levels of formal and informal care support and more flexible approaches to their housing circumstances are likely to be required to meet their needs;

ii. *the increasing acceptance that the majority of elderly and disabled people wish to remain in their current homes.* Research has shown that most elderly people wish to remain in their own homes and that this is the most cost-effective solution to their needs (Tinker, 1984, Challis and Davies, 1986). Staying at home has been encouraged by Government and housing providers through various schemes, including home improvement agencies, which provide advice and support to elderly and disabled people carrying out repairs and adaptations to their homes. The new community care arrangements are also likely to create some additional demand for social housing from elderly and disabled people retained in the community who would previously have gone to residential care, and from those transferred from long-stay institutions into the community. It has, however, proved difficult so far to predict with any accuracy the extra resources for housing that will be required as a result of the new community care arrangements.

iii. *growing evidence of inappropriate allocation of housing resources to elderly people in the social rented sector.* Several studies have shown a significant number of elderly residents of sheltered housing have no physical or mental disability or dependency (Butler, Oldman and Greve 1983, Clapham and Munro, 1988, Tinker, 1989). It has also been demonstrated that many of those re-housed in sheltered housing would have preferred to remain in their previous homes (Butler, Oldman and Greve, 1983, Tinker, 1989). Other studies have concentrated on the growing phenomenon of difficult-to-let sheltered housing and have shown that providers are finding it increasingly problematic to let certain types of accommodation in schemes in less attractive locations (Barelli, 1992, Micallef, 1994). The extent of under-occupation by elderly households in mainstream housing in the local authority and housing association sectors has also been highlighted (Barelli, 1992). Lastly, some research has examined elderly residents' attitudes towards the sheltered housing they live in and their use of facilities in schemes and found that satisfaction is more often related to the housing itself rather than the communal facilities and warden support (Butler, Oldman and Greve 1983, Wirz, 1981, Clapham and Munro, 1988). All of this has led to a growing recognition on the part of providers that there is a potential mismatch between the needs of elderly people for subsidised housing provision and the type and characteristics of the stock available to meet them (NFHA, 1993);

iv. *representations from disability organisations on the need for extending the Part M Building Regulations `Access and Facilities for Disabled People'* to cover all new housing (Part M Approved Document 1992, Access Committee for England, 1992). The objective being to ensure a stock of new dwellings which are more easily accessible and provide a measure of independent living for disabled people who do not need or want specialised housing provision;

v. *the need to ensure that future planning addresses the issue of the most cost-effective methods of providing subsidised housing and housing with care options for elderly and disabled people.* Several studies have shown that there is a wide variation in the costs of options for elderly people, even with the same levels and types of assessed housing needs (Clapham and Munro 1988, Tinker, 1984, 1989);

vi. *the continuing problems faced by a small but significant group of relatively poor elderly owner-occupiers and private renters in housing in the worst condition.* Single elderly households are more likely than any other group in the population to live in private housing in the worst condition. The houses they occupy are usually the oldest (pre-1919) stock (English House Conditions Survey 1991, HMSO/DoE, 1993). There are, however, fewer elderly households in the worst condition housing since the last English House Conditions Survey in 1986. In absolute terms, the number of single elderly people and two-person older households living in housing in the worst condition fell by 6% and 10% respectively;

vii. *concern about the indicators of need for subsidised housing provision by elderly and disabled people in the compound statistical indices used to allocate capital resources for subsidised housing provision* to Government regional offices and the Housing Corporation. These compound statistical indices are known as the General Needs Index and the Housing Needs Indicator. At the time of the study, these indices took account of a range of measures of need including overcrowding, concealed and sharing households, private sector stock condition as well as need amongst elderly and disabled people based on eligibility for income support in order to identify the `poor elderly' and prevalence rates of disability amongst the population as a whole. As such, they did not take into account severity of disability or level of dependency, need for specialised housing options, current receipt of adaptations, elderly and disabled peoples' housing aspirations, social circumstances or the relative costs of different housing and housing with care options. It was one of the main objectives of this study to produce revised indicators of need for subsidised housing provision by elderly and disabled people to be used in the GNI and HNI. In carrying out a study to address this issue, however, several of the other policy interests outlined above have also been covered.

Housing and housing with care options for elderly and disabled people

1.4   The housing needs of elderly and disabled people are catered for, to some extent, by design and access requirements in housing association new build mainstream or non-specialised housing. All new-build housing association accommodation should now be built to mobility standards, designed for people who can walk but only with difficulty. As indicated above, disability organisations would like to see this approach adopted for all new housing, irrespective of tenure. The present regulations, however, are much more limited in scope and, even if building regulations were introduced to cover all new housing, the vast majority of existing housing would have no particular design features to enable better access. Moreover, this would be a possible long-term solution to the housing needs of elderly and disabled people not dependent upon 'their' individual wishes or aspirations.

1.5   There are, however, five basic housing and housing with care options for elderly and disabled people that do depend, to a large extent, upon their wishes. They are as follows:

● staying put with no additional support;

● staying put with necessary repairs only;

● staying put with repairs and adaptations only or with domiciliary care support as well;

22

- a move to smaller, ordinary or mainstream housing; and,

- a move to specialised housing, such as sheltered and wheelchair housing.

Most of these housing and housing with care options are defined in paragraphs 2.5 and 8.13 of Chapters 2 and 8 respectively. The only one not covered is staying put with necessary repairs. The reason for this is given in paragraph 1.25 below.

Staying put options

1.6   The policy of enabling elderly and disabled people to remain at home arose out of the recognition that, wherever possible, most elderly and disabled people wish to remain in their own home rather than move to any other form of housing to meet their needs. A number of initiatives have been taken by housing providers and Government to support elderly and disabled people in their decision to stay at home. Most notably, the development of home improvement agencies which provide help and support to elderly and disabled people in carrying out repairs and improvements to their homes. In 1993, the Department allocated £3.9 million to home improvement agencies in England. In 1992, elderly and disabled people had access to home improvement agencies in one in three (118 out of 365) local authority areas in England. Care and Repair Ltd. is the national co-ordinating body for all these home improvement agencies in England. The essential point about all of these initiatives, however, is that the ability of elderly people to remain in their own homes is often only partly determined by the housing they occupy. Solutions to their needs require a combination of house adaptations and health and social care support such as home care aides, district nurses, occupational therapists and so on.

1.7   Having said that, staying put as an option need not involve or require any form of support. The majority of elderly and disabled people have no need for any form of specialised housing or care provision. Some elderly and disabled people may, moreover, choose not to receive any housing, health or social care support, even though they are physically dependent and/or mentally impaired. Staying at home options involving adaptations and domiciliary support are, nevertheless, important ways in which frail elderly and disabled people can be enabled to live independently in mainstream housing for as long as it is practicable for them to do so. Not all, however, will need or want domiciliary care support to remain at home. For example, to some extent, aids and adaptations and health and social care services are interchangeable, and some informal carers may not want any help from formal care support services.

Specialised housing options

1.8   There are six main types of specialised housing for elderly and disabled people:

- Category 1 accommodation (specially designed housing without warden support);

- Category 1.5 accommodation (specially designed housing with warden support but no communal facilities);

- Category 2 accommodation (specially designed housing with warden support and communal facilities);

- Category 2.5 accommodation (specially designed housing with warden support, enhanced communal facilities and extra care staff);

- Wheelchair housing (for those who regularly use or are confined to a wheelchair); and,

- Mobility housing/housing adapted for disabled people (for those who can walk but with difficulty). This type of housing is also often referred to as "accessible" housing.

The first four of these types of specialised housing are normally provided for elderly (disabled or non-disabled) people. The last two are usually only made available for non-elderly disabled adults.

The present study

Aims and objectives

1.9   The overall objectives of the programme of research were to:

i. provide reliable national and regional estimates of the housing needs of elderly people requiring subsidised provision by local authorities, housing associations and other voluntary sector providers e.g. Almshouse and Abbeyfield societies, in England;

ii. provide reliable national estimates of the housing needs of non-elderly disabled adults requiring subsidised provision by local authorities and housing associations;

iii. identify more accurate indicators of need for subsidised housing provision for elderly and disabled people for use in determining the allocation of capital resources to local authorities and, through the Housing Corporation, to housing associations; and,

iv. examine the extent to which any unmet need for subsidised provision by elderly people can be most cost-effectively met through housing options.

The choice of approach

1.10   Like all similar studies, this programme of research faced a number of key decisions at the outset and, perhaps the most fundamental, was whether primary data or fresh information was actually required. Data from regular and ad hoc surveys such as the General Household Survey, the Labour Force Survey, the English House Conditions Survey, the 1991 Census and the OPCS surveys of disability in Great Britain (published in 1988) covered several of the topics that would be included in any assessment of the housing needs of elderly and disabled people. None of these sources, however, had all of the information required and it was impossible to piece the relevant items of data together to form the necessary dataset. Even if it had been possible the combined dataset would still have lacked crucial evidence on elderly and disabled peoples' housing and care aspirations. The essential point here is that the assessment of housing needs, even at the planning level, requires information on a wide range of different aspects of housing, social and financial circumstances, health and level of dependency and aspirations. In order to collect this information for a sufficiently large sample of elderly and disabled adult households, a new survey was required.

1.11   The next major decision was how to define the target populations for interviews. For the elderly population, it was decided to include all those aged 65 or over. In doing so, this excludes women pensioners aged 60 to 64. This decision was made in order to ensure that this study was consistent with definitions of elderly people used in previous major studies. For the disabled population, it was decided to follow as closely as possible the definition used in the OPCS surveys of disability in Great Britain. This approach is discussed in more detail in Chapter 7 on the survey of non-elderly disabled adults. The definition mainly consisted of a checklist of twelve long-term illnesses or disabilities which was used to identify potential respondents.

1.12   It was also decided at the outset that any estimates of need produced would be estimates of the number of households in need rather than individuals in need of subsidised housing provision. This is necessary because it is households that are rehoused not individuals, except where the household is a single person. For instance, a household may contain one physically fit elderly person and one physically frail person, if the assessment were based purely on the needs of the fit person this household might be denied access to sheltered housing. Taking into account the needs of both people should lead to a more balanced judgement. Only in relation to residential care, is it possible that an elderly couple might be rehoused separately. For example, a person might suffer from severe senile dementia whilst their spouse/partner is perfectly fit. In this situation, it might be necessary to consider separate re-housing options. Staying at home options also require a household approach, as a fit spouse/partner might be in a position to offer informal care support to a frail elderly person. It should be noted, however, that whilst household needs were assessed in this study, the information on which to base these assessments was gathered from one respondent in the household (each of the individual reports on the main interview surveys contain sections on the survey design and fieldwork which explain how these respondents were selected – see Appendix 1). The respondent answered questions about the housing aspirations of the household as a whole and provided information on the physical/mental abilities and disabilities of one other household member. In the vast majority of cases, this was their spouse/partner.

1.13   At the start of the study, there was also considerable discussion about the inclusion of elderly peoples' housing and housing with care aspirations in any assessment of needs. It was decided that preferences should be taken into account and the research shows that most elderly and disabled people have reasonably clear views on the broad characteristics of different options to meet their needs. Taking into account preferences is in line with the emphasis in the new community care arrangements (introduced through the National Health Service and Community Care Act 1990 and re-inforced in `Care Management and Assessment: Practitioners' Guide SSI/Dept. of Health, 1991) towards greater user or client involvement in assessments for health and social care services and housing provision. It is also essential to producing realistic estimates of need as elderly and disabled households cannot be forced to move against their will, neither can they be compelled to install adaptations in their homes. For example, as this study shows, a small but significant `core' of elderly people refuse help despite their objective circumstances. They are also less likely to be encouraged to undertake repairs and improvements by the offer of advice and support throughout the building process than any other group in the elderly population (see paragraphs 8.38 – 8.39, Chapter 8). Paragraphs 8.5 – 8.8 in Chapter 8 describe in detail some of the methodological issues and problems involved in asking about housing preferences.

1.14   Another important decision at the outset of the study was the choice of dependency measure. After consideration of a range of possible measures including the Crichton Royal Behavioural Rating Scale, the Clifton Assessment Procedures for the Elderly, the York Guttman and Hereford Scales, it was decided to use the Townsend/Clackmannan Model of Dependency as the principal measure and the Leeds Scale of Dependency as a secondary measure and for comparison with previous studies (see Appendix 2 for a full description of the different elements in these two scales).

1.15   The Townsend/Clackmannan scale of dependency was developed and used by Bond and Carstairs (1982) as part of a survey of 5,000 elderly people in the Clackmannan District of Scotland. They divided the content of the measure on functional and clinical criteria as shown in Figure 1.1. Bond and Carstairs took the original sixteen-point Townsend Index, which is the basis of all recent major dependency measures, and developed a uni-dimensional scale for functional criteria. The chosen scale was based on Guttman logic, from work by Sainsbury (1973) and inter-item correlations. This means that mobility, self-care and house-care capacity are all scored on a hierarchical scale of ability and hence an explicit assumption of dependency gradation. For example, within the scale for self-care tasks, the questions are designed so that ability to do shopping also assumes no requirement for assistance for getting in and out of a chair (Table 1.2). The clinical criteria are incontinence and mental state. The mental state is further sub-divided into intellectual functioning and emotional disorders. They are scored on an additive scale, and banded accordingly into no, mild or severe dependency. The final outcome is to place individuals in a Clackmannan Grouping A to G, where A represents nil/zero dependency or full independence and G represents the highest level of physical and/or mental frailty.

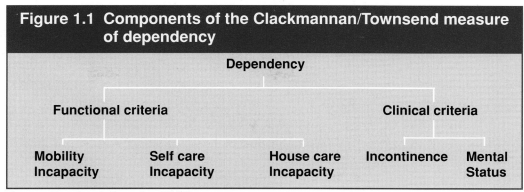

Figure 1.1 Components of the Clackmannan/Townsend measure of dependency

Source: Bond and Carstairs (1982)

1.16 The Townsend/Clackmannan scale of dependency was designed for use in residential settings and to be completed by an interviewer using a structured schedule. The interviewers do not require professional training in care assessment. The main strengths of the Townsend/Clackmannan scale of dependency are:

i. the detailed research on inter-item correlations that went into its development;

ii. it was specifically designed for assessing the physical/ mental frailty of elderly people and for residential or non-communal establishment populations;

Table 1.2 Hierarchical scales for mobility, self-care and house care incapacities		
Mobility incapacity	**Self care incapacity**	**House care incapacity**
1. Difficulty travelling by bus 2. Difficulty walking outside 3. Unable to travel by bus 4. Unable to walk outside 5. Difficulty walking inside 6. Unable to get up from chair 7. Unable to walk outside chair	1. Difficulty washing hair 2. Unable to wash hair 3. Unable to wash all over or bath 4. Difficulty dressing 5. Difficulty washing hands and face 6. Unable to put on shoes or socks or stockings 7. Unable to dress 8. Unable to wash hands and face	1. Unable to do heavy shopping 2. Difficulty washing clothes 3. Difficulty ironing clothes 4. Unable to wash clothes 5. Difficulty preparing and cooking meals 6. Unable to iron clothes 7. Difficulty with light housework 8. Unable to prepare and cook meals 9. Unable to make bed 10. Unable to do light housework.
Coefficient of reproducibility 0.97 *Coefficient of scalability 0.71*	*Coefficient of reproducibility 0.99* *Coefficient of scalability 0.69*	*Coefficient of reproducibility 0.96* *Coefficient of scalability 0.62*

Source: Bond and Carstairs (1982)

iii. the scale is progressive, higher categories always indicate higher levels of dependency;

iv. elderly people with the same dependency score are more likely to have similar dependency characteristics.

The main weaknesses, each of which was overcome in the present study, of the Townsend/Clackmannan scale are:

i. it requires a longer interviewing process than other scales;

ii. the measure had not been used on a national basis before this survey;

iii. the relatively large number of `non-scale types', because of missing information on relevant questions.

1.17   The second dependency measure was developed by researchers at Leeds University, from which it derived its name. The Leeds scale is a twelve-point dependency score covering mobility, self-care and domestic activities. One point is scored for each activity an elderly or disabled person has difficulty in performing or is unable to do without help. On average, the higher the score the higher the level of dependency. Thus, a score of zero equates to `fully independent'. Scores are usually combined to produce ranges equivalent to low, medium and high dependency.

1.18   As with the Townsend/ Clackmannan scale, the Leeds measure of dependency was designed for use in residential settings and to be completed by an interviewer using a structured questionnaire. The main strengths of the Leeds scale are:

i. it was specifically designed for assessing the physical/ mental frailty of elderly people and for non-communal establishment populations;

ii. it has been used in other large-scale studies and so its results can be used for comparative analysis of findings.

The main weaknesses of the Leeds scale are:

i. it does not include any measure of mental state;

ii. there is an absence of any grading within scale elements and, as a consequence;

iii. elderly people with the same dependency score are much less likely to have similar dependency characteristics.

Different elements of the study

1.19   The study began with a qualitative exercise involving group discussions with elderly people living in three areas of England – West Wickham, Eastbourne and Derby . These group discussions were intended to help with the design of the main questionnaires to be used in the study by identifying issues of concern to elderly people in relation to their housing needs. This was followed by a conference, held in October 1990, involving housing, health and social services academics and practitioners to discuss the research design and, specifically, proposals for the costings, dependency and needs assessment methodologies.

1.20   After these preliminary stages, the ten main elements to the study were established as follows[5]:

i. A national survey of the provision of subsidised specialised housing for elderly and disabled people;

ii. A national survey of the costs of specialised housing for elderly people;

iii. A national survey of the costs of maintaining an elderly person at home;

iv. A study of the comparative costs of housing and housing with care options for elderly people;

v. A national and regional survey of elderly people in the community;

vi. A national survey of elderly residents of specialised housing;

vii. A national survey of informal carers to elderly people;

viii. A national survey of non-elderly disabled adults;

ix. An allocation model and estimates of need for subsidised housing provision; and,

x. An investigation of potential indicators of need for subsidised housing provision.

1.21   In order to address the objectives set out in paragraph 1.9, the study sought answers to four key questions (the elements of the research, referred to above, designed to provide answers to each question are shown in brackets):

● What is the current provision of subsidised specialised housing for elderly and disabled people? (i);

● What are the most cost-effective forms of subsidised housing and housing with care provision for elderly people? (ii, iii and iv);

---

[5]   Individual reports on all of these main elements were produced plus two further reports on minor surveys of the cost of aids and adaptations and allocations policies and practices for specialised housing for elderly people. Details of the reports are given in Appendix 1.

- What is the current need at national and regional level for additional subsidised housing and housing with care provision for elderly and disabled people? (v, vi, vii, viii and ix); and,

- What are the best indicators of need by elderly people for subsidised housing and housing with care provision for planning local housing strategies? (x).

1.22   Issues relating to methodological approaches, sample sizes, fieldwork dates and so on, for each of the ten main elements of the study are summarised in relevant chapters and given detailed descriptions in the individual reports of the study. The remainder of this section of the introductory chapter looks at some groups and topics that were not examined in the study and reasons for doing so. It also explains why non-elderly disabled adults were not covered in the same depth as elderly people.

1.23   This study of the housing needs of elderly and disabled people did not cover one potential source of need for subsidised housing provision which may become increasingly important as community care policies settle down. No data was collected to enable estimates of housing need to be produced for elderly and disabled people being transferred out of long-stay hospitals into the community. Whilst this is not an omission of any great significance at present, it may become increasingly important as the new arrangements for community care become more established towards the end of this century. This source of need, however, was outside the scope of the study.

1.24   Another omission is information on the costs of residential care and hospitals. Here, however, there is evidence from two previous Departmental studies of the costs of housing and care for elderly people (Tinker, 1984, 1989) that residential care and hospital places are considerably more expensive than most housing and housing with care options. Although based on relatively small numbers, the current study does provide costings for sheltered housing schemes registered as residential care homes under the Registered Homes Act 1984, which confirm this finding. It should also be noted that the costs of short stays in respite residential care homes have not been included in calculations of the unit costs of staying at home options. This service would, however, only be used by the most dependent elderly people in the community and would probably not significantly alter the comparison of the relative costs of staying at home for the highly dependent and a place in very sheltered housing (see paragraph 3.44 in Chapter 3).

1.25   It was decided at the outset that the study would not produce estimates of need for staying at home options simply requiring repairs. Whilst some basic information about state of repair was collected in interviews, the topic was not covered in great depth in the study because to have properly surveyed the physical condition of a representative sample of homes occupied by elderly and disabled people would have doubled the cost of the research. This topic, moreover, was already being more than adequately covered by the 1991 English House Conditions Survey and data from the EHCS has been used in the costings exercises to derive estimates of costs of repair for this research. It is arguable, moreover, that because repairs problems are faced by all types of household, they are not a housing need solely of elderly and disabled people in the same sense as sheltered housing, adaptations or wheelchair housing. Instead, this study concentrated on staying at home options involving house adaptations as well as repairs and domiciliary care support.

1.26   Lastly, the study did not examine the housing needs of non-elderly disabled adults from as many angles or in as much depth as it did the housing needs of elderly people. (Where data is not available for non-elderly disabled adults this is clearly sign-posted in Chapters.) The prime motivation for the study was to refine the elderly indicators in the General Needs and Housing Needs indices and improving the disabled indicators was a secondary and later objective. Having said that, sufficient information has been collected on the housing circumstances of non-elderly disabled adults to produce useful findings with regard to their needs, particularly for wheelchair housing.

The questionnaire

1.27   A copy of the main questionnaire designed for the study is available on request from the Department of the Environment. This questionnaire was used in the survey of 9,000 elderly households and 850 non-elderly disabled adults. It had five parts – the main section, a dependency form, a short form, a mental state form and a proxy filter. The dependency form contained the detailed questions on ability to perform mobility, self-care and domestic tasks required for the Townsend/Clackmannan scale of dependency. It was only completed for approximately 4,100 of the 9,000 elderly respondents. A simple filter in the main questionnaire determined whether the respondent and other household members were physically fully independent or not and the mental/health status questions were part of the main questionnaire. The mental state and proxy filters were introduced into the interview if the respondent appeared confused or unsure of her/his answers during the first section of the main questionnaire. The mental state filter was used to determine whether the respondent could proceed with the interview; the purpose of the proxy filter was to identify an appropriate proxy respondent. In the absence of a proxy respondent, the interviewer was instructed to complete a short form. Short forms collected basic information such as the type and age of property, shared facilities, adaptations installed and repairs needed, and were designed to be completed by observation, with limited help from the respondent. In the event, only 3% of the interviews in the main survey of approximately 9,000 elderly households were with proxies, 3.5% of respondents required a mental state test and, of these, only 38% (1.3% of the total sample) could not continue with the full interview. In these cases a short form was completed.

Table 1.3 Age and gender profile of respondents to the main survey compared with 1991 Census data on elderly people (Column %'s in bold)

Age group	Male Main survey	Census	Female Main survey	Census	All Respondents Main survey	Census
65-74	**63%**	**61%**	**54%**	**52%**	**58%**	**56%**
	45%	44%	55%	56%		
75-84	**31%**	**33%**	**36%**	**38%**	**34%**	**36%**
	38%	36%	62%	64%		
85+	**6%**	**6%**	**10%**	**10%**	**8%**	**8%**
	28%	29%	72%	71%		
All	41%	40%	59%	60%		

Comparisons with the Census

1.28   Finally, Table 1.3 compares the age and gender profile of respondents in the main sample of 9,000 elderly households with the same profile of elderly people from the 1991 Census. It is encouraging to see that there is very little difference between the two sets of row and column percentages. This study has a very slight bias towards elderly people aged between 75 and 84 years old, but this is only in the order of 2% more than the Census. Age and sex are two important characteristics of elderly respondents in the present study and the close match to the 1991 Census results adds, to a large extent, to the confidence that can be placed in its findings.

The structure of the report

1.29   This report is a summary of the whole programme of research. It concentrates on the main elements of the study and is divided into four broad sections as follows:

a. *The stock*: this deals with the nature and extent of subsidised specialised housing for elderly and disabled people (Chapter 2);

b. *Comparative costs of housing and housing with care options*: this describes the findings from an analysis of the cost-effectiveness of different types of specialised accommodation for elderly people and staying put options (Chapter 3);

c. *Characteristics of elderly and disabled people and their carers:* this describes results from all the interview surveys of the study including the housing, social and financial circumstances of elderly and disabled people, their health and level of dependency and housing aspirations (Chapters 4,5,6 and 7);

d. *The allocation model and estimates of need*: this final section, describes the national and regional estimates of need for subsidised housing provision by elderly and disabled people produced from an allocation model based on the survey data collected in the study (Chapter 8).

2 The current stock of specialised housing provision for elderly and disabled people

2.1   In order to address the housing needs of elderly and disabled people properly, it is first necessary to examine the current stock of any specialised housing provision for these groups. This is important to any basic attempt to describe the relationship between supply and assessed need and it helps to identify what specific types of accommodation are available for particular sub-groups within the elderly and disabled populations. Specialised housing, moreover, is the only housing or housing with care option for which there is a fixed stock of provision specifically designated for elderly and disabled people, as opposed to provision, such as health and social care support, that is also regularly supplied to other client groups.

2.2   With this in mind, this study of the housing needs of elderly and disabled people included a national survey of the current and planned stock of subsidised specialised housing for elderly people as at 31 March 1990. (As was pointed out in the previous chapter, provision for non-elderly disabled adults was not covered in as much detail as that for elderly people throughout this study. It is, nevertheless, possible to present some details of provision for this group based on other published data sources). The national survey was conducted between October 1990 and August 1991 and postal questionnaires[6] were sent to approximately 3,000 providers of specialised housing for elderly people in England, including all local housing authorities, housing associations, Abbeyfield and Almshouse societies providing subsidised specialised housing for elderly people. Whilst full coverage was not entirely achieved, the lowest response was 71% of all housing associations and the highest was 91% of Abbeyfield societies. It was also possible through using published data in conjunction with the survey data to produce grossed-up national and regional figures for the current supply of specialised housing. Some information was also collected on planned[7] provision of subsidised specialised housing for elderly people.

What is specialised housing?

2.3   Specialised housing was defined as property specifically designed or adapted and intended for use by elderly or disabled people, which may be let on

---

[6]   Copies of the questionnaires used and other detailed methodological issues are covered in Report 1 of the individual reports on different elements of this programme of research.

[7]   Planned provision was defined as increases in the housing stock for which sites have been found and which have received design, capital and revenue approval or decreases in the housing stock which have received the approval of the housing committee or equivalent.

tenancy or licence agreement. In the survey, information was collected on the number and type of different specialised units of accommodation for elderly people owned and managed by each organisation. By contrast, all of the data on the number of units of specialised accommodation for non-elderly disabled adults comes from the existing stock data on Housing Investment Programme returns supplied annually to the Department of the Environment by local authorities[8]. The following sections of this chapter use this information to present a profile of the nature and extent of the specialised stock and compare provision with assessed need. Before doing so, however, it is worthwhile briefly examining the different types of specialised housing for elderly and disabled people.

Types of specialised housing provision for elderly and disabled people

2.4   First of all, it is important to point out that the specialised housing options available for elderly and non-elderly disabled people differ considerably. The former group are mainly covered by specialised housing options for all elderly people, such as sheltered housing. Non- elderly disabled adults are housed in forms of specialised housing, such as wheelchair housing, which are mostly provided to meet their housing needs only.

2.5 Having said that, there are *four* main types of specialised housing provision for elderly people. These are:-

> *Category 1 accommodation* – contains specially-designed units of accommodation for elderly people of the more active kind. Communal facilities such as a common room, a laundry room or a guest room may also be provided, although these are optional;

> *Category 1.5 accommodation* – is broadly similar to Category 1 housing, but it must have an alarm system and warden support. No communal facilities are provided in this form of accommodation;

> *Category 2 accommodation* – are schemes with units of accommodation for less active elderly people. They must have a resident or non-resident warden and a system for calling him or her. Communal facilities such as a common room, a laundry room or a guest room must also be provided;

> *Category 2.5 accommodation* – these are also known as either 'very sheltered' or 'extra care' schemes. They are for frail elderly people and have more provision or a greater level of care than Category 2 schemes. They may, for example, provide meals, extra wardens, care assistants and additional communal facilities such as special bathrooms, sluice rooms etc.

---

[8]   In the absence of primary research data on wheelchair and mobility housing/housing adapted for disabled people, HIP1 returns for 1 April 1993 are the best available source. It should be noted, however, that this may significantly undercount the amount of mobility housing/housing adapted for disabled people. It should also be pointed out that, according to the rules for completing the HIP1 form, mobility housing should not be included in these figures. It is extremely difficult, however, for local authorities to separate mobility housing from all housing specially designed or adapted for use by disabled people in their stock. It is highly likely, therefore, that most, if not all, of stock built to mobility standard is still included in HIP figures. Annual returns collected by the Housing Corporation from registered housing associations (HAR10/1) also contain information on the stock of wheelchair dwellings but not mobility housing/housing adapted for disabled people. The exclusion of the latter form of provision prompted the decision to rely only on HIP1 data.

[Category 1.5, 2 and 2.5 accommodation can be grouped as sheltered housing under the definition provided in Schedule 5, paragraph 10 of the 1985 Housing Act]

And there are *two* main types of specialised housing provision for non-elderly disabled people. These are:-

Wheelchair housing – this is housing generally designed or converted according to the standards in HDD Occasional Paper 2/75 for people confined or totally dependent on wheelchairs. Essential features include entrances accessible for wheelchair users, internal space planning for the easy movement of wheelchairs and wheelchair access to the bathroom, lavatory, kitchen and at least one bedroom at entrance level;

Mobility housing/housing adapted for disabled people – this covers all accommodation built to mobility standards, that is, it is designed to conform with standards set out in HDD Occasional Paper 2/74, for people who can walk but with difficulty. It also includes all accommodation that has been adapted specifically for use by disabled people.

Whilst these two broad sets of specialised housing options are not exclusively for elderly and non-elderly disabled people respectively, only relatively small numbers of non-elderly disabled people are housed in specialised housing for elderly people and vice-versa.

2.6   Apart from these main specialised housing options, there is a wide range of less numerically significant or clearly distinguishable forms of housing or housing with care provision for elderly and disabled people. Some are linked to particular providers such as Abbeyfield societies, whilst others are rarely available for the sole use of one group of people with special needs. They are as follows:

- Granny Annexes

- Supportive Houses

- Intermediate Care Schemes

- Hostels

- Shared Houses/Group Homes

The detailed report of the survey of specialised housing for elderly people (Report 1 – see Appendix 1) contains definitions and individual results for each of these forms of accommodation. Throughout this summary report, however, they will be collectively referred to as `other specialised housing'.

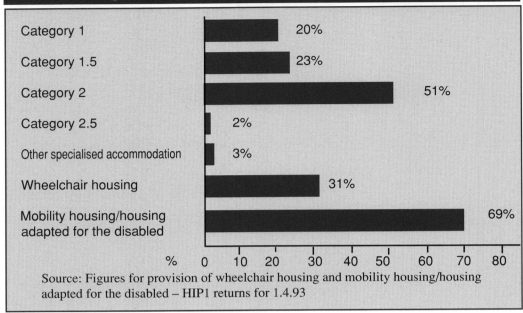

Figure 2.1 National provision of subsidised specialised housing for elderly and disabled people by Category of accommodation (percentages based on grossed-up figures)

Category 1	20%
Category 1.5	23%
Category 2	51%
Category 2.5	2%
Other specialised accommodation	3%
Wheelchair housing	31%
Mobility housing/housing adapted for the disabled	69%

%   0   10   20   30   40   50   60   70   80

Source: Figures for provision of wheelchair housing and mobility housing/housing adapted for the disabled – HIP1 returns for 1.4.93

The extent of current provision

Nationally

2.7　Figure 2.1 shows the national profile of subsidised housing provision for elderly people. Sheltered housing, in various forms, accounts for just over three-quarters of all specialised units of accommodation and Category 1 or specially designed units without warden support accounts for a further fifth. The remaining units are spread across a wide spectrum of 'other specialised housing', none of which amounts to more than 1% or 2% of accommodation for elderly people nationally. Figure 2.1 also shows the national profile of subsidised specialised housing for disabled people. There are twice as many units of mobility housing/housing adapted for disabled people as units of wheelchair housing.

2.8　Ordinary sheltered housing with at least one communal facility and resident or non-resident warden support is still the main form of subsidised specialised housing provision for elderly people in England, accounting for just over half (51%) of the grossed-up figure for provision. Very sheltered or extra-care housing only accounts for a small proportion of the total stock (2%) but, as will be shown later in this chapter, it is proportionately the fastest growing form of provision. Amongst `other specialised housing', it was also found that there is very little hostel or wheelchair housing provision exclusively for elderly people.

2.9　These grossed-up figures of provision based on the survey data also reveal that, in comparison with other data sources, there is significantly more specialised housing for elderly people than previously estimated. In fact, for sheltered housing, the combined figure for the current stock of Category 1.5, 2 and 2.5 accommodation – 494,243 – is 16% greater (67,366 units of

Table 2.1 Regional distribution of units of subsidised specialised housing for elderly people by Category of accommodation (grossed-up figures)

Row %s	Category of accommodation					Total
	1	1.5	2	2.5	Other	
S. East	14,864 17%	14,596 17%	49,449 58%	2,943 3%	3,408 4%	85,260 100%
S. West	9,121 16%	9,067 16%	35,178 62%	2,064 4%	1,717 3%	57,147 100%
London	6,941 12%	6,620 12%	38,023 67%	2,776 5%	2,106 4%	56,466 100%
Eastern	15,842 22%	7,461 10%	44,828 62%	1,789 2%	1,845 3%	71,765 100%
W. Mids	24,717 33%	18,572 25%	28,228 38%	2,185 3%	1,281 2%	74,983 100%
E. Mids	17,360 24%	20,068 28%	31,329 43%	758 1%	3,442 5%	72,957 100%
N. West	21,164 21%	21,966 22%	50,143 50%	1,137 1%	5,651 6%	100,061 100%
Yorks & Humb.	8,498 12%	32,665 47%	27,549 39%	761 1%	475 1%	69,948 100%
Northern	8,356 16%	19,699 37%	24,019 45%	369 1%	464 1%	52,907 100%
England	126,863 20%	150,715 23%	328,746 51%	14,782 2%	20,389 3%	641,494 100%

accommodation) than the figure produced from Housing Investment Programme returns for 1 April 1990. There are several possible reasons for this, including the difference in the treatment of bedsits between the national survey and HIP1 data. The Housing Investment Programme return for 1990 treated each group of bedsits as one dwelling, whereas this survey counted each bedsit as one unit of accommodation. More detailed analysis of the data showed, however, that this could not be the only explanation for the discrepancy. Another explanation for some but not all of the difference is the inclusion of Almshouse and Abbeyfield society providers not registered with the Housing Corporation in this survey. Such providers are not included in HIP1 estimates. Even if all of these non-registered voluntary sector providers were included in the HIP figures, however, their total sheltered housing stock could only account for just under a fifth of the additional units identified by this survey. Lastly, it is possible that some of the variation is due to the different approaches providers took to completing the survey and HIP1 returns.

Regionally

2.10 Table 2.1 shows the distribution of subsidised specialised housing provision for elderly people across the nine DoE regions. North-West region has the largest number of specialised units of all the regions and Northern the smallest number of units. It is also clear from the Table, that the dominance of sheltered housing among specialised accommodation for elderly people is not uniform across the country. For instance, in West Midlands region over 30% of all specialised housing is Category 1 accommodation, i.e. specially-designed without warden support. This compares with London and with Yorkshire and Humberside where just over 10% of accommodation falls into this category. Table 2.1 also shows that there is wide variation in the profile of sheltered housing provision across DoE regions. Looking at the two most extreme positions, only 38% of specialised housing in West Midlands is Category 2 accommodation, i.e. warden support and communal facilities, compared with 67% of specialised housing in London. In contrast, whereas 12% of provision in London is Category 1.5 accommodation comprising warden support only, 47% of specialised housing in Yorkshire and Humberside falls into this category.

2.11   There seems to be a clear difference between the pattern of provision in the northern (West Midlands, East Midlands, North-West, Yorkshire and Humberside and Northern) DoE regions and the southern (South-East, South-West, London and Eastern) DoE regions. Within the former group, the amount of Category 1.5 housing is significantly greater than in the latter group, where the more traditional model of ordinary sheltered housing is the predominant form of provision. The proportion of the stock that is very sheltered is also greater in southern than in northern regions. Part of the reason for this, as will be shown in the next section, is the greater presence of housing associations, Abbeyfield and almshouse providers in the South.

Table 2.2 Regional distribution of units of subsidised specialised housing for disabled people by Category of accommodation (grossed-up figures)

Row %s	Wheelchair housing	Mobility housing/housing adapted for disabled people	Total
N. West	5,717 32%	12,123 68%	17,840 100%
W. Midlands	2,627 44%	3,382 56%	6,009 100%
E. Midlands	2,047 32%	4,321 68%	6,368 100%
S. West	2,340 42%	3,243 58%	5,583 100%
S. East	2,751 30%	6,502 70%	9,253 100%
London	4,884 45%	5,854 55%	10,738 100%
Eastern	3,327 62%	2,018 38%	5,345 100%
Yorks & Humberside	2,111 16%	11,282 84%	13,393 100%
Northern	1,858 12%	13,415 88%	15,273 100%
England	27,662 31%	62,140 69%	89,802 100%

2.12   Table 2.2 shows the distribution of specialised units for non-elderly disabled people across the DoE regions. As with elderly persons specialised housing, North-West region has the greatest number of units but this time it is Eastern region that has the lowest level of provision. The balance between wheelchair and mobility housing/housing adapted for disabled people is extremely variable at the regional level with few regions coming close to the 2:1 national ratio of mobility/adapted to wheelchair units. In Yorkshire and Humberside and Northern regions, for example, mobility/adapted units out-number wheelchair units by approximately five and seven to one. There is also a striking difference in the total amount of mobility housing/housing adapted for disabled people provided in these regions and the North-West region compared with the rest of the country. Whilst the North-West, however, has the highest number of wheelchair units, Yorkshire and Humberside and Northern regions have amongst the lowest levels of provision of this form of accommodation. As will be shown in the next section, much of this variability in provision is attributable to the presence of housing associations as major providers of specialised housing for disabled people in some regions but not in others.

Type of Provider

2.13   The largest providers of subsidised specialised housing overall for elderly people are local housing authorities, accounting for almost three-quarters (73%) of all units in England. Housing associations supply 23% of all specialised accommodation and, of the remaining provision, almshouses account for 3% and Abbeyfields 1% of the total stock in the social rented sector. However, local housing authorities are not the major provider of all forms of specialised housing for elderly people. For example, they account for only 45% of very sheltered housing units nationally with housing associations providing an equivalent proportion and Abbeyfield and almshouse societies supplying the remaining 10% of the extra-care stock.

Table 2.3 Units of subsidised specialised housing for elderly people by Category of accommodation and type of provider (grossed-up figures)

	Category of accommodation					
Col%s/Row%s	1	1.5	2	2.5	Other	Total
Local	94,488	131,487	222,297	6,618	11,031	465,920
authorities	74%	87%	68%	45%	54%	73%
	20%	28%	48%	1%	2%	100%
Housing	24,852	15,214	98,847	6,675	2,998	148,586
associations	20%	10%	30%	45%	15%	23%
	17%	11%	65%	4%	3%	100%
Abbeyfield	0	10	12	656	5,552	6,230
	0	0	0	4%	27%	1%
	0	0	0	11%	89%	100%
Almshouse	7,523	4,004	7,590	833	808	20,758
	6%	3%	2%	6%	4%	3%
	36%	19%	37%	4%	4%	100%
Base	126,863	150,715	328,746	14,782	20,389	641,494

2.14   Table 2.3 compares the profile of specialised housing provision between these groups of providers. Housing associations are more likely than any other provider to offer sheltered housing with both warden support and one or more communal facilities. Local housing authorities have a higher proportion of Category 1.5 sheltered accommodation than any other provider and almshouse societies are most likely to have Category 1 housing amongst their stock. Abbeyfield societies are the only providers of supportive houses and this form of specialised housing represents over four-fifths of their total specialised housing provision for elderly people. Overall, housing associations, Abbeyfield societies and almshouse providers have a greater proportion of their stock in very sheltered housing schemes for frail elderly people than local authorities.

2.15   The proportion of the total stock owned and managed by each provider also varies by DoE region. For instance, housing associations provide over a quarter of the stock (27%) in southern regions (South- East, South-West, Greater London, and Eastern regions) but only a sixth of stock (17%) in northern regions (West Midlands, East Midlands, North-West, Yorkshire and Humberside and Northern regions). This geographical bias towards southern regions also applies, to a lesser extent, to Abbeyfield societies and almshouse providers. This partly explains the higher proportion of very sheltered housing in the specialised stock for elderly people in regions in the south of the country.

2.16   Local authorities are also the largest providers of subsidised specialised housing for disabled people in England, they account for well over four-fifths (84%) of the stock with almost all of the remainder (16%) being provided by housing associations. A very small number of units are provided by organisations such as Regional Health Authorities, County Councils, New Towns and Government Departments, but these units do not comprise a significant percentage share of the total stock.

Table 2.4 Units of subsidised specialised housing for disabled people by Category of accommodation and type of provider (grossed-up figures)

Col%s/ Row%s	Wheelchair housing	Mobility housing/housing adapted for disabled people	Total
Local authorities	18,898 68% 25%	56,212 90% 75%	75,110 84% 100%
Housing associations	8,291 30% 59%	5,780 9% 41%	14,071 16% 100%
Other public sector	473 2% 76%	146 1% 24%	619 0 100%
Base	27,662	62,138	89,800

2.17   Table 2.4 shows the type of specialised housing provided by local authorities and housing associations, and reveals an interesting difference in emphasis. Housing associations are more likely to provide wheelchair housing than mobility housing/housing adapted for disabled people. The opposite is true for the local authority stock where mobility/adapted homes outnumber wheelchair dwellings by approximately three to one. Some caution should be exercised with this finding, however, which is based on HIP1 data. All new build housing association units are generally developed to mobility standards and there has been a considerable house adaptations programme for housing association tenants over the last decade. The importance of housing associations as providers of wheelchair housing is also reflected in their share of the national stock of this type of accommodation, which at 30% is almost twice their share (16%) of the stock of all specialised dwellings for disabled people. In contrast, housing associations' share of the mobility housing/housing adapted for disabled people stock (9%) is approximately half their share of the stock of all dwellings.

2.18   As with specialised units for elderly people, there is considerable regional variation in the contribution of different providers to the stock of dwellings for disabled people. For example, the proportion of the stock owned and managed by housing associations varies from 31% in London and 27% in Eastern regions to 4% in Northern region and 8% in Yorkshire and Humberside. This may go some way to explaining, moreover, why there is relatively little wheelchair housing provision in these latter two regions.

Type of Local Authority

2.19   Table 2.5 in Appendix 3 shows the distribution of specialised housing stock for elderly people by type of local authority. The main difference appears to be between London and the rest of the country. Whilst in all three types of authorities provision is largely dominated by Category 2 sheltered housing, the spread of different forms of specialised housing is greater in MDCs and DCs. For instance, District Councils outside London (metropolitan or non-metropolitan) are approximately twice as likely to have Category 1 and 1.5 housing than London Boroughs.

2.20   One of the possible reasons for the different profile of provision in London is that over two-fifths (43%) of all specialised units of accommodation for elderly people in London are owned and managed by housing associations, Abbeyfield and almshouse societies. This is a much higher proportion than elsewhere in the country.

2.21   Table 2.6 in Appendix 3 shows that, as with specialised housing for elderly people, London has a different profile of provision for non-elderly disabled adults than MDCs and DCs. The proportion of the specialised stock for disabled people in the form of wheelchair housing is greater in London than for District Councils and over twice the figure for Metropolitan District Councils. This, once again, illustrates the importance of housing association provision of specialised housing in the Capital.

Type of Accommodation

2.22   The following sections of this chapter look at different characteristics of the stock of specialised housing for elderly people such as size, self-containment, floor level etc. No such information was collected for non-elderly disabled persons' specialised housing and, as far as is known, there is no data on the size, self-containment and floor level in published sources (see also paragraph 1.26 in Chapter 1).

Housing type

2.23   Figure 2.2 shows the type of accommodation available in specialised housing schemes for elderly people. Three-fifths of units are self-contained flats, a third are bungalows and, of the small remainder, non self-contained flats figure prominently.

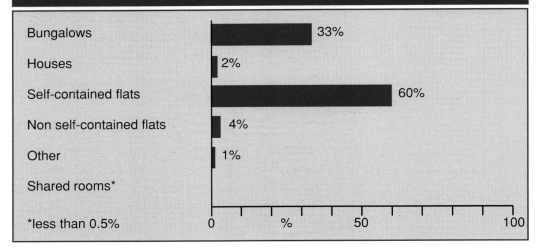

Figure 2.2 National provision of subsidised specialised housing for elderly people by housing type (percentages based on un-grossed figures)

Bungalows — 33%
Houses — 2%
Self-contained flats — 60%
Non self-contained flats — 4%
Other — 1%
Shared rooms*
*less than 0.5%

2.24   Within category of accommodation, as Table 2.7 shows, ordinary and very sheltered schemes consist mostly of flats, although 7% of Category 2 flats and 35% of Category 2.5 flats are non self-contained. Flats also form a significant proportion of Category 1 and 1.5 units, but, not to the same extent, as nearly a half of all units in these schemes are bungalows.

2.25   By type of provider, the pattern is quite distinct (Table 2.8). The majority of the housing association and Abbeyfield societies stock is in the form of flats, with the former concentrating on self-contained flats and the latter, non self-contained flats. For local authorities and almshouse societies, there is a greater spread of different types of housing. For example, over two-fifths of local authority and nearly a third of almshouse stock is in the form of bungalows.

2.26   Table 2.9 in Appendix 3 puts category of accommodation together with the two main types of providers – local authorities and housing associations. This reveals that for some categories of accommodation – such as Category 2.5 – there are clear differences in the types of housing being provided for potentially the same group of elderly people. Almost all units in local authority extra-care housing are self-contained flats, whereas nearly a half of the housing association frail elderly stock is in the form of non self-contained flats. (This finding confirms previous research undertaken by the Department on very sheltered housing (Tinker, 1989)). This difference may be due to several factors, such as the influence of capital and revenue funding regimes encouraging non self-contained dwellings and the requirements of registration as residential care homes. It is not likely to be due to differences in the frailty of local authority and housing association residents, as will be shown in Chapter 5.

2.27   Whilst the profile of housing types is more or less consistent across the regions, there is one major exception. Even though bungalows represent a third (33%) of the specialised stock for elderly people nationally, only a twentieth (5%) of specialised units in London are bungalows. Similarly, whilst almost two-thirds of all units nationally are flats (self-contained or non-self contained), nine-tenths of units in London fall into this category. Possible explanations for this are three-fold: firstly, the relative importance of housing associations as providers in London; secondly, the lower provision of Category 1 and 1.5 schemes in the Capital and, thirdly, housing densities in most forms of accommodation are notably higher in London.

Table 2.7 Units of subsidised specialised housing for elderly people by Category of accommodation and housing type (un-grossed figures)

Col%s/ Row%s	Category of accommodation					
	1	1.5	2	2.5	Other	Total
Bungalows	57,237	62,386	48,864	423	5,229	174,139
	48%	52%	19%	4%	26%	33%
	33%	36%	28%	0	3%	100%
Houses	4,931	1,850	1,467	36	146	8,430
	4%	2%	1%	0	1%	2%
	58%	22%	17%	0	2%	100%
Self-contained flats	57,328	54,615	185,852	6,701	9,290	313,786
	48%	46%	74%	59%	46%	60%
	18%	17%	59%	2%	3%	100%
Non self-contained flats	0	456	13,952	3,633	5,347	23,388
	0	0	6%	32%	26%	4%
	0	2%	60%	16%	23%	100%
Other	607	173	838	618	377	2,613
	1%	0	0	5%	2%	1%
	23%	7%	32%	24%	14%	100%
Shared rooms	0	0	18	236	158	412
	0	0	0	2%	1%	0
	0	0	4%	57%	38%	100%
Base	120,103	119,480	250,973	11,411	20,389	522,356

Table 2.8 Units of subsidised specialised housing for elderly people by type of provider and housing type (un-grossed figures)

Col%s/ Row%s	Local authority	Abbeyfield	Housing Association	Almshouse	Total
Bungalows	160,182	0	7,503	6,454	174,139
	41%	0	7%	31%	33%
	92%	0	4%	4%	100%
Houses	5,112	1	602	2,715	8,430
	1%	0	1%	13%	2%
	61%	0	7%	32%	100%
Self-contained flats	207,285	1,996	94,471	10,034	313,786
	54%	32%	87%	48%	60%
	66%	1%	30%	3%	100%
Non self-contained flats	12,057	4,154	5,664	1,513	23,388
	3%	67%	5%	7%	4%
	52%	18%	24%	6%	100%
Other	1,583	79	909	42	2,613
	0	1%	1%	0	1%
	61%	3%	35%	2%	100%
Shared rooms	70	43	257	42	412
	0	1%	0	0	0
	17%	10%	62%	10%	100%
Base	386,219	6,230	109,149	20,758	522,356

Size

2.28   Figure 2.3 shows that the 1-bed unit is the dominant size of dwelling in specialised housing schemes for elderly people nationally. Bedsit and 2-bed units account for roughly one-sixth and one-fifth of the stock respectively and the remainder is made up of 3 and more bedroom units.

2.29   By category of accommodation, Table 2.10 shows that as the frailty of intended residents increases so the size of units decreases. Bedsits are commonest in very sheltered housing, 'other specialised housing' – mostly, Abbeyfield supportive houses – and ordinary sheltered housing. In contrast, the provision of 2 and 3 + units, as a proportion of the total stock of each type of accommodation, is greatest in Category 1 and 1.5 schemes.

Figure 2.3 National provision of subsidised specialised housing for elderly people by size of units (percentages based on un-grossed figures)

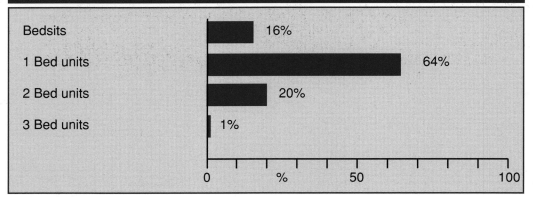

Bedsits	16%
1 Bed units	64%
2 Bed units	20%
3 Bed units	1%

Table 2.10 Units of subsidised specialised housing for elderly people by Category of accommodation and size of units (un-grossed figures)

Col%s/ Row%s	Category of accommodation					Total
	1	1.5	2	2.5	Other	
Bedsits	4,466	3,496	61,626	4,859	7,225	81,672
	4%	3%	25%	43%	35%	16%
	5%	4%	75%	6%	9%	100%
1-bed units	80,746	76,338	160,407	5,947	10,416	333,854
	67%	64%	64%	52%	51%	64%
	24%	23%	48%	2%	3%	100%
2-bed units	32,096	39,013	28,595	579	2,636	102,919
	27%	33%	11%	5%	13%	20%
	31%	38%	28%	1%	3%	100%
3+ bed units	2,795	633	345	26	112	3,911
	2%	1%	0	0	1%	1%
	71%	16%	9%	1%	3%	100%
Base	120,103	119,480	250,973	11,411	20,389	522,356

2.30 As a proportion of their total stock of specialised housing, local authorities supply more two and three plus bedroom accommodation than any other provider and Abbeyfield societies have more bedsits (see Table 2.11 in Appendix 3). Whilst local authorities, moreover, are the major provider for all sizes of accommodation in absolute terms, their share of the stock goes down as size decreases. For instance, whereas local authorities supply over nine-tenths of all three or more bedroom units, they only account for just over a half of all bedsits.

2.31 As with housing type, combining categories of accommodation and type of provider yields some interesting findings (Table 2.12 in Appendix 3). Concentrating, once again, on Category 2.5 provision by local authorities and housing associations, the former are much more likely to provide one-bed units than bedsits in their schemes and the latter are more likely to provide bedsits than one-bed units. As pointed out above, this could be due to a number of reasons, but one possible explanation is that housing associations and local authorities have different policies on the appropriate type of accommodation for frail elderly people.

2.32 London stands out amongst the regions in terms of the size profile of units. London has the highest proportion of bedsits amongst its specialised stock (33%) and, together with one-bed flats, these two sizes of accommodation account for 95% of all provision in the Capital. In contrast, bedsits only represent, on average, 14% of the stock in most other regions and, together with one-bed flats, roughly 80% of all provision.

Floor level

2.33   This aspect of the type of accommodation provided in specialised housing schemes for elderly people is important for several reasons, including providing estimates of the amount of the stock that requires lifts and the extent of conversion of multi-storey blocks into sheltered housing. It is only relevant, however, for flats (self and non-self contained) and shared rooms. The following sections, therefore, describe results for a subset (65%) of the full dataset of units of accommodation in specialised housing for elderly people.

2.34   Figure 2.4 divides the stock of specialised housing with the potential for being on more than the ground floor into three groupings – units on the ground floor, units on the 1st – 5th floors and units on the 6th floor or above. This shows that the majority of flats and shared rooms are in ground floor schemes or low-rise blocks. Only a small minority of units are in high-rise blocks; a form of provision which evolved from the need to provide support to elderly tenants in blocks which had been designated, for example, as suitable for people aged 50 or above.

2.35   Category 1.5 accommodation has the most high-rise units as a proportion of the stock, although these dwellings still represent only a small share of the total national provision of warden supported housing without communal facilities. Ground floor flats are the most common form of provision in Category 1, 1.5 and 'other specialised' accommodation and there is a roughly equal split of ground floor and low-rise units in Category 2 and 2.5 schemes (Table 2.13 in Appendix 3).

2.36   Local authorities are the only significant providers of high-rise or multi-storey flats; 2.4% of their specialised housing stock for elderly people is at or above the sixth floor. For all providers, however, the vast majority of their flats and/or shared rooms are on the ground floor or in low-rise blocks. Lastly, unlike some other aspects of the type of accommodation in specialised housing schemes, the distribution of high-rise Category 1.5 accommodation is quite regionally specific. Multi-storey units only form a relatively significant part of provision in London (3%), West Midlands (4%) and Northern regions (4%).

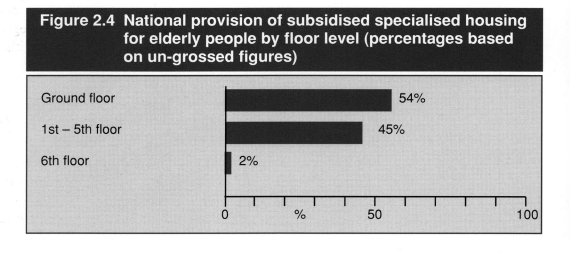

Figure 2.4 National provision of subsidised specialised housing for elderly people by floor level (percentages based on un-grossed figures)

Ground floor — 54%
1st – 5th floor — 45%
6th floor — 2%

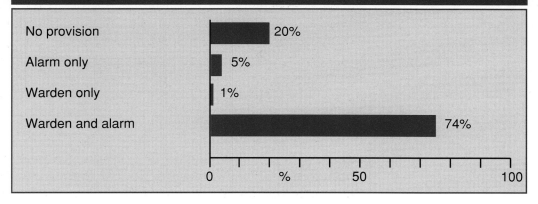

Figure 2.5 National provision of subsidised specialised housing for elderly people by Alarm and Warden support (percentages based on un-grossed figures)

Alarm and warden support

2.37 Most units and schemes for which information was collected could be placed into one of four groupings – alarm and warden provision, alarm only, warden only and units with no warden support or alarm system. The following findings relate to local authority, housing association and Abbeyfield schemes as no information was available on this subject for almshouse schemes.

2.38 Figure 2.5 shows that almost three-quarters of specialised units are covered by both an alarm system and warden support. Nearly all of this is in sheltered housing schemes which require a warden and a system for calling him or her. Wardens only (1%) and alarm only (5%) schemes are rare, and the remaining fifth (20%) of the stock is not covered by any form of support or emergency cover. Almost all of this is in Category 1 schemes where warden support and alarm systems are optional.

Type of provider

2.39 Just over nine-tenths of Abbeyfield schemes are covered by both warden and alarm support, with most of the remainder being warden only (Table 2.14 in Appendix 3). In contrast, a fifth of local authority and 13% of housing association specialised units have no warden or alarm cover at all. Both these providers, however, have substantial amounts of Category 1 accommodation and over three-quarters (77%) of Category 1 housing has no warden or alarm support.

Scheme-based and centrally-based alarm and warden provision

2.40 An alarm system can be either scheme based or centrally based or some combination of the two, depending upon when a warden is on or off duty. Scheme-based alarms tend to be connected to the accommodation occupied by a resident warden on a scheme-by-scheme basis and centrally-based alarms are

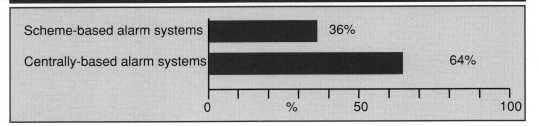

Figure 2.6 National provision of subsidised specialised housing for elderly people by Type of alarm (percentages based on un-grossed figures)

Scheme-based alarm systems — 36%

Centrally-based alarm systems — 64%

connected to a central control unit, covering a large number of schemes in a local area with mobile wardens. (In those few cases, where there is a combination of the two types of alarm systems, these have been counted as scheme-based).

2.41   Figure 2.6 shows that schemes that are linked to centrally-based systems outnumber those linked to scheme-based systems by approximately two to one. This varies, however, by type of provider (see Table 2.15 in Appendix 3) with local authorities being much more likely to have centrally-based alarm systems than any other type of provider and Abbeyfields relying almost exclusively on scheme-based alarm systems. Between the two extremes, roughly a third of housing association schemes are covered by centrally-based alarm systems, with the majority still being supported by a scheme-based warden.

Planned provision

Nationally

2.42   On the basis of responses from providers, national provision was projected to increase by 13,440 units in 1990/91, which is equivalent to an annual 2.6% expansion in the stock of specialised dwellings for elderly people.

2.43   Of this planned change in provision, the largest proportion (45%) of new units are in Category 2 schemes, 24% are in Category 1.5 and 18% in Category 2.5 accommodation. Thus, by definition, over four- fifths of new accommodation will be provided with alarm and warden support of some kind (with or without communal facilities). If, however, these planned increases are looked at in terms of what they represent as a proportion of the current stock in each category of accommodation, the picture is very different. Very sheltered housing emerges as the type of accommodation with the largest increase in provision (21%) and Category 1 accommodation with the smallest (1%). In between, Category 1.5 housing shows a 2.7% increase on its current stock and Category 2 a 2.4% expansion in provision.

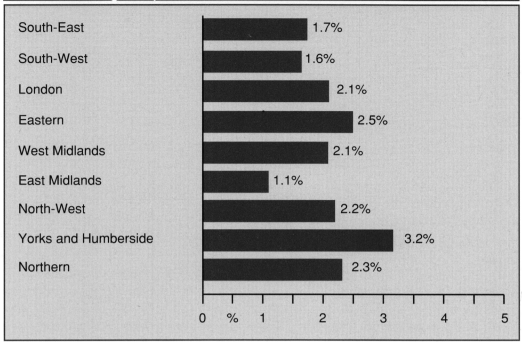

Figure 2.7 Regional planned provision of subsidised specialised housing for elderly people: percentage increases in the total stock (percentages based on un-grossed figures)

South-East	1.7%
South-West	1.6%
London	2.1%
Eastern	2.5%
West Midlands	2.1%
East Midlands	1.1%
North-West	2.2%
Yorks and Humberside	3.2%
Northern	2.3%

Regionally

2.44   At the regional level, Yorkshire and Humberside has the largest percentage increase in its current stock and East Midlands the smallest amount of growth (Figure 2.7). Planned increase in provision also varies by type of accommodation within region. As Table 2.16 shows, Category 1 accommodation accounts for almost a quarter of all expansion in the numbers of dwellings in Eastern region, but none of the planned increase in North-West region.

2.45   In terms of growth in the numbers of dwellings in a particular type of accommodation, very sheltered or Category 2.5 accommodation demonstrates the most rapid expansion across all regions. In fact, Yorkshire and Humberside is increasing its supply of very sheltered housing in one year by 50% and the North-West by 36%. In both cases, however, this is from a small base. In contrast, in London and South- West where provision is, by comparison, much higher, there is significantly less growth in the stock (11% and 9% respectively).

Table 2.16 Regional planned provision of subsidised specialised housing for elderly people by Category of accommodation (percentages based on un-grossed figures)

Col%s/ Row%s	Category of accommodation					Total
	1	1.5	2	2.5	Other	
S. East	88	269	562	442	87	1,448
	7%	8%	9%	19%	18%	11%
	6%	19%	39%	31%	6%	100%
S. West	58	71	617	139	54	939
	5%	2%	10%	6%	11%	7%
	6%	8%	66%	15%	6%	100%
London	158	182	516	213	95	1,164
	13%	6%	9%	9%	19%	9%
	14%	16%	44%	18%	8%	100%
Eastern	401	41	915	398	30	1,785
	32%	1%	15%	17%	6%	13%
	23%	2%	51%	22%	2%	100%
W. Mids	42	407	689	431	34	1,603
	3%	13%	11%	18%	7%	12%
	3%	25%	43%	27%	2%	100%
E. Mids	94	49	459	138	28	768
	8%	2%	8%	6%	6%	6%
	12%	6%	60%	18%	4%	100%
N. West	-5	585	1,270	284	114	2,248
	0	18%	21%	12%	23%	17%
	0	26%	57%	13%	5%	100%
Yorks & Humb.	230	1,087	632	290	3	2,242
	18%	34%	10%	12%	1%	17%
	10%	49%	28%	13%	0	100%
Northern	192	538	430	35	48	1,243
	15%	17%	7%	2%	10%	9%
	15%	43%	35%	3%	4%	100%
England	1,258	3,229	6,090	2,370	493	13,440

Type of provider

2.46   Local authorities are likely to supply just over a half of the new provision (52%), housing associations just over two-fifths (41%) and the remainder is divided equally between Abbeyfield and almshouse societies. This shows, to some extent, a change in the profile of providers of specialised housing with registered housing associations becoming increasingly important as providers of newly-built or converted specialised housing for elderly people. Whereas, housing associations provide just under a quarter of all current specialised housing for elderly people, they represent two-fifths of all planned units in 1990/91.

2.47   Table 2.17 shows the planned provision of new units by provider organisation and type of accommodation. The largest share of the planned increase for most providers is taken up by Category 2 accommodation. Abbeyfield societies being the exception to this in that the largest part of their planned increase is in supported housing. In fact, housing associations and Abbeyfield societies are the organisations most likely to be planning to provide very sheltered or extra-care housing. Abbeyfield societies plan a 38% increase on their current stock of very sheltered units and housing associations 24% expansion. In contrast, local authorities and almshouse societies do not appear to perceive the same need for rapid expansion, with plans to increase very sheltered housing as a proportion of their current stock by 17% and 12% respectively.

Table 2.17 Planned units of subsidised specialised housing for elderly people by Category of accommodation and Type of provider (percentages based on un-grossed figures)						
	Category of accommodation					
Col%s/ Row%s	1	1.5	2	2.5	Other	Total
Local Authority	-321	2,819	3,524	830	89	6,941
	-26%	87%	58%	35%	18%	52%
	-5%	41%	51%	12%	1%	100%
Abbey- field	0	0	0	251	216	467
	0	0	0	11%	44%	4%
	0	0	0	54%	46%	100%
Housing Associa- tion	1,465	302	2,414	1,189	157	5,527
	117%	9%	40%	50%	32%	41%
	27%	6%	44%	22%	3%	100%
Alms- house	114	108	152	100	31	505
	9%	3%	3%	4%	6%	4%
	23%	21%	30%	20%	6%	100%
Total	1,258	3,229	6,090	2,370	493	13,440

2.48   There are also regional variations in planned increases by types of provider (Table 2.18). Housing associations have the largest share of the planned increase in the stock in London, the North-West and Northern regions. In fact, the dominance of non-local authority providers, including Abbeyfield and almshouse societies, is so great as to reduce the local authority contribution to the planned stock to only 18% in London. Local authorities are the major provider in all other regions, except the West Midlands, where the proportion of the planned stock to be provided by local authorities is the same as that of housing associations.

Type of accommodation

2.49   Local authorities appear to be planning to build proportionately more bungalows and fewer self-contained flats than any other provider, and almshouses seem to be moving in the opposite direction with a greater emphasis on self-contained flats at the expense of bungalows. (Table 2.19 in Appendix 3).

Table 2.18 Regional planned provision of subsidised specialised housing for elderly people by Type of provider (percentages based on un-grossed figures)

Col%s/ Row%s	Local authority	Abbeyfield	Housing Association	Almshouse	Total
S. East	904	105	340	99	1,448
	13%	23%	6%	20%	11%
	62%	7%	24%	7%	100%
S. West	580	47	234	78	939
	8%	10%	4%	15%	7%
	62%	5%	25%	8%	100%
London	213	112	721	118	1,164
	3%	24%	13%	23%	9%
	18%	10%	62%	10%	100%
Eastern	1,213	87	417	68	1,785
	18%	19%	8%	14%	13%
	68%	5%	23%	4%	100%
W. Mids	732	10	734	127	1,603
	11%	2%	13%	25%	12%
	46%	1%	46%	8%	100%
E. Mids	419	37	289	23	768
	6%	8%	5%	5%	6%
	55%	5%	38%	3%	100%
N. West	941	54	1,251	2	2,248
	14%	12%	23%	0	17%
	42%	2%	56%	0	100%
Yorks & Humb.	1,409	0	819	14	2,242
	20%	0	15%	3%	17%
	63%	0	37%	1%	100%
Northern	530	15	722	-24	1,243
	8%	3%	13%	-5%	9%
	43%	1%	58%	-2%	100%
England	6,941	467	5,527	505	13,440

2.50   There is also evidence of a change in attitudes towards non-self contained accommodation. For both Category 2 and 2.5 sheltered housing, a much higher proportion of planned provision is in the form of self-contained flats than is found in the current stock, and there is a correspondingly lower proportion of non-self contained accommodation. This would seem to be in line with residents' own preferences (Tinker, 1989 paragraph 13, p120).

The current stock compared with assessed needs

2.51   As was described in the introductory chapter, one of the main objectives of the study was to produce regionally representative estimates of need by elderly people for different housing and housing with care options. The process and data used to produce these estimates is covered in Chapter 8 – the allocation model and estimates of need. Estimates of need for various forms of specialised housing for elderly people were calculated as part of this exercise and this section compares these estimates with current levels of provision per 100 elderly households (DoE Household Projections 1993/94). Tables 2.20 and 2.21 compare the current stock of subsidised Category 2 and 2.5 housing with assessed need for these forms of accommodation amongst elderly households (similar tables are not presented for Category 1 and 1.5 accommodation, but can be easily compiled from estimates of need presented in Chapter 8).

Table 2.20 The current regional stock of subsidised Category 2 accommodation compared with assessed need (grossed-up figures)

DoE Region	1. No. of Cat. 2 units	2. No. of elderly households	3. 1. as a % of 2.	4. % of 9,000 elderly households requiring OSH	5. % difference i.e. % of house-holds in 2. with unmet need
South-East	49,449	818,385	6.04	3.0	+3.04
South-West	35,178	591,747	5.94	1.0	+4.94
London	38,023	735,802	5.17	1.7	+3.47
Eastern	44,828	627,418	7.14	2.3	+5.44
West Mids	28,228	586,016	4.82	2.0	+2.82
East Mids	31,329	431,705	7.26	2.7	+4.56
North-West	50,143	778,430	6.44	3.1	+3.34
Yorks & Humberside	27,549	571,859	4.82	2.6	+2.22
Northern	24,019	285,764	8.41	3.1	+5.31
England	328,746	5,427,127	6.06	2.4	+3.66

2.52 There is evidence of a significant over-supply of ordinary sheltered housing both nationally and in each region. For England as a whole, there are almost 4 units per 100 elderly households more than estimates of assessed need would suggest are required. For some regions – South-West, East Midlands, Eastern and Northern – this figure goes up to 5 units in excess of assessed need, but for others – Yorkshire and Humberside and West Midlands – it is lower at 2 and 3 units in excess of demand. Not all of the units counted in the national survey will be easy to let, there is growing evidence that many schemes have difficulty finding new tenants because of problems associated with their location, non-self contained accommodation and low-grade communal facilities (Barelli, 1992, Micallef, 1994). A proportion of most providers' stocks of ordinary sheltered housing is now quite old, having been constructed in the early 1960s, and needs renovation to ensure its continued use. Some allowance might be made, therefore, for possible reductions in the numbers of Category 2 sheltered housing units presented in Table 2.20 for these reasons. It is extremely doubtful, nevertheless, that this would significantly close the gap between supply and demand at the national and regional levels. It should be borne in mind, however, that this study did not specifically look at the balance of supply and assessed need for specialised housing at the local level.

Table 2.21 The current regional stock of subsidised Category 2.5 accommodation compared with assessed need (grossed-up figures)

DoE Region	1. No. of Cat. 2.5 units	2. No. of elderly households	3. 1. as a % of 2.	4. % of 9,000 elderly households requiring VSH	5. % difference i.e. % of households in 2. with unmet need
South-East	2,943	818,385	0.36	0.8	-0.45
South-West	2,064	591,747	0.35	1.2	-0.85
London	2,776	735,802	0.38	1.5	-1.12
Eastern	1,789	627,418	0.29	0.5	-0.19
West Mids	2,185	586,016	0.37	1.5	-1.13
East Mids	758	431,705	0.18	2.0	-1.82
North-West	1,137	778,430	0.15	0.7	-0.55
Yorks & Humberside	761	571,859	0.13	2.6	-2.47
Northern	369	285,764	0.13	1.3	-1.17
England	14,782	5,427,127	0.27	1.3	-1.03

2.53   In contrast to ordinary sheltered housing, there appears to be a shortage of very sheltered housing at both national and regional levels. For England, there is roughly a shortage of 1 unit per 100 elderly households. With the exception of the North-West, northern regions – Northern, Yorkshire and Humberside, East and West Midlands – seem to have a significantly greater shortage of Category 2.5 accommodation than southern regions -South-East, South-West, London and Eastern. This reflects, to a large extent, the current regional bias in the provision of very sheltered housing towards southern regions, in that some northern regions have very small amounts of very sheltered housing. It is also, however, probably a reflection of the greater numbers of households with an assessed need for very sheltered housing in Yorkshire and Humberside and the East Midlands.

2.54   One way of providing very sheltered housing is to up-grade ordinary sheltered housing with the addition of care staff and enhanced communal facilities. Several examples of this type of conversion were included in research the Department conducted on very sheltered housing in the late 1980s (Tinker, 1989). This study showed that up- grading schemes gradually by giving additional help to residents as soon as their level of physical and/or mental dependency warranted it rather than moving them on, could be successful. It may be, therefore, that one approach to overcoming the shortages of very sheltered housing would be to up-grade some under-used or surplus ordinary sheltered housing stock. This would probably require, however, significant capital and revenue investment both in terms of improving standards of accommodation and in the level of care and support services provided.

2.55   Finally, it is also possible to compare estimates of need for specialised accommodation by non-elderly disabled adults with current levels of provision of subsidised wheelchair and mobility housing/housing adapted for disabled people. Caution should be exercised, however, with these estimates – produced

Table 2.22	The current national stock of subsidised specialised housing for disabled people compared with assessed need (grossed-up figures)				
England	1. No. of units	2. No. of households containing non-elderly disabled adults	3. 1. as a % of 2.	4. % of 850 non-elderly disabled adults requiring provision	5. % difference i.e. % of house-holds in 2. with unmet need
Wheelchair housing	27,662	2,032,491	1.36	2.0	-0.64
Mobility	62,138	2,032,491	3.06	3.4	-0.34

using the allocation model described in Chapter 8 – as they are based on a relatively modest national sample of 850 households containing non-elderly disabled adults.

2.56   Table 2.22 shows these national estimates of need for subsidised wheelchair and mobility housing/housing adapted for disabled people and compares them with the proportion of all households containing non-elderly disabled people covered by current provision in England. This shows a slight shortfall in the availability of places in wheelchair housing of 0.6 units for every 100 households containing non-elderly disabled adults. There is not, however, the same degree of shortfall in the supply of other disabled dwellings – mobility housing/housing adapted for disabled people. It should be noted, however, that the actual shortfalls in wheelchair and mobility/adapted housing are probably slightly lower than these estimates. This is because any limitation in activity is counted within the national estimate of numbers of households containing non-elderly disabled adults taken from the Census and used in Table 2.20. In contrast, as is discussed in Chapter 7, this study used a more focused definition of disability based on limitations in performing a specific set of activities. Unfortunately, there are no published national estimates of the number of non-elderly disabled adult households using this more focused definition.

3 Comparative costs of housing provision for elderly people

Introduction

3.1 It is advisable to consider the cost-effectiveness of different options for meeting housing or housing with care needs in order to ensure that limited capital and revenue resources are used to the maximum advantage. For example, it is important to establish the broad range of costs of options for elderly people at the same level of physical or mental frailty, so that expensive solutions are not automatically provided without looking at equally effective and cheaper alternatives. It was with this in mind, that the study included specific costings exercises to examine the comparative costs of different types of specialised housing for elderly people and maintaining an elderly person in non-specialised or mainstream housing in the community. No equivalent information was collected on the costs of housing and housing with care options for disabled people. Since the research was also only concerned with the costs of subsidised housing provision for elderly people, no information was collected on the costs of sheltered housing for sale.

3.2 Before describing the results of these costings exercises in detail, it is necessary to discuss some methodological issues which cut across the analysis of the data collected.

Methodological issues relating to costs

Previous research

3.3 The methodology used for producing estimates of the costs of different housing and housing with care options for elderly people was based upon costings methodologies used in two previous Departmental studies – 'Staying at Home: Helping Elderly people' (Tinker, 1984) and 'An Evaluation of Very Sheltered Housing' (Tinker, 1989). This study sought to build on and develop these methodologies by incorporating the following modifications:

i. the capital cost of mainstream housing occupied by elderly people in the community was calculated by using information from the DoE/Halifax indices for market valuations, a secondary analysis of data from the English House Condition Survey 1986 (up-rated to 1992/93 costs – see paragraph 3.9) for costs of major repairs required to bring homes up to an acceptable standard and a specially commissioned study of benchmark costs of house adaptations to enable an elderly person to remain at home;

ii. the revenue costs of mainstream housing were obtained through asking elderly occupants themselves about their expenditure on items such as heating, lighting, minor repairs and rates;

iii. costs of informal care received by elderly people in mainstream housing were produced using estimates of time spent in providing care given by carers themselves in combination with a `notional' housing wage based on wardens' and home helps' salaries. These figures have been included in the analysis of the costs of maintaining an elderly person at home;

iv. lastly, a different dependency or physical/mental frailty scaling mechanism was used for this study. Instead of using the Leeds dependency scale it was decided to adopt the Clackmannan/Townsend scale of dependency. Descriptions of both of these scales are given in the introductory chapter.

The components of costs

3.4   In order to identify the costs of various housing and housing with care options, it was decided to look at *five* broad components of expenditure, which together represent the total cost of provision. These were the:

i. *capital cost* of the accommodation occupied by elderly people, converted to an annual `notional' rent figure. This included acquisition and works costs, professional fees and the capital cost of major repairs and adaptations to enable elderly people to remain at home;

ii. *annual revenue expenditure* (i.e. maintenance and running costs) for housing lived in by elderly people. This included the revenue cost of staff in specialised housing schemes, standard maintenance and repair costs, heating, electricity and food costs;

iii. *cost of the health and social care services* consumed by elderly people;

iv. *cost of informal care* received by elderly people living in general as opposed to specialised housing in the community; and,

v. *value of state benefits and allowances* paid to elderly people.

3.5   Data on all of these sources of costs was collected for elderly people living in general housing in the community. For elderly people living in specialised housing no data was obtained on the costs of any informal care they received for the reasons given in paragraph 3.8v (a) below. More detailed information about what was included under each of these five expenditure headings and how it was obtained can be found in reports no. 2, 3 and 4 (see Appendix 1) on the costings exercises for the study. The capital cost or `notional' rent figure, however, needs some further explanation here. To derive 'notional' rent, the capital cost per person of the dwelling occupied plus any necessary repairs and adaptations was discounted using a standard interest rate of 8% and an expected property life of 60 years if properties were built post 1914, and 40 years for pre-1919 dwellings. This method of valuation was intended to be consistent with two previous costings exercises on housing options for elderly people carried out by the Department and referred to in paragraph 3.3 above.

Cost measurement

3.6   All costs presented within this chapter and most of those within the individual reports on the costings exercises are based on 'per elderly person per annum' figures. The costs associated with maintaining an elderly person at home are divided by all elderly members of the household to produce per person per annum figures. This is to ensure comparability with per person per annum figures for specialised housing options which are produced through dividing costs by all residents of schemes as opposed to all households within schemes.

3.7   The two main costs measures of housing options used throughout this study are the:

    a. *Gross Resource Cost* (the sum of paragraph 3.4 i, ii and iii); and

    b. *Gross Resource Cost plus Transfer payments plus Informal Care costs.*

3.8   The reasons for choosing to examine gross resource costs instead of simply public sector costs are as follows:

    i. gross resource costs allow the most straightforward comparisons to be made of the total costs of provision, irrespective of who is paying;

    ii. although public sector costs can be calculated on the basis of the information collected these would show overwhelmingly that, in the majority of cases, the costs of options enabling elderly people to stay at home are considerably cheaper to the public purse than the costs of specialised housing options;

    iii. there was considerable variation in the extent of financial assistance elderly people received towards their housing and care costs and this made it difficult to disentangle expenditure through private or public funds at the level of the individual. This was particularly true for expenditure by elderly people living at home on heating, lighting, rates and food. Net costs of provision were, therefore, difficult to produce;

Certain types of costs, however, have to be looked at separately either because they create double-counting or because they are difficult to measure accurately:

iv.　　gross resource costs plus transfer payments or welfare benefits enable comparisons to be made of the different amounts of financial support elderly people receive in different forms of housing and housing with care. Transfer payments, moreover, can be a costly element of housing and housing with care options for elderly people. They have to be looked at separately from gross resource costs, however, since to include them would result in double-counting. Most of the revenue costs of running specialised housing schemes are paid for through rent which, in turn, is paid for through benefits received by elderly residents. To have included welfare benefits in gross resource costs would have meant that running costs were accounted for twice in the costs of schemes;

v.　　gross resource costs plus transfer payments and informal care can be considered to approximate the full economic cost of options to enable an elderly person to remain at home. Informal care costs are, however, not readily identifiable and cannot be easily measured. They should, therefore, be examined separately from capital, revenue and domiciliary care costs. There are three further reasons, moreover, why informal care costs should be treated with extreme caution, and certainly differently from the other elements of costs in each of the housing options:

a. it is very difficult to make true like-for-like comparisons between informal care taking place in specialised housing schemes and informal care received by elderly people in ordinary, mainstream housing in the community. Although informal care is received by residents in sheltered housing schemes, it can come from a wide variety of sources, ranging from relatives to the resident or non-resident warden. It can also be restricted in a way that informal care provided to elderly people in mainstream or ordinary housing is not. For instance, wardens may not be allowed to do anything more than collect pensions or some shopping for their residents, leaving formal care services to provide personal support. Therefore, simply looking at the costs of informal care in staying at home options for elderly people may be misleading, since it overstates the costs of these options in comparison with specialised housing;

b. some elements of informal care costs do involve direct expenditure on the part of the carer or the person being cared for. For example, carers can often pay bills, buy household items, such as fridges or cookers, or pay for repairs and maintenance. Elderly people can also use attendance allowances to pay for their informal care. Many elements, however, such as the vast majority of the time spent in providing support by a carer, do not involve any direct monetary cost in the same way as public expenditure on health and social care support services or welfare benefits. The opportunity cost of lost career earnings by carers has been taken into account in informal care costs, but it is difficult to quantify what `economic good' they would have produced in non-work time they currently spend in providing care;

c. there is no generally accepted method for producing informal care costs, unlike some of the other costings in the exercise. One of the main problems covered in some detail in Appendix 3 of the individual report on the costs of maintaining an elderly person at home (no. 3), is in reconciling statements made by carers about the support they provide with statements made by elderly dependants about the amount of care they receive. In this study, carers' estimates of support were up to 88% greater than the estimates given by elderly dependants. Some attempts was made to reconcile these two perceptions of the amount of care provided and received, but inevitably they had to be very imprecise.

For these reasons, while gross resource costs plus state benefits and informal care costs are commented upon in this Chapter, it is proposed that the more reliable basis for comparison of the relative costs of different housing and housing with care options for elderly people is the gross resource cost only.

3.9   Finally, it should be noted that all costs presented in this chapter are for 1992-93. Details of the methods for up-rating historical costs are given in the individual reports on the costings exercises.

Housing and care costs

3.10   The costings exercises within this study were designed to answer the broad question of what are the most cost-effective forms of housing provision for elderly people, irrespective of who is paying. The study, therefore, usually refers to the costs of housing options for elderly people rather than to housing costs and care costs. Some of these options will involve purely housing inputs (although, even in these cases, it is difficult to be certain as some of the capital costs of schemes can be paid for by social services or health), others will require a combination of housing and care inputs. In the combined housing with care options, it would not be easy to separate fully housing and care costs for, say, revenue expenditure. Both housing associations and local authorities have some permanent staff – primarily care assistants – performing nursing and personal care support tasks, often funded through social services budgets. Both housing associations and local authorities also have wardens who undertake landlord/caretaker, counselling and support and nursing/personal care tasks. What proportion of their time, however, is spent in performing these activities and, therefore, how expenditure on staff costs should be allocated between housing and care functions is extremely difficult to ascertain.

Non-quantifiable costs and benefits

3.11   In any costings analysis there will be sources and aspects of expenditure which are extremely difficult to quantify, and some which cannot be quantified because relevant data is not collected. In this study, a decision was taken early on not to attempt to quantify central management costs or to measure the quality of care on offer in schemes as part of any assessment of cost-effectiveness.

Central management costs: these were excluded from this costings analysis for two main reasons -

a. what is included in general supervision and management costs is extremely variable from one local authority or housing association to another. For example, Departmental research on the costs of local authority housing management (Price Waterhouse, 1992) found that allocated central costs e.g. relating to services supplied to the housing department by other parts of the local authority, could vary from 11% to 46% of general supervision and management costs. The research found that the degree to which central costs bear upon direct housing management costs is related to the way in which a local authority is organised to deliver services. Some housing departments, for example, buy in computing services but others have them in-house. In some cases, activities such as the maintenance of the waiting lists can be undertaken outside the housing department. It is extremely difficult, therefore, to compare central management costs on a consistent basis within providers, let alone across providers. Added to this, are the difficulties of separating central management costs for the general purpose stock from supervision and management costs for the specialised stock;

b. it is debateable if the inclusion of central management costs would significantly (if at all) change the conclusion of the comparison between the relative revenue costs of local authority sheltered housing schemes and housing association sheltered housing schemes. Apart from the largest housing association providers of sheltered housing (which probably have reasonably large staffing, office equipment and premises overheads), most housing associations are small in scale and, therefore, would not benefit from the same economies of scale that local authorities enjoy.

Quality of care offered to elderly people: the quality of care on offer in specialised housing schemes was not looked at primarily because of the inherent difficulties in measuring standards of care. One measure might be satisfaction but, from interviews with residents conducted at the same time as costings exercise (see Chapter 5), there is no major difference in overall satisfaction levels between tenants of housing association and local authority schemes. Another measure might be the numbers of hours spent by wardens and carers with each resident. However, a recent study (DoE unpublished) of the activities performed by wardens in local authority sheltered housing and the average time taken to perform these functions, found that only 6% of a warden's time was taken up with nursing and personal care tasks. It is unlikely that the situation for housing association sheltered housing wardens would be very different. It would also be surprising if the amount of time devoted by each care assistant to each tenant (say, on average, 2-3 hours per week) in housing association schemes would be very different from the combined amount of time offered by health and social care services (e.g. two hours of a home help once a week and one hour of a district nurse once a fortnight) for tenants of local authority schemes. Lastly, what one elderly person might call a high standard of care, another might view as too intensive and oppressive, denying them privacy and independence. It would be extremely difficult to reconcile these two opposing views of the quality of care.

The costs of specialised housing

Methodology and response rates

3.12   Figures for the costs of providing different forms of subsidised specialised housing are derived from two main sources:

> a. financial questionnaires were sent to providers of 940 subsidised specialised housing schemes for elderly people. Half were local authority run schemes and the remainder were housing association, Abbeyfield and almshouse society schemes. In total, some 73% of providers responded with costs data for their schemes. Not all questionnaires, however, were fully completed and, in particular, the capital section was poorly completed by all types of provider. The main reasons for this were that:

> > i.   the data was not available because of the way capital is accounted for in organisations, particularly local authorities;

> > ii.   there was limited staff time to track down the financial information, a great proportion of which would have been either archived or (in some cases) destroyed;

> > iii. collecting the information required for local authority schemes sometimes required considerable co-ordination of input between housing, social services and health authorities.

> Despite this, two-thirds of respondents were able to supply fully completed questionnaires, resulting in a sample size of approximately 460 schemes. This breaks down by DoE region, type of scheme and provider as follows:

Region		Type of provider	
South-East	16%	Local authorities	33%
South-West	10%	Housing associations	45%
London	9%	Abbeyfield societies	16%
Eastern	13%	Almshouse societies	6%
West Midlands	10%	**Category of scheme**	
East Midlands	11%	Category 1	11%
North-West	12%	Category 1.5	5%
Yorks & Humberside	9%	Category 2	61%
Northern	10%	Category 2.5	8%
		Other spec. housing	15%

The sample is, therefore, reasonably representative of the stock of subsidised specialised housing, as judged by these three aspects of provision. The schemes studied, however, are a cross-section and included varying proportions of large and small, purpose- built and converted, new and old schemes. In view of this, some caution must be exercised in applying findings based on average costs to particular schemes or types of schemes. Some caution should also be exercised with results broken down by type of provider for categories of schemes where there is a small sample size e.g. Category 2.5. Having said that, the sample of very sheltered schemes in this study is slightly larger than the previous Departmental study of extra-care housing for both local authority and housing association/Abbeyfield society providers. Whilst capital and revenue costs were collected for Category 1.5 and 'other' specialised housing schemes, moreover, findings below are only presented for Category 1, 2 and 2.5 accommodation. These three forms of provision represent the full range of specialised housing for elderly people. They are also more likely to encompass schemes with broadly similar characteristics than Category 1.5 and 'other' specialised accommodation, where extremes in provision are more common and may unduly influence average costs;

b. interview surveys with approximately 3,600 residents of the specialised housing schemes where cost information was obtained through the financial questionnaire. These interviews were designed to collect data on the type and frequency of health and social care services residents consumed and the level of state benefits they received. Details of this sample are given in Chapter 5.

Capital costs or 'notional' rents

3.13   Capital costs or notional rents per person per annum rise steadily from £4,289 for Category 1 accommodation to £4,843 for Category 2 and £5,379 for Category 2.5 or very sheltered housing. This pattern of increasing costs, however, becomes less clear when looked at by type of provider (Table 3.1). Housing associations and Almshouses seem to be building schemes with more communal facilities and catering for elderly people with a higher level of dependency, at a lower cost than schemes for elderly people who are fully independent. For the most part, moreover, local authorities appear to have built specialised accommodation at a lower unit capital cost than other providers.

Table 3.1 Notional rent (£ per person per annum) by Category of accommodation and Type of provider				
	Local authority	Housing Association	Abbeyfield	Almshouse
Cat. 1 housing	3,717	4,539	0	4,788
Cat. 2 housing	4,565	5,052	3,341	4,376
Cat 2.5 housing	5,041	4,529	7,073	0
All schemes	4,440	5,060	4,613	4,719

3.14   Some explanations for these differences can be found in the profile of the housing stock within the sample of schemes covered by the study. Tables 3.2 and 3.3 in Appendix 3 show the type and size of accommodation provided by local authorities, housing associations, Abbeyfield and almshouse societies within the three categories of specialised housing. Almshouse Category 1 accommodation is more likely to contain 2 and 3-bed units, houses and bungalows than Almshouse Category 2 accommodation and this size difference might be part of the explanation for the higher capital costs of the former in comparison with the latter type of provision. Although, clearly, it is not the only explanation, as the scale of the difference in the size of Almshouse Category 1 and 2 stock, would suggest that there should be a much greater difference in costs than approximately £400 per person per annum.

3.15   A similar size-related explanation might be offered for the marginal difference in costs between housing association Category 1 and 2.5 accommodation. A problem arises, however, in relation to Category 1 and 2 schemes. Whilst housing association Category 1 accommodation contains more 2-bed units than Category 2 accommodation, the latter schemes are more costly on a per person per annum basis than the former. This requires a further explanation and the answer may lie in the age of the stock under consideration since space standards differ between schemes built pre-1980 and those built post-1980, when the standards set out in Circular 82/69 Housing Standards and Costs: accommodation specially designed for old people ceased to be mandatory. All capital costs were up-rated to 1992-93 prices, but if average costs were lower because schemes were generally smaller in the 60s and 70s, then the up-rating mechanism does not allow for this. The age-profile of housing association Category 1 accommodation is likely to be slightly older than the age profile of housing association Category 2 accommodation. Thus, despite differences in the numbers of large 2-bed units in each stock, the lower space standards would tend to pull down the average capital costs of Category 1 schemes. By itself, however, this is probably still not an adequate explanation of the higher capital cost of housing association Category 2 accommodation.

3.16   It is suggested, therefore, that a further factor in the capital cost of schemes is the type of accommodation and communal facilities provided. Schemes consisting of bungalows, although generally more expensive than flats, can sometimes be cheaper than flats with lifts. This factor could be at work in increasing the unit capital costs of housing association Category 2 schemes, along with the requirement to provide costly communal facilities in ordinary sheltered housing: this is something which is optional in Category 1 accommodation. The influence of this factor and lower space standards could also be the reason for the lower than expected difference in the capital costs of Almshouse Category 1 and 2 accommodation and the only marginal difference in costs between housing association Category 1 and 2.5 housing.

3.17   Turning to the finding that local authorities have, on the whole, built specialised housing at a lower unit cost than other providers, it seems likely that all three of these factors have a part to play in explanation. This finding changes, therefore, to some extent, depending upon the type and age of accommodation being considered. For example, the annual capital cost or notional rent (see paragraph 3.5) of a place in housing association very sheltered housing is approximately £500 cheaper than the capital cost of a place in local authority very sheltered housing. In comparison with housing associations, moreover, the older profile of the local authority stock (Table 3.4 in Appendix 3) probably makes a significant difference to costs through lower space standards: almost one in five local authority Category 2 schemes were built before 1971 compared with one in twenty-five housing association Category 2 schemes.

Revenue costs

3.18   As with capital costs, there is a clear pattern of rising revenue costs with increases in the physical or mental frailty of the elderly people for which schemes are designed. Average costs per person per annum increase from £709 in Category 1 schemes to £1,023 for Category 2 and £5,237 for Category 2.5 or very sheltered housing.

3.19   These differences in revenue costs are mainly related to the level of emergency cover and care support and, hence, the staff resources required for each category of accommodation. The main difference between Category 1 and 2 accommodation is the support and emergency cover provided by a resident or non-resident warden. In Category 2.5 or very sheltered housing, there are additional costs for care staff and the provision of meals to add to the average revenue expenditure for Category 2 schemes. These differences in staffing requirements are well illustrated by Table 3.5, which shows average full-time equivalent staff numbers per 100 residents.

Table 3.5 Average number of full-time equivalent staff per 100 residents by Category of accommodation						
Category of accommodation						
	Cat 1	**Cat 1.5**	**Cat 2**	**Cat 2.5**	**Other**	**Nat. avge**
Average staff per 100 elderly people	3.9	5.4	9.0	43	31	14

3.20   Unlike capital costs, however, a pattern of rising revenue costs with the increased frailty of elderly people being catered for applies to all providers (Table 3.6). The scale of the increase in costs between categories of accommodation is, nevertheless, very different for local authorities compared with housing associations and Abbeyfield societies. Whereas local authority very sheltered schemes cost approximately £1,700 per person per annum more to run than local authority ordinary sheltered schemes, the difference in costs between these two types of provision for housing associations and Abbeyfield societies is in the order of £6,000. Having said that, these revenue costs figures for housing association and Abbeyfield society Category 2.5 accommodation

---

[9]   Many housing association and Abbeyfield society very sheltered or extra-care schemes are registered as residential care homes with the local social services under the Registered Homes Act 1984.

are distorted by mixing registered with non-registered schemes[9] – registration imposes higher than normal staffing levels. Based on the limited data available, the adjusted figures (Table 3.6) show that non-registered housing association very sheltered or Category 2.5 schemes are only, in fact, £1,900 more expensive than housing association ordinary sheltered or Category 2 schemes.

3.21   Table 3.6 also shows that local authorities have lower revenue costs per person per annum for their specialised accommodation for elderly people than other providers. For instance, the revenue cost of a place in local authority ordinary or Category 2 sheltered housing is roughly £290 less than equivalent housing association accommodation, £770 less than almshouses and £2,740 less than Abbeyfield societies. There is an even greater difference for very sheltered housing although, as pointed out above, other providers' average revenue costs are affected by schemes registered as residential homes. Once again, based on the limited data available, the figure for housing association schemes, excluding registered homes, is, nevertheless, still £500 more expensive per person per annum than local authority schemes. This finding confirms the results of earlier research by the Department into very sheltered housing (Tinker, 1989, p112, Table 10.3).

Table 3.6 Revenue costs (£ per person per annum) by Category of accommodation and Type of provider

	Local Authority	Housing Association	Abbeyfield	Almshouse
Cat. 1 housing	291	669	0	1,040
Cat. 2 housing	838	1,125	3,574	1,603
All Cat. 2.5 housing	2,514	7,276	9,929	0
Non Regd. Cat 2.5 housing	0	3,026	[1]	0

[1] All Abbeyfield Category 2.5 schemes in the sample were registered as residential care homes.

3.22   The main reason local authority revenue costs are lower than those of other providers is because of lower staffing levels in their schemes. Table 3.7 in Appendix 3 shows average numbers of full-time equivalent staff per 100 residents for local authority and housing association providers by category of accommodation. It is clear from this, that, even for those categories of accommodation not affected by the staffing requirements of registration as a residential home, housing associations are likely to have a higher staff to resident ratio than local authorities. For example, within ordinary sheltered or Category 2 accommodation, housing associations employ, on average, three more full-time equivalent staff members per 100 residents than local authorities.

3.23   There could be a number of explanations for this difference in staffing levels: firstly, levels of care may be lower in local authority schemes; secondly, local authorities may obtain care and support for their residents from other sources; thirdly, local authority residents are generally less frail and require a lower level of support; and, fourthly, local authority wardens are allocated to larger schemes. On the first of these possible explanations, from other elements of this study (see Chapter 5 on the residents survey) there is no reason to believe that local authorities are providing a lower level of care. Data from interviews with residents of all types of specialised housing also shows that local authority tenants tend to be slightly more frail than their counterparts in housing association schemes and just as frail as elderly people in Abbeyfield and almshouse society schemes. If, moreover, reasonably dependent elderly people can be supported or provided with emergency cover by one warden working in a large scheme of 30-40 units, this would seem to be a more efficient use of resources than one warden covering 10-20 units. One further possible explanation is addressed in the next section of this chapter.

Health and social care services

3.24   Table 3.8 shows the costs of health and social services such as home helps, district nurses and occupational therapists provided to residents of specialised housing on a per person per annum basis. Normally, these services visit residents in schemes and are, therefore, not provided by permanent members of staff. It should also be noted that health services are provided free of charge and, whilst social care services can be charged for, this is normally done on a non-means tested basis, such as a flat rate charge for meals.

Table 3.8 Costs of health and social care services received by elderly residents (£ per person per annum) of specialised housing: Category of accommodation by Type of provider				
	Local Authority	Housing Association	Abbeyfield	Almshouse
Cat. 1 housing	448	397	0	408
Cat. 2 housing	890	469	0	433
All Cat. 2.5 housing	923	1,359	684	0
Total	836	532	367	415

3.25   Average annual costs of health and social care services, not surprisingly, rise with the increasing frailty of residents being catered for by different categories of accommodation. Average annual costs per resident go up from £431 in Category 1 schemes to £1,014 in Category 2.5 or very sheltered schemes. There is no change in this pattern across the four providers.

3.26   There are, however, several differences between the providers in the amount of health and social care services consumed by residents. Overall, local authority residents of specialised housing take up the most health and social care services and Abbeyfield residents the least. Within type of accommodation, the costs of statutory care services consumed by residents are also higher for local authority Category 1 and 2 accommodation than for any other provider. In fact, the average cost of services received by local authority residents of ordinary sheltered housing is almost twice as much as the cost of services received by residents of other providers. This tends to support the possibility that local authorities are able to achieve lower annual revenue costs per person through substitution of on-site or permanent care staff costs with visiting domiciliary carers. The only exception to this pattern is housing association Category 2.5 or very sheltered housing where the average annual costs of health and social care services taken up by residents is £1,359 per person. This compares with a figure of £923 for local authority very sheltered housing schemes.

State benefits

3.27   Table 3.9 in Appendix 3 shows the cost of state benefits received by elderly residents of specialised housing. State benefits include basic state pensions, low and high rate attendance allowances, severe disability premium, mobility and invalid care allowance[10]. The Table shows that, whilst the receipt of state benefits is related to level of dependency, the increase in average costs is not very significant across different categories of accommodation. For example, residents of very sheltered housing appear to receive benefits worth 6% more in cost terms than elderly people in Category 1 accommodation. This picture is more or less the same at every level of physical and/or mental dependency, that is, no particular advantage is enjoyed by residents at the same level of dependency across different types of specialised housing. As might be expected, however, there is a reasonably large difference in the value of state benefits received by elderly people at different levels of dependency in the same scheme. For example, tenants of very sheltered housing in the Clackmannan G grouping receive benefits worth almost a third (32%) more than very sheltered tenants in the Clackmannan C grouping.

The costs of maintaining an elderly person at home

Methodology and response rates

3.28   Figures for the costs of maintaining and elderly person at home come from two main sources:

> a. an interview survey covering a regionally representative sample of 8,969 elderly households living in the community. This collected information on the type of housing in which elderly people live, the

---

[10]   Data on receipt of housing benefit and income support was collected but the numbers of residents saying they received these benefits were so low as to suggest some misunderstanding by those providing this information. This also applied in the elderly in the community survey data used for the costs of state benefits as an element of maintaining elderly people at home.

running costs of their housing, the range and frequency of health and social care services which they receive and benefit payments;

b. an interview survey covering a nationally representative sample of 832 informal carers. These carers were asked about the level of physical, financial and other care support they provided to elderly dependants. From their responses, it was possible to produce broad estimates of the cost of their care. Because of significant differences, however, in estimates of the amount of financial and physical support provided by carers in their interviews and similar estimates for the amount of support received by elderly people given in their interviews, these cost figures should be treated with caution. Similar problems with major discrepancies in reported help and support have been experienced in other studies, (Perkins, Berthoud and Marsh, 1994 forthcoming).

Other information – most notably a benchmark study of the costs of aids and adaptations – was collected as part of this research, but these two surveys provided the main bulk of the costing data used.

Capital costs or `notional' rents

3.29   There appear to be three main drivers of notional rent or average capital cost per elderly person per annum: the type of dwelling, the size of the household and the tenure of the accommodation.

3.30   The notional rent or average capital cost per person per annum of housing occupied by elderly people varies significantly from £6,555 for a detached house to £3,047 for a terraced house and £2,661 for a flat. These capital costs are derived from calculating the combined value of the accommodation occupied plus the repairs and adaptations required to enable an elderly person to remain at home. The vast majority of the cost, however, is the cost of the dwelling itself – between 95% and 97% – rather than any repairs or adaptations required.

3.31   Figure 3.1 shows the average notional rent of accommodation occupied by single elderly people compared with elderly couples and the national average. It reveals that elderly couples live in more expensive accommodation than single elderly people. The notional rent for an elderly couple (£2,712) is almost half the notional rent or average annual capital cost of housing occupied by single elderly people (£4,073). The implied notional rent if a single person were living in accommodation occupied by elderly couples is £5,424, which is roughly a third more expensive than the average cost of the accommodation actually occupied by single elderly people. This is explained, to a large extent, by the form of housing occupied by these two types of household and its tenure. More than twice as many single elderly people live in flats and maisonettes than elderly couples, and three-fifths of elderly couples live in houses compared with two-fifths of single elderly people. A significantly lower proportion of single

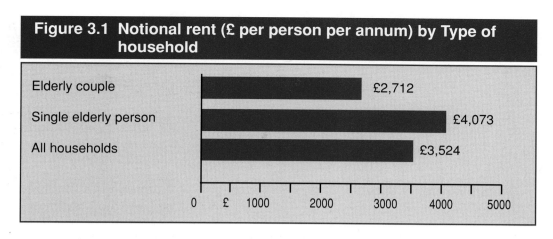

Figure 3.1 Notional rent (£ per person per annum) by Type of household

Elderly couple	£2,712
Single elderly person	£4,073
All households	£3,524

elderly people, moreover, are owner-occupiers (see paragraphs 4.26 and 4.29 in Chapter 4).

3.32   Figure 3.2 shows the average notional rent of housing lived in by elderly people by tenure. In general, council rented properties have the lowest market value, with an average notional rent of £2,316 per person per annum. In contrast, owner occupied properties have the highest capital values and, therefore, the highest notional rent at £4,321 per person per annum. In part, these differences will be due to the type and size of housing within each form of tenure. For example, the local authority stock tends to include a lower proportion of houses and a higher proportion of purpose-built flats than the owner-occupied sector. Average dwelling size as measured by the internal floor area and number of habitable rooms is also slightly higher in the owner-occupied and private rented sectors.

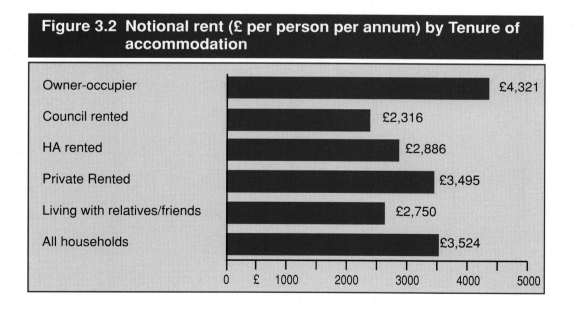

Figure 3.2 Notional rent (£ per person per annum) by Tenure of accommodation

Owner-occupier	£4,321
Council rented	£2,316
HA rented	£2,886
Private Rented	£3,495
Living with relatives/friends	£2,750
All households	£3,524

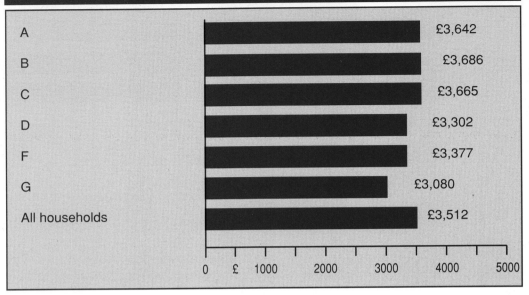

Figure 3.3 Notional rent (£ per person per annum) by level of dependency

A	£3,642
B	£3,686
C	£3,665
D	£3,302
F	£3,377
G	£3,080
All households	£3,512

3.33 Figure 3.3 shows the average notional rent of property occupied by elderly people at each level of dependency. It is clear that, whilst there is some variation in notional rents, the differences from one level of dependency to another are smaller than exist from one tenure or household type to another. The findings from a closer investigation of the profile of housing occupied by elderly people at different levels of dependency are described in the individual report (no. 3 – see Appendix 1). This more detailed analysis, however, found no clear relationship between dependency and the cost of housing occupied by the sample. A higher proportion of elderly people in dependency groups A and B live in owner occupied properties than other dependency groups (Table 3.10 in Appendix 3). Whilst approximately three-fifths (65%) of fully independent elderly people live in owner-occupied accommodation, only 46% of elderly people with some degree of dependency are owner- occupiers. A slightly higher proportion (57%) of elderly people in dependency groups A and B, moreover, live in the most expensive properties – detached houses, bungalows and semi-detached houses – compared with other dependency groups (49%). Most variations in the housing circumstances of elderly people in the different dependency groups, however, are quite small and tend also to balance each other out. For example, whilst a high proportion of elderly people in dependency group C live in the least expensive properties – terraced houses and flats/maisonettes – they are much more likely to be single person households.

Revenue costs

3.34 Similar trends emerge for housing revenue costs with the type of dwelling and the type of household being greater influences upon costs per person per annum than the dependency level of elderly people.

3.35   Revenue costs range from £725 per person per annum for a detached house to £546 for a terraced house. Electricity and gas account for almost a half (45%) of revenue costs, and larger detached houses will often require higher expenditure on heating costs than smaller flats and terraced houses. Single elderly people also incur greater expenditure per person per annum on revenue items than elderly couples. The average revenue cost of housing occupied by single elderly people is £667 per person per annum compared with £486 per person per annum for elderly couples.

3.36   There appears to be no direct link between dependency and the running costs which elderly people incur (Table 3.11 in Appendix 3). This is probably because revenue costs are more directly linked to the household type and the accommodation occupied and these two factors are balancing each other out within dependency groups. For example, low dependency elderly people are slightly more likely to live in larger detached/semi-detached houses, with associated higher revenue costs such as heating bills and minor repairs costs. They are also more likely, however, to be living with a spouse/partner which considerably reduces unit costs. In comparison, dependent elderly people have a tendency to live in smaller properties and are marginally more likely to be single person households.

Health and social care services

3.37   Figure 3.4 compares the average costs per person per annum of health and social care services consumed by single elderly people and elderly couples. Elderly people living alone are receiving more formal health and social care support than elderly people living with spouses/partners. This finding will be explored further in the next Chapter and in Chapter 6 on the survey of informal carers. Here it is simply necessary to note that the average annual cost of health and social care services received by single elderly people (£385) is roughly two and a half times more than the cost of services received by elderly couples (£149). Thus, even allowing for the effect of calculating costs on a per person per annum basis, there is still a gap between these two main types of elderly household. This is probably accounted for by the higher level of informal care

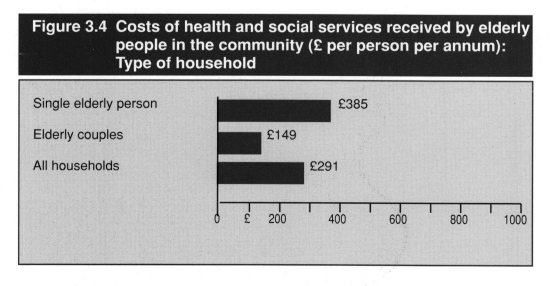

Figure 3.4 Costs of health and social services received by elderly people in the community (£ per person per annum): Type of household

Single elderly person £385
Elderly couples £149
All households £291

being undertaken by spouses and partners of elderly people. This is confirmed within the findings from the survey of informal carers (Chapter 5). Resident carers were providing much more time in care support to their dependant than non-resident carers.

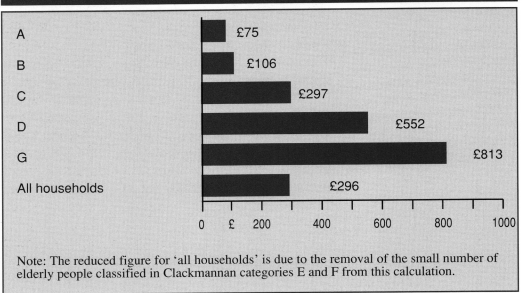

Figure 3.5 Costs of health and social services received by elderly people in the community (£ per person per annum): Level of dependency

Note: The reduced figure for 'all households' is due to the removal of the small number of elderly people classified in Clackmannan categories E and F from this calculation.

3.38   As might be expected, moreover, the unit cost of health and social care services received rises in line with increasing frailty or dependency amongst elderly people (Figure 3.5). Fully independent elderly people annually consume, on average, £75 of health and social care services, such as chiropodists and social workers, compared with £552 for elderly people in Clackmannan group D.

Informal care

3.39   As was stated earlier, this study attempted to cost informal care inputs to maintaining an elderly person at home from those inside and outside the household, such as relatives, friends and neighbours. There are three main sources of costs: firstly, the time spent in providing informal care; secondly, the direct expenditure by the carer on household goods, bills, etc.; and, thirdly, the opportunity of cost of lost career earnings. A full account of the methodology is given in individual report (no. 3 – see Appendix 1), including a description of the problems encountered in producing these costs.

3.40   The three main determinants of informal care costs are the level of dependency of the person receiving care, the type of informal carer and the type of household of which the dependant is part. On the first of these, Table 3.12 shows the cost components of informal care by a selection of different levels of

Table 3.12 Costs of informal care (£ per person per annum) by the level of dependency of the dependant

	Level of Dependency							
	C		D		G		Total	
	£	%	£	%	£	%	£	%
Time cost	2,466	88.0	4,248	94.2	5,339	97.1	4,062	93.9
Direct costs	77	2.7	74	1.6	44	0.8	70	1.6
Career costs	260	9.3	187	4.1	116	2.1	192	4.4
Total costs	2,803	100	4,509	100	5,500	100	4,324	100
Base	171		506		133		815	

physical frailty or dependency. Elderly dependants in Clackmannan group D receive informal care costing approximately £1,700 more per person per annum than those in Clackmannan group C. It is also apparent that the amount of time spent in providing informal care rises with increasing dependency. Costs associated with direct expenditure and lost career earnings, however, appear to move in the opposite direction. At a first glance, it might be thought that this is related to the type of informal carer looking after elderly people at higher levels of dependency. A higher proportion of those with extremely frail dependants might be resident – elderly spouses and partners in the same household as the dependant are more likely to be in a position to offer more time in care support than external carers. Chapter 6 describes findings which shed light on this. These findings suggest that resident carers are no more likely to be looking after elderly people at higher dependency levels than non- resident carers. Instead, at all levels of dependency, resident carers are providing more time in care support to their dependant than non- resident carers.

3.41   Table 3.13 in Appendix 3 confirms this from the viewpoint of costs. The costs of informal care received by elderly dependants of spouses or partners are significantly greater per person per annum than the costs of informal care received by elderly dependants of relatives, neighbours and friends, at all levels of dependency. In fact, elderly dependants of spouses and partners in the Clackmannan G grouping are receiving informal care costing approximately three and a half times more than elderly dependants of relatives, friends and neighbours in the same Clackmannan grouping.

3.42   Lastly, the costs of informal care by household type further confirm this finding. The costs of informal care support offered in households consisting of elderly couples (£6,149 per person per annum) is almost double that of single elderly households (£3,375 per person per annum).

State benefits

3.43   Figure 3.6 in Appendix 3 shows the average annual cost of state benefits received by elderly people in the community at different levels of dependency. It demonstrates that there is a clear relationship between the two variables – as dependency rises the cost of state benefits received also increases. The differences in costs are, however, not substantial. At the two extremes, an elderly person in Clackmannan group G received, on average, £3,461 of state benefits in 1992 compared with £2,798 for a fully independent elderly person in Clackmannan group A. (These figures do not include income support or housing benefit payments[11].) This is not surprising given that as elderly people become more frail they are increasingly eligible for benefits which are tied to severity of disability, such as attendance allowance and the severe disablement premium.

A comparison of the relative costs of housing and housing with care options for elderly people

Gross resource costs for all housing options

3.44   At all levels of dependency and assessed need, staying at home options for elderly people are considerably cheaper (as measured by gross resource costs per person per annum, excluding informal care costs and state benefits) than a move to specialised accommodation (Table 3.14 in Appendix 3). For low dependency elderly people (Clackmannan C), the specialised housing option available to them – Category 1 accommodation – is approximately £1,100 more expensive per person per annum than staying at home. For medium and high dependency elderly people, the costs of some specialised housing options, e.g. very sheltered or Category 2.5 accommodation, could be as much as £7,500 per person per annum more expensive than the costs of staying at home options.

3.45   The picture is radically different, however, for medium and high-dependency elderly people when informal carers costs and state benefits are included. Staying at home options then become more expensive than most specialised housing options, although very sheltered housing still remains the most costly option whichever measure of costs is used. Staying at home options also start to vary significantly by the level of dependency of elderly people, having previously been dominated by the notional rent of accommodation occupied. The addition of these non-accommodation costs results in the annual gross cost of maintaining an elderly person at home rising by as much as two-thirds to roughly £7,140 per annum for someone with no dependency and doubling to £13,390 for a highly dependent elderly person. This finding should be treated with extreme caution, however, for the reasons given in paragraph 3.8v above.

3.46   Table 3.14 in Appendix 3 also shows that the annual gross cost of providing a place in specialised housing increases significantly from low-to-high dependency accommodation for elderly people. For example, the annual gross resource cost of a place in very sheltered or Category 2.5 accommodation is over 75% greater than the cost of a place in ordinary or Category 2 sheltered housing. Not surprisingly, there is also considerable variation in the proportion of the gross resource costs represented by capital and revenue expenditure. Table 3.15 in Appendix 3 illustrates this and shows that revenue costs, which are principally staff costs for higher care support in accommodation, rise from 13% of gross resource costs in Category 1 accommodation to 45% in very sheltered housing. Lastly, this overall cost comparison reveals that, at comparable levels of dependency, residents of specialised housing are receiving

---

[11]   See earlier footnote 10.

health and social care services costing twice as much, and for some forms of provision three times as much, as health and social care support obtained by elderly people in ordinary, mainstream housing in the community.

Gross resource costs for specialised accommodation

3.47   Gross resource costs for specialised accommodation by type of provider are shown in Table 3.16. This demonstrates that, as far as it is practicable to make a like-for-like comparison, local authority provision is consistently cheaper across all specialised housing options for elderly people. The only exception being where almshouse Category 2 provision appears to be the cheapest, but this finding is based on a sample of two almshouse schemes compared with a sample of 120 local authority Category 2 schemes.

3.48   Table 3.17 in Appendix 3 looks at this finding in relation to elderly people at medium and high levels of dependency. It shows that the difference between the major providers – local authorities and housing associations – ranges from £540 per person per annum for elderly residents in Clackmannan group C to £445 for those in Clackmannan group D/E. Finally, Table 3.18 in Appendix 3 compares the costs of local authority Category 2 sheltered housing with housing association Category 2 accommodation for elderly people at the same level of dependency. Category 2 or ordinary sheltered housing is the dominant form of specialised housing provision for elderly people, and this shows that local authorities are able to house dependent elderly people in this type of accommodation at a cost which is £580 less expensive than housing associations.

Gross resource costs for maintaining an elderly person at home

3.49   Gross resource costs for maintaining an elderly person at home by type of dwelling occupied and household type are shown in Table 3.19 in Appendix 3. This shows that it is considerably more expensive to maintain an elderly person in detached housing. The costs of the other accommodation options are broadly comparable, although flats have a slightly lower cost due to the notional rent figure for this type of accommodation. Table A3.19 also demonstrates that the average annual gross resource cost of maintaining an elderly couple at home is approximately a third less than the costs for a single elderly person.

Table 3.16 Average gross resource cost (£ per person per annum) of subsidised specialised housing for elderly people: Category of accommodation by Type of provider

Category of accommodation	Local authorities			Housing associations			Abbeyfield societies		Almshouse societies	
	1	2	2.5	1	2	2.5	2	2.5	1	2
Notional rent	3,717	4,565	5,041	4,539	5,052	4,529	3,341	7,073	4,788	4,376
Revenue costs	291	838	2,514	669	1,125	7,276	3,574	9,926	1,040	1,063
Health and social care costs	448	890	923	397	469	1,359	684	684	408	433
Gross resource costs	4,456	6,293	8,478	5,605	6,646	13,164	7,599	17,683	6,236	5,872
State benefits	3,007	3,077	3,195	3,007	3,077	3,195	3,077	3,195	3,007	3,007
Total costs	7,463	9,370	11,673	8,612	9,723	16,359	10,676	20,878	9,243	8,949

4 A national and regional survey of elderly people in the community

4.1   At the core of any study of housing needs is a survey of the characteristics, circumstances and aspirations of the group under investigation. This programme of research contained a major interview survey with elderly people in private households to provide regionally representative data on their housing, social and financial circumstances, their state of health and level of dependency and their housing aspirations. This chapter describes the main findings from the survey and is divided into five sections: the research methodology and survey sample; the characteristics of elderly people and their households; their housing circumstances; their housing aspirations; and, their receipt of health and social care services.

4.2   The data collected on these topics has been used to allocate households to housing options appropriate to their assessed needs. This information, therefore, provides the basis for producing estimates of need for subsidised housing and housing with care provision (see Chapter 8). Before describing the findings in detail, it should be pointed out that regional level data is only reported where it is of interest and significance to the main thrust of the comments under a section heading in the chapter. Regional results are reported in greater detail in the individual report (no. 7 – see Appendix 1) for this element of the study.

Research methodology and the survey sample

4.3   The survey of elderly people in the community was conducted between August 1991 and January 1992. It was based on achieving a total of 9,000 interviews with elderly people, comprising 1,000 interviews in each of the nine DoE regions; two-thirds of the interviews were to be with people aged 75 years and over and one-third with those aged 65-74 years. This was done to avoid having a sample with insufficient numbers of households containing old elderly people i.e. those aged 75 and over, and which over-represented the young elderly i.e. those aged between 65 and 74 years old. The survey sample was then re-weighted using data on elderly households from the Labour Force Survey to restore these two age groups into the correct proportions both nationally and regionally. All tables are based on re- weighted data.

4.4   Sampling was based on a large-scale screening of randomly selected addresses drawn from the Postal Address File (PAF) in order to identify elderly household for interview. It was based on selecting a total of 500 sampling points (plus 85 reserves), with 56 sampling points in each DoE region. A total of 14,013 households were identified as containing eligible elderly respondents to represent their households. 8,969 interviews were completed, including 5,734 with elderly people aged 75 years and over. More detail about the research methodology and survey sample can be found in the individual report on this element of the programme of research.

Age and sex

4.5   Table 4.1 shows the age profile within gender of the elderly people sampled. The majority of elderly people in private households are aged between 65 and 74 years old, although over a third are aged between 75 and 84. Three-fifths of elderly people are female and this must be related to their longer life expectancy. This is also borne out by the age breakdown of elderly men and women. There are 9% fewer elderly women than elderly men aged between 65 and 74 in the survey sample but 5% more elderly women aged between 75 and 84 and 4% more aged 85 and over.

Table 4.1 Age and gender profile of elderly respondents				
Col%s/ Row%s	65-74	75-84	85+	All
Male	44	36	29	40
	61	33	6	100
Female	56	64	71	60
	52	38	10	100
Base	4,989	3,166	746	8,901
	56	36	8	100

Marital status

4.6   Just over half of elderly people (55%) are single, widowed, divorced or separated. Elderly women are more than twice as likely to be widowed (58%) than elderly men (24%). 44% of elderly people are married or co-habiting and, here the situation is reversed, with men being more than twice as likely to be married (66%) than women (30%). These findings illustrate two things, firstly, the longer life expectancy of women and, secondly, a greater likelihood for men to marry women younger than themselves.

Household type

4.7   The vast majority of elderly people (91%) live in single or two- person households (Table 4.2). In fact, overall, elderly people are just as likely to live on their own as they are to live with one other person. This varies, however, by the age and sex of elderly people. Two-thirds of elderly people aged 85 and over (68%) live alone, compared with around a third of 65-74 year olds (36%) and just over half of 75-84 year olds (55%). Women are also twice as likely to live alone (57%) than men (28%).

Row%s	Single adult aged 65-74	Single adult aged 75+	2 adults: at least 1 aged 65-74 none 75+	2 adults: at least 1 aged 75+	3 or more adults at least one aged 65+
Gender:					
Male	13	15	39	22	11
Female	25	32	18	17	7
Age of respondent:					
65-74	36	0	47	6	10
75-84	0	55	0	38	6
85+	0	68	0	22	10
Base	1,806	2,256	2,366	1,686	773
	20	25	27	19	9

Employment, income and savings, pensions and state benefits

4.8   Not surprisingly, over four-fifths of elderly people are retired (85%). Very few are in full (1%) or part-time employment (2%). Amongst those who are married or co-habiting, 4% have partners in full or part- time employment.

4.9   Table 4.3 in Appendix 3 shows the profile of household weekly income at the time of the survey by gender, age, household type and tenure. Just over a half of the households interviewed have a weekly income of £85 or less. Elderly people living on their own are much more likely to be low-income households than households with two or more people – roughly seven in ten single elderly households have a weekly income of up to £85 compared with approximately three in ten elderly people in two adult households. Income is also related to **age** – 70% of elderly people aged 85 and over have incomes of up to £85 per week compared with 58% of those aged 75-84 and 43% of elderly aged 65-74 – and **gender** – 61% of women have incomes of up to £85 per week compared with 37% of men. In contrast, just over a quarter (29%) of elderly households have a weekly income of over £115 and these tend to be two person households, where both or at least one of the household members are aged 65-74. Lastly, not surprisingly, elderly households renting their property are more likely to have lower weekly incomes of up to £85 than owner-occupiers, two-fifths of whom have weekly incomes in excess of £115.

4.10   Three-quarters of elderly respondents say that they and/or their spouse or partner have savings and investments. (Table 4.4 in Appendix 3). One in five either have none or are unwilling to talk about the extent of their savings. As with income, the amount of savings and investments elderly people possess is related to the age and gender of household members and the household type itself. Single elderly households, elderly people aged 75 or over and women are more likely to have savings and investments under £5,000. In contrast, two and three or more person elderly households, elderly people aged 65-74 and elderly men are more likely to have savings and investments worth over £5,000.

4.11   Over half the elderly households covered in the survey have someone receiving a pension from a former employer (51%). Men are more likely than women to collect pensions from a former employer (60% versus 44% of female respondents), as are people aged 65-74 compared with those aged 85 or over (57% versus 35% of respondents aged 85 plus). Occupational pensions boost the household income significantly – over twice as many elderly households with weekly incomes of more than £115 receive a pension from a former employer compared with 35% of households with incomes of up to £85 per week. Overall, the pension most frequently received, by nine in ten elderly people (91%), is the state retirement pension. Apart from this, relatively small proportions of respondents benefit from any other pensions: 5% receive a widow's state pension or private pension, 3% an invalidity pension and 2% a war disablement pension.

4.12   Table 4.5 in Appendix 3 shows the state benefits or allowances other than pensions received by age of respondent, household type and level of dependency. Just 8% of the elderly households surveyed receive income from state allowances, excluding housing benefit and income support. Some caution, however, should be exercised with regard to this finding as elderly respondents may not have been fully aware of the types and names of the allowances they received. At least two of these benefits – mobility allowance and the severe disablement allowance, moreover, are not available to those whose needs arise after retirement age. Having said that, elderly people with a high dependency level (21%), those living with friends or relatives (17%) and those aged 85 or over (15%) are most likely to receive these state allowances.

4.13   Approximately one in eight elderly households receive income support and two-thirds of those who rent their homes obtain housing benefit (Table Table 4.5 in Appendix 3)[12]. Most likely to receive income support and housing benefit are single elderly people aged 75 and over and those with medium to high dependency levels.

Health

4.14   The health and level of physical and/or mental frailty of elderly people are important considerations in their ability to cope with different housing and housing with care solutions to their needs. The survey, therefore, asked several questions designed to obtain information on these topics, some of which are based on respondents' own assessment of their state of health and others based on specific measures of performance in carrying out mobility, self-care and domestic tasks.

4.15   Three in ten elderly people are registered as disabled or have long-term illnesses or disabilities which handicap or prevent them from doing things for

---

[12]   See, however, earlier footnote 10.

themselves (Table 4.6 in Appendix 3). Registration as disabled does not vary by age, gender or household type. Instead, a clear determinant of registration seems to be the level of dependency of elderly people, with just under a third (32%) of the most frail stating they are registered compared with less than a twentieth of the least frail (4%).

4.16   By comparison, elderly peoples' perceptions of their own state of health do vary by the age of the respondent (but not by gender) and their household type as well as by their level of dependency. For example, elderly respondents aged 85 or over (not registered as disabled) are twice as likely (32%) to say they have long-term illnesses or disabilities than those aged 65-74 (16%), and those in the highest dependency grouping are approximately five times more likely to state that they have health problems than those who are fully independent.

4.17   Table 4.6 in Appendix 3 also shows that only a very small percentage of elderly people who say they are registered as disabled or have long-term illnesses or disabilities are permanently confined to a bed or chair.

4.18   Two further questions explored the nature of respondents' health problems and disabilities. Both questions required self-assessment of health problems, so some caution must be exercised, as respondents may have been unaware of medical conditions or unwilling to tell the interviewer about them. Respondents were first of all shown a list of twelve possible difficulties due to long-term health problems (Table 4.7 in Appendix 3) and then, a list of six specific illnesses and disabilities.

4.19   Three in ten elderly people say they have difficulty with steps and stairs and one in four experience breathlessness, wheezing and coughing or have difficulty bending or straightening. Similar proportions mention difficulty hearing someone talking or deafness and falling or keeping balance. Around two in five say they have none of the difficulties listed in the long term. Table 4.7 in Appendix 3 shows that many of these difficulties are more likely to be experienced by elderly people aged 85 than elderly people aged 65-74. For example, whereas nearly a half of younger elderly respondents say they have none of the difficulties listed, only one-eighth of older elderly people fall into the same category. Older elderly people seem particularly prone to falling over, experiencing difficulty hearing someone talking or deafness and having difficulty coping with steps and stairs.

4.20   The most common long-term health problem among respondents is painful joints, mentioned by two in five (40%). This problem is more likely to be found amongst women than men (46% versus 31% respectively) and amongst the very elderly (51% of those aged 85 and over). One in eight (13%) said they regularly felt pains in their chest on effort and one in twenty had sugar diabetes (5%). Almost half of the elderly people (49%) surveyed, however, had none of the long-term illnesses or disabilities listed.

Table 4.8 The Dependency profile of elderly people: by age and household type

Row%s	Clackmannan dependency					Leeds dependency				
	A/B	C	D/E	F/G	Base*	0	1-3	4-7	8-12	Base
All households	58	9	26	8	8,645	72	7	9	12	8,901
Age of respondent:										
65-74	70	6	18	7	4,866	82	6	5	7	4,989
75-84	47	11	33	8	3,050	64	9	12	15	3,166
85+	20	14	51	15	721	39	9	19	33	746
Household type:										
Single adult aged 65-74	69	8	17	6	1,746	79	7	6	7	1,806
Single adult aged 75+	42	16	35	6	2,151	57	11	14	18	2,256
2 adults: at least 1 aged 65-74 none 75+	71	4	18	7	2,307	85	5	4	7	2,366
2 adults: at least 1 aged 75+	48	7	33	12	1,647	67	8	10	15	1,686
3 adults: at least 1 aged 65+	55	4	29	12	790	70	4	8	17	773

Note *256 of the respondents could not be classified on the more complex Clackmannan scale because of missing data on their dependency forms. This applies to the base figures for Clackmannan dependency used in other tables. 8 respondents refused to state their age and 4 households could not be classified into these household types.

Dependency levels

4.21   As mentioned in the introductory chapter, the study used two measures of dependency covering the ability or inability of elderly people to perform mobility, self-care and domestic tasks, their state of mental health and whether they suffered from incontinence. They were the Clackmannan/Townsend and the Leeds scales of dependency.

4.22   Table 4.8 shows the distribution of the elderly people sampled across these two measures of dependency by the age of the respondent and the type of household. Both measures indicate that there are substantial numbers of elderly people who have no physical dependency or disability, although they differ on the proportion of the elderly population that falls into this group. For the reasons given in the introductory chapter, it is suggested that the Clackmannan/Townsend scale is probably the more accurate of the two measures. Having said that, for both measures there is a direct correlation with age: the older the elderly person, the more likely he or she is to be in higher dependency groupings. For example, whereas just over a half of those aged 85 or over are in the Clackmannan group D/E, only a third of those aged 75-84 and a sixth of those 65-74 have the same level of physical and/or mental frailty. In contrast, over a half (52%) of those elderly people aged below 75 are fully independent – Clackmannan group A – compared with a third (33%) of those aged between 75 and 84 and a seventh (14%) of those aged 85 and over.

4.23 This pattern by age is reflected in terms of household type, whereby single elderly people and respondents within two or more person households containing elderly people aged under 75 are more likely to be fully independent than those with older respondents.

Housing circumstances

Type of property

4.24 Just over half of elderly people (54%) occupy a house, a quarter (25%) live in a bungalow, and a further fifth (20%) live in a flat or maisonette, or

Table 4.9 Housing occupied by elderly people: by age, household type, tenure, region and level of dependency

Row%s	House	Bungalow	Flat/maisonette	Base
All households	54	25	20	8,901
Age of respondent:				
65-74	58	23	17	4,989
75-84	48	26	24	3,166
85+	42	29	28	746
Household type:				
Single adult aged 65-74	45	23	30	1,806
Single adult aged 75+	38	27	33	2,256
2 adults: at least 1 aged 65-74 none 75+	64	24	10	2,366
2 adults: at least 1 aged 75+	54	29	16	1,686
3 adults: at least 1 aged 65+	81	15	3	773
Tenure:				
Owner-occupier	63	28	8	4,952
LA rented	36	24	39	2,620
HA rented	16	13	69	378
Private rented	60	15	23	423
Living with friends/rels.	80	14	4	270
DoE Region:				
South-East	48	26	24	1,417
South-West	51	28	19	956
London	43	14	41	1,058
Eastern	49	33	16	1,017
W. Mids	59	22	16	1,008
E. Mids	55	31	13	752
N. West	65	19	16	1,236
Yorks & Humberside	54	27	18	957
Northern	56	28	15	500
Level of Dependency:				
A	58	24	17	3,715
B	57	24	18	1,281
C	46	25	28	738
D	47	27	26	2,218
F	48	25	25	77
G	51	29	18	608

occupy part of a house. Very few respondents described their home as a dwelling with business premises or a mobile home or caravan (Table 4.9).

4.25   The type of accommodation occupied by elderly people varies according to their age, household type, the tenure of the property they live in and their level of dependency. (Table 4.9). Younger elderly people aged 65-74 are more likely to live in houses and older elderly people, particularly those aged 85 and over, are more likely to occupy flats and maisonettes. Similarly, dependent elderly people are more likely than independent elderly people to occupy flats, maisonettes or bungalows. More than twice as many single elderly people of all ages, moreover, live in flats and maisonettes than elderly couples. This position is reversed, to some extent, for houses: three-fifths of elderly couples live in this type of accommodation compared with two-fifths of single elderly people. There are also some interesting differences by tenure and region. Elderly people renting privately are more likely to be occupying terraced housing (see Report No 7 – Appendix 1) than any other tenure group and three-quarters of elderly people occupying flats or maisonettes rent them from a local authority or housing association. In London, more than twice as many elderly people live in flats or maisonettes as in other regions (41% versus 18% on average), and correspondingly lower proportions live in houses or bungalows (43% and 14% respectively). A higher than average number of elderly people live in houses in the North-West (65%) and in the West Midlands (59%), whereas bungalows are more popular to the east of England (33% in DoE Eastern region and 31% in the East Midlands).

Tenure

4.26   Just over half of elderly people live in property that they own outright or which they pay for through a mortgage (Table 4.10a). Around two in five elderly people rent their homes, whether from the council or a new town/development corporation (29%), a housing association (4%) or privately (5%). Two per cent live in rent-free accommodation and a further three per cent live with relatives or friends in their home as part of their household.

4.27   Tenure varies by the age, household type and degree of physical and/or mental frailty of elderly people (Table 4.10a). Very elderly people aged 85 and over are less likely to own the property they live in than any other age group within the elderly or non-elderly population, except those aged under 25. They are also more likely to live with friends and relatives, although the numbers of such households are quite small. Elderly people aged 75-84 also have a lower level of owner- occupation than exists within the country as a whole (65% – GHS 1991), and it is only those aged 65-74 who have levels of owner-occupation roughly comparable to the rest of the population. All elderly respondents aged 75 or over are more likely to rent their accommodation than younger elderly people, although not from any particular landlord.

Table 4.10a	Tenure of dwellings occupied by elderly people: by age, household type and level of dependency				
Row%s	Owner-occupier	Council rented	Housing Association rented	Private rented	Base
All households	55	29	4	5	8,901
Age of respondent: *					
Under 25	36	31	5	25	404
25-29	59	27	3	10	857
30-44	75	17	2	4	2,750
45-59	75	18	2	3	2,414
60-64	69	23	2	4	760
65-74	60	29	3	3	4,989
75-84	51	30	5	5	3,166
85+	44	30	5	5	746
Household type:					
Single adult aged 65-74	51	38	5	3	1,806
Single adult aged 75+	45	36	7	6	2,256
2 adults: at least 1 aged 65-74 none 75+	69	25	2	2	2,366
2 adults: at least 1 aged 75+	59	24	4	4	1,686
3 adults: at least 1 aged 65+	49	18	2	3	773
Level of Dependency:					
A	65	23	3	4	3,715
B	60	27	4	3	1,281
C	41	41	7	6	738
D	46	36	5	4	2,218
F	49	34	12	1	77
G	47	33	4	3	608

Note	* The figures for the tenure profiles of heads of household aged between 16 and 64 years old are taken from the General Household Survey 1991 published by OPCS/HMSO, 1993.

4.28   A significantly lower proportion of single elderly people, and particularly those aged 75 or over, are owner-occupiers in comparison with elderly couples. Those living alone are also more likely to rent from social landlords, especially from local authorities. Only single elderly people aged 75 or over show any greater tendency to rent from private landlords. In fact, they represent two-fifths of all elderly people in that sector (Table 4.10a). Tenure also varies noticeably according to the level of dependency of elderly people, with those classified as 'fully independent' more likely to be owner-occupiers (65% versus 48% of elderly people in the highest dependency groupings) and frail elderly people tending to rent, particularly from local authorities (34% versus 23% of 'fully independent' elderly people).

Table 4.10b Characteristics of elderly people occupying dwellings within tenure: by age, household type and level of dependency

Col%s	Owner-occupier	Council rented	Housing association rented	Private rented
Age of respondent:				
65-74	61	56	46	40
75-84	33	36	43	49
85+	7	9	10	11
Household type:				
Single adult aged 65-74	18	26	25	16
Single adult aged 75+	21	31	39	39
2 adults: at least 1 aged 65-74 none 75+	33	23	14	16
2 adults: at least 1 aged 75+	20	15	18	21
Base	4,952	2,620	378	423
Level of Dependency:				
A/B	64	46	47	51
C	6	12	14	13
D/E	21	31	27	25
F/G	7	9	10	6
Base	4,950	2,604	377	346

4.29 Table 4.10b looks at these factors – age, household type and level of dependency – within as opposed to across tenure. It shows that housing associations and private renters have the oldest tenant profile and these tenures contain proportionately more single elderly people aged 75 or over than any other tenure. It also shows that a slightly higher proportion of private renters are 'fully independent' than local authority and housing association tenants and marginally fewer private renters are in the highest dependency groupings.

4.30 There are also some pronounced differences in tenure by region. Approximately three in five elderly people in the South East, South West and Eastern regions are owner-occupiers, compared with 55% of elderly households in the sample as a whole. Fewer elderly people own their property in the Northern region (41%) or in London (47%). There is also a greater tendency for elderly people to rent council property in the Northern (45%), London and East Midlands regions (both 35%), whilst the number of private renters is highest in London (8%).

4.31 Taking some of these findings together, it might be thought frail elderly owner-occupiers and private renters have been specifically targeted by local authorities for re-housing. The high proportion of older, frail and single elderly people who are local authority tenants may be simply due, however, to an ageing elderly population within local authority housing. Many of the elderly households in local authority accommodation were first housed as families in three-bedroom accommodation in the immediate post-war era. Children have grown up and left home, while elderly parents have continued as local authority tenants. Some elderly renters have moved to smaller, mainstream or sheltered accommodation, others have remained in the same home and now under occupy (see paragraphs 4.39 – 4.41). These elderly people will now be aged in their mid-to-late seventies and eighties.

Age of property and length of residence

4.32   Almost one-fifth of elderly people live in properties built before 1919, which is slightly lower than the national figure for the proportion of households living in pre-1919 housing (22% – English House Conditions Survey 1991, HMSO, 1993) (Table 4.11 in Appendix 3). Just over a half live in housing built after the second World War, whether before or after 1964 (26% and 30% respectively), and the remaining fifth of elderly people occupy accommodation built between the two world wars – 1919-1945.

4.33   Successive English House Condition Surveys have shown that the majority of unfit dwellings are to be found in the pre-1919 stock, and that privately rented housing built before 1919 is more likely to be unfit than owner-occupied housing of this age. In this survey, just over a half (56%) of the elderly tenants in the private rented sector were living in pre-1919 housing, which is just below the proportion of the private rented stock built before the end of the First World War (61% – English House Conditions Survey 1991 HMSO/DoE, 1993). The latest English House Condition Survey (1991) has also revealed that of all household types single elderly households are most likely to live in the worst private rented housing – almost one in two (46%) experiencing poor conditions. This is not confined, moreover, to elderly households headed by someone aged 85 or over – 46% of whom were in the worst dwellings in the private rented sector – but applies equally to those aged 65-74 (42%) and 75-84 (48%).

4.34   By region, London has the highest proportion of elderly people living in pre-1945 properties (56%) and, conversely, the lowest proportion of people living in post-war properties (38%). It also has the highest proportion of elderly

Row%s	Less than 5 yrs	5-10 yrs	10-20 yrs	20+ yrs	Base
Table 4.12 Length of residence of elderly people: by tenure					
All house-holds	17	14	20	48	8,901
Tenure:					
Owner-occupier	12	13	18	56	4,952
LA rented	22	16	24	38	2,620
HA rented	41	22	24	13	378
Private rented	11	7	12	68	423
Living with friends/rels	38	21	19	23	270

people living in pre-1919 properties (25%). Respondents living in Eastern, South East and South West DoE regions were more likely to live in properties built after 1945 (66%, 64% and 62% respectively).

4.35   Turning to length of residence, approximately seven in ten elderly people have lived in their present homes for ten years or more, with around half (48%) having lived there for 20 years or more. (Table 4.12). The latter figure compares with one-third of the population as a whole (33% – English House Conditions Survey 1991 DoE/HMSO, 1993). Housing association tenants and those living with friends and relatives are most likely to have moved in the last five years. Conversely, elderly people living in privately rented accommodation and owner-occupiers are more likely to have lived in their present home for ten years or more.

Amenities and shared facilities

4.36   Very small numbers of people either share or lack basic household facilities – 1% share a bedroom/shower room, an inside toilet or their hot water supply, with less than half of 1% sharing a kitchen and wash-hand basin. Sharing facilities is more common in privately rented and housing association property.

4.37   One per cent of elderly people do not have a fixed bathroom/shower room, a wash-hand basin or an inside toilet, with less than half of one per cent lacking a kitchen and a supply of hot water. (Table 4.13 in Appendix 3). Privately rented accommodation and very old properties (pre-1919) are considerably more likely to lack these amenities than any other type of housing lived in by elderly people. Some care should be exercised here, however, because the absence of these amenities was only established through respondents' answers as opposed to an independent survey of properties. Those aged 85 and over and single elderly adults aged 75 and over appear to be the groups with fewest essential amenities.

House size

4.38   Around one in five elderly people have one bedroom in their home, whilst approximately two in five have either two or three bedrooms (Table 4.14). 6% live in accommodation with four or more bedrooms.

4.39   Respondents living in one-bedroom accommodation are most likely to be council and housing association tenants (39% and 67% respectively) and to live in a flat or maisonette (59%). Elderly people living in privately rented accommodation and bungalows are most likely to have two bedrooms; respondents living in houses (particularly semi-detached or detached – 78%), owner occupiers (57%), and those living with relatives or friends (85%) are more likely to have three or more bedrooms. By region, London has the highest proportion of elderly people living in one-bedroom accommodation (24% versus 18% on average).

Table 4.14 Numbers of bedrooms in accommodation occupied by elderly people: by tenure, type of housing and region

Row%s	1-Bed	2-Bed	3+ Bed	Base
All households	18	36	45	8,901
Tenure:				
Owner-occupier	4	39	57	4,952
Council rented	39	34	26	2,620
Housing association rented	67	22	10	378
Private rented	12	45	42	423
Live with relatives/ friends	2	14	85	270
Type of housing:				
Bungalow	19	52	29	2,213
Terraced house	2	43	55	1,668
Semi-detached/ detached house	1	20	78	3,061
Flat/ maisonette	59	36	4	1,829
DoE Region:				
South-East	17	38	45	1,417
South-West	15	38	47	956
London	24	31	44	1,058
Eastern	16	35	49	1,017
West Midlands	15	34	50	1,008
East Midlands	16	35	49	752
North West	17	34	49	1,236
Yorks & Humberside	21	38	40	957
Northern	21	42	37	500

4.40   Data on the number of bedrooms in properties can also be used in conjunction with the measure of under-occupation reported in the General Household Survey (OPCS/HMSO, 1993). This measure is called the Bedroom Standard and the rules it uses to assess the number of bedrooms required by each household are presented in Appendix 5. Households are classified as occupying property at the bedroom standard and one, two or three or more bedrooms above (or below) the standard. The following paragraph concentrates upon under-occupation amongst single elderly households and elderly couples as these two types of household account for over four-fifths (84%) of elderly households in the sample and are probably of greatest interest with regard to policies on under-occupation.

4.41   Table 4.15 shows the level of under-occupation by tenure amongst all single elderly households and elderly couples in the survey sample and compares this with equivalent data from the English House Condition Survey 1991 for the population as a whole. It is clear that levels of under-occupation in the combined sample of single elderly households and elderly couples renting from local authorities and housing associations are, more or less, the same as

Table 4.15 Under-occupation amongst elderly couples and single elderly person households: by tenure

Row%s	At Bedroom standard	EHCS 1991	1-Bed over	EHCS 1991	2 or more Beds over	EHCS 1991	Base: present study	Base: EHCS 1991
All households	24	29	38	38	33	30	7,271	19,111
Elderly owner-occupiers:								
All	5	21	42	41	52	37	4,017	12,872
Single	8		47		45		2,029	
Couples	2		37		60		1,988	
Elderly council tenants:								
All	48	47	33	33	19	16	2,470	3,877
Single	56		30		14		1,699	
Couples	28		40		31		771	
Elderly housing association tenants:								
All	75	67	18	22	6	8	372	662
Single	81		14		5		276	
Couples	59		29		11		96	
Elderly private rented tenants:								
All	15	37	48	36	37	25	412	1,700
Single	17		48		35		288	
Couples	8		49		42		124	

those for all households renting from local authorities and housing associations. This is probably not surprising, however, since elderly households headed by people above retirement age form almost a half (49%) of all those under-occupying local authority and housing association accommodation (EHCS, 1991). When this overall picture is broken down, however, it emerges that levels of under-occupation amongst single elderly tenants are much closer to the norm for local authority and housing association accommodation than under-occupation amongst elderly couples. For example, almost twice as many elderly couples renting local authority accommodation under-occupy their property by two or more above the standard (31%) than local authority tenants as a whole (16%). In contrast, elderly owner-occupiers and those renting from private landlords have much higher levels of under- occupation than households in general within these tenure groupings, irrespective of household type.

House condition

4.42   No physical survey of house condition was conducted as part of this study, but information was collected on respondents' views on the state of repair of their homes. As such, these are not professional assessments of disrepair and, therefore, should be treated cautiously. Respondents were also asked about their expenditure on minor repairs and improvements in the 12 months preceding the survey.

4.43   Approximately one in two of the elderly people surveyed said they had undertaken repairs and improvements to their homes in the 12 months prior to the survey (49%). A quarter (23%) had spent up to £100, a half (49%) had spent between £100 and £999 and the remainder had spent £1,000 or more. Not surprisingly, owner-occupiers and those with high weekly incomes – £115 or more – are most likely to have carried our repairs in the 12 months prior to the survey (63% and 62% respectively).

4.44   Just over three in five elderly people think their home does not need any repairs or improvements to make it easier for them to live there (Table 4.16a in Appendix 3). These tend to be those living in properties built since 1964, renting from housing association, or living with friends and relatives. In contrast, elderly private renters, those living in terraced houses (see Report No 7 – Appendix 1) and those who would like to remain in their own homes are particularly likely to cite at least one repair need. External windows are most frequently referred to as needing repairs or improvements (13%). One in five respondents (21%) mention just one repair or improvement, one in eight (12%) mention two or three, and three per cent mention four or more. Respondents were also asked what types of support and advice it would be helpful to have with regard to repairs and improvements. Help with raising finance and support and reassurance while repair work is being carried out, are the most frequently mentioned by approximately one in ten respondents (9%) for each form of support. There is no particular pattern to this response by age of respondent, tenure or household type, although as is shown in paragraph 8.39 of Chapter 8, one group of respondents are significantly less likely to want any advice or support, even though their objective circumstances suggest they need adaptations and improvements to continue living in their homes (Table 4.16b in Appendix 3).

4.45   People living in privately rented accommodation are particularly concerned with their damp proofing (15% versus 4% on average) and damp/condensation (15% versus 6% on average). Electrics and wiring are also thought more likely to need attention in privately rented accommodation (13% versus 5% on average). Lastly, respondents living in terraced houses are almost twice as likely to cite two or more repair needs than the sample as whole (see Report No 7 – Appendix 1).

Adaptations and alterations

4.46   Almost two-fifths (38%) of elderly people have adaptations in their homes in order to make it easier for them to live there. (Table 4.17). The most frequently fitted adaptations include additional hand rails (both inside and outside) and a warden/emergency alarm system. Council and housing association tenants are more likely to benefit from adaptations and alterations in general than other tenure groups but, in particular, from a warden/emergency alarm system and additional hand- rails. Overall, adaptations seem to be reasonably well targeted[13] – the presence of adaptations is strongly related to age, household type and level of dependency of elderly people (Table 4.17). For example, whereas almost three in five high dependency elderly people have at least one of the adaptations/alterations listed, only one in four fully independent elderly have them. Within these two sub-groups, moreover, five times as many high dependency people say they have two or more of the adaptations listed than zero dependency elderly people. Income levels make little difference to the presence of adaptations – those with incomes of more than £115 per week at the time of the survey are just as likely to have adaptations in their homes as households with incomes up to £85 per week.

4.47   When asked whether they or other elderly members of their household need any other adaptations at present only three in ten respondents say they do, and no one adaptation is mentioned as being needed by more than one in thirteen (Table 4.18 in Appendix 3). The most frequently requested adaptation is an adapted bath/shower, particularly by dependent elderly people and those who want to remain in their own homes with adaptations to make it easier to live there. In fact, the more dependent elderly people are the more likely they are to state they need adaptations. The interest in obtaining adaptations shown by those who would like to remain in their own homes is also consistent with the response this group gave to the need for major repairs and improvements (see paragraph 4.44 above). By tenure, owner-occupiers seem to be less interested than other tenure groups. One in four owner-occupiers say they need

---

[13]   'Targeted' as a term is used in its broadest sense here. It refers not only to the means-tested allocation of renovation grants to pay for adaptations for those most in need, but also to the likelihood that privately obtained aids and adaptations were also to be found in elderly households with these specific characteristics. This broad definition also applies to the same section within Chapter 7 on the survey of non-elderly disabled adults.

Table 4.17 Adaptations in homes occupied by elderly people: by age of respondent, household type, level of dependency and household income

Col%s	All households Base = 8,901	Row%s	Presence of adaptations	1-mentioned	2 + mentioned	Base
Ramps outside	3					
Additional handrails outside	8					
Ramps inside	1	**Age of respondent:**				
Additional handrails inside	16	65-74	32	17	14	4,989
Any doors altered for better access	2	75-84	45	21	23	3,166
Any other alterations for better access	*	85+	56	22	32	746
Stairlift	1	**Household type:**				
Specially designed or adapted kitchen	1	Single adult aged 65-74	37	18	18	1,806
Specially designed or adapted bath/shower	6	Single adult aged 75+	51	22	28	2,256
Relocated bath	1	2 adults: at least 1 aged 65-74 none aged 75+	27	16	11	2,366
Relocated shower	1	2 adults: at least 1 aged 75+	43	21	21	1,686
Specially designed or adapted toilet	3	3 adults: at least 1 aged 65+	31	18	13	773
Relocated toilet	1	**Level of dependency:**				
Hoist	1	A/B	26	16	9	4,996
Electrical modifications	4	C	49	20	29	738
Door entry phone	4	D/E	56	25	31	2,226
Extra locks/safety gates	7	F/G	57	21	36	685
Warden/emergency alarm system	11	**Household weekly income:**				
Additional heating	1	Up to £54	41	20	21	1,645
Other	3	£54-£84	40	19	22	2,912
None of these	62	£85-£115	38	20	17	1,795
		£115+	36	18	18	2,549

Note * – Less than 0.5%.

95

adaptations (24%) compared with one in three private renters and almost two in five local authority and housing association tenants.

Satisfaction with home

4.48   As numerous other studies have found, elderly people express a very high level of satisfaction with their home: a majority of 92% say they are very or fairly satisfied with their present home, two-thirds (65%) saying they were very satisfied. Most likely to be very satisfied with their home are elderly people living with relatives or friends (79%), owner-occupiers (71%) and respondents aged 85 or over (71%). Respondents living in bungalows are more positive (72% say they are very satisfied) than those living in other types of housing, particularly those in flats or maisonettes (56%). Elderly people living in private rented accommodation are the group least likely to be very satisfied (45%).

Housing aspirations

4.49   An important element of the study was to investigate elderly peoples' housing aspirations. A series of questions were asked which did not ask about any specific option such as very sheltered or extra- care housing, but were designed in such a way that when responses were combined, a clear indication would be given of particular housing preferences. This was done in order to avoid the problems posed by respondents' lack of awareness of specific housing options or, when elderly people did know of some types of specialised accommodation, confusion over what housing care support and communal facilities it provided.

Housing preferences

4.50   Respondents were initially shown a list of six broad housing options, and asked which they thought would best suit them (and other elderly members of their households, where appropriate) at present (Table 4.19). Over four-fifths of elderly people say that their present home is the most suitable type of accommodation for them: 69% opt for their home exactly as it is, and 15% require repairs and adaptations to be carried out to make it easier for them to live there. A further one in seven express a desire for other alternative accommodation: 8% want a smaller property, 4% want alternative accommodation of the same size and 2% wish to live somewhere larger. Lastly, 1% want to move to live with relatives or friends as part of their household.

4.51   There is a small but steady increase in the proportions of households wishing to remain in their present homes by the age of the respondent and a decrease in the number of those wanting smaller accommodation. Council tenants, private renters and elderly people with a high dependency score are more likely than other groups to opt to stay in their present home with repairs and adaptations. Elderly private renters are also the group most likely to want to move, in particular, to somewhere smaller.

Table 4.19 Housing aspirations of elderly households: by age of respondent, tenure and level of dependency

Row%s	Present home as it is	Present home with repairs /adaptations	Other accomm: same size	Other accomm: smaller	Other accomm: larger	Move to live with friends/rels	Base
Age of respondent:							
65-74	69	14	4	9	2	*	4,989
75-84	69	17	3	8	1	1	3,166
85+	71	18	2	4	1	2	746
Tenure:							
Owner-occupier	72	13	3	10	1	*	4,952
Council rented	65	20	5	6	3	*	2,620
Housing association rented	72	16	3	4	5	*	378
Private rented	59	22	4	13	1	*	423
Living with rels/friends	63	14	2	5	2	13	270
Level of dependency:							
A/B	76	10	4	8	2	0	4,996
C	65	19	3	9	3	1	738
D/E	61	24	3	8	2	1	2,226
F/G	52	28	5	12	1	2	685

Note * – Less than 0.5%.

Preferred type of property

4.52   Two-thirds of those who wish to live in alternative accommodation would prefer a bungalow and approximately one-sixth would like to live in a flat or maisonette (Table 4.20). A flat or maisonette is more popular with private renters, single elderly people (particularly those aged 75 and over) and those already in flats and maisonettes. A bungalow is more likely to be sought by two person elderly households, those in detached/semi-detached houses, elderly men and owner-occupiers.

4.53   Further questioning to gauge the type of accommodation preferred covered home ownership, number of bedrooms, specially- designed accommodation for easy access, for example, by wheelchairs, floor level and willingness to share facilities (Table 4.21 in Appendix 3). Respondents are fairly equally divided between those who would wish to own their home (47%) and those would prefer to rent (45%). As may be expected, current owner-occupiers are most likely to want to own their property (73%) and renters to rent (88%). Three in five respondents (61%) say they would prefer a property with a minimum of two bedrooms and 26% would seriously consider a property with just one bedroom. One in ten (10%) would prefer three or more bedrooms. In fact, the number of bedrooms respondents are prepared to accept is closely related to respondents' household type and age. Over two-fifths (44%) of single elderly people say they would accept one bedroom compared with only 13% of two-person elderly households. In contrast, whereas almost three-quarters (72%) of two-person households express a preference for two bedrooms, only a half of single elderly people said this is their minimum requirement. Within the single elderly group, however, this does vary by age with those aged 75 and over more likely to accept one-bed accommodation (51%) than those aged 65-74 (39%).

4.54   In terms of specially-designed accommodation for easy access, two in five (41%) say they would not prefer this option, almost twice as many say they would (24%). Three in ten (30%) said they had no preference either way. Respondents with a high dependency score, housing association tenants and the very elderly are the most likely to prefer to live in housing specially designed for easy access (38%, 41% and 46% respectively). Very small percentages of respondents say they would seriously consider moving to a flat or maisonette where they shared the bathroom (3%), the kitchen (2%) or the toilet (1%). Finally, the majority of those who wish to move and want a flat or maisonette (85%) prefer an entrance on the ground floor. Slightly fewer (69%) say they would consider one with an entrance on the first floor if the block had a lift.

Help and support needed

4.55   Respondents were shown a list of five broad types of help and asked whether they or other elderly members of their household needed any of these types of support to enable them to remain in their present home or to live in alternative accommodation. Some caution should be exercised in these results

Table 4.20 Preferred type of property: by tenure, household type, current accommodation and gender

Col%s	All house-holds	Gender		Household type					Tenure					Current accommodation			
		Male	Female	Single adult 65-74	Single adult 75+	2 adults 1 aged 65-74 none 75+	2 adults 1 aged 75+	3+ adults 1 aged 65+	Owner-occupier	Council rented	Housing assoc. rented	Private rented	Living with friends/rels	Bun-galow	Ter-rraced house	Semi det/det-ached house	Maison-ette/flat
House	9	8	9	9	5	9	5	23	8	10	9	5	16	7	9	9	8
Bunga-low	66	72	61	56	49	80	77	59	72	61	49	58	49	73	62	77	46
Purpose-built flat	17	14	20	26	33	8	9	8	13	21	26	33	16	13	20	9	32
Conver-ted flat	1	*	1	1	1	0	2	0	1	*	0	1	0	*	*	*	2
Other	3	2	5	4	6	1	3	6	3	4	3	1	13	2	4	1	7
Base	1,226	552	674	284	234	392	219	97	704	352	44	75	24	209	285	466	243

Note * – Less than 0.5%.

because they are based on respondents' perceptions of their needs as opposed to professional assessment by a social work or occupational therapist.

4.56   Those wishing to remain in their home are less likely overall to feel they need outside help and support: three-quarters say they do not need any of the services listed compared with just under two-fifths of those who would find other accommodation more suitable (Table 4.22 in Appendix 3). Moreover, whilst the two groups place help with household chores at or close to the top of the list of types of support, almost three times as many of those wanting alternative accommodation wish to be able to call on a warden in emergencies than those wanting to stay in their present homes.

4.57   Amongst those who wish to remain in their present homes, there are also some significant variations by the age, household type and level of dependency of respondents (Table 4.22 in Appendix 3). Those aged 85 and over are roughly three times more likely to cite a need for one or more of the types of help as those aged 65-74. Single elderly people aged 75 or over are particularly interested in obtaining help with household chores and being able to call a warden in emergencies. For all of the types of support, there are greater numbers of elderly people interested in obtaining the help at each successive increase in frailty or dependency. Table 4.22 in Appendix 3 also shows that twice as many of those elderly households wishing to remain in their present homes but with repairs and adaptations require each of these forms of support, than those who are content with their home exactly as it is. Not surprisingly, this is also a group that shows clear interest in carrying out repairs and adaptations to their homes as described in earlier sections. Turning to the group that would like to move to alternative accommodation, similar patterns emerge. Those aged 85 and over and with a high level of dependency are more interested in each of these types of support than younger elderly and more physically independent people in this group.

Table 4.23 Expect to move within 12 months of the survey: by tenure and preferred tenure

Col%s	Very/fairly likely to move	Not very/not at all likely to move
Current tenure:		
Owner-occupier	53	56
Council rented	34	29
Housing Assoc. rented	4	4
Private rented	5	5
Living with friends/ relatives	3	3
Base[1]	744	7,859
Preferred tenure:		
Own	41	53
Rent	53	38
Base[2]	532	630

[1]   This base does not include those who said 'don't know'.
[2]   This base covers only those who said they wished to move to other accommodation when asked about their housing aspirations.

Desire to move

4.58   Only 8% of respondents say they are very or fairly likely to move within twelve months of being interviewed. Elderly people living in flats/maisonettes (11%) and those aged 65-74 (10%) are more likely than average to expect to move. There is no difference by tenure: elderly owner-occupiers are just as likely to expect to move in the next 12 months as elderly renters. It is, however, interesting to compare this response with the answer given by all those who wish to move to alternative accommodation, whether in the short or long-term. Returning to the preferred type of property, Table 4.23 shows that, elderly people expecting to move within a year of the survey are more likely to want to rent than own their new property. In fact, there is a degree of proposed tenure switching apparent. Whereas owner- occupiers form just over half (53%) of those saying they are very or fairly likely to move within a year of the survey, only two-fifths (41%) of those moving would want to own their new homes.

Receipt of health and social care services

Care and support services received

4.59   Formal care and support services received by elderly people appear overall to be well targeted (Table 4.24 in Appendix 3). Respondents with higher dependency scores and those living alone and aged 75 or over are generally the most likely to receive visits from health and social care services. There is also some evidence that elderly couples, where at least one is aged 75 or over, are more likely to receive services than single elderly people and elderly couples aged under 75. This suggests that more support is also going to carers for older and potentially frailer elderly people and this is in line with community care objectives. It is interesting to see, however, that owner-occupiers and private tenants consistently seem to have slightly lower level of receipt of these services than those living with friends of relatives, local authority and housing association tenants. Part of the reason for this might be that, overall, there are lower proportions of older elderly (85 or over), single and high dependency people in the private rented and owner-occupied sectors. It may also be because social services, community and health organisations are more aware of the needs of local authority and housing association tenants through referrals from other statutory and voluntary agencies. For most services, nevertheless, the older and frailer the elderly person the more frequent are the visits from health and social care services.

4.60   Looking at one particular important service – the local authority home help/care aide The very elderly aged 85 and over, and particular those living alone, are most likely to receive help in the home. Council and housing association tenants are also more likely than average to have a home help (16% and 17% respectively compared with 7% of owner-occupiers, 11% of private renters and 5% of those living with friends and relatives).

Care and support services requested by elderly people

4.61   Latent demand for care and support services amongst elderly people appears to be extremely low (Table 4.25 in Appendix 3). The most frequently mentioned service – home visits from chiropodists – is requested by no more than one in seventeen respondents (6%). Even fewer (3%) of respondents would like to have a local authority home help, and just 2% say they need visits from a doctor or social worker. Those already in receipt of care and support services, the very elderly (those aged 85 and over) and the highly dependent are most likely to request visits.

5 A national survey of elderly residents of specialised housing

Introduction

5.1   Chapter 3 showed that specialised housing for elderly people is a relatively expensive form of provision and, as such, it is important to ensure that it is used effectively. There has been increasing concern, in recent years, over evidence of mismatches in the subsidised sector between the needs and wants of elderly households for particular types of accommodation and the characteristics of the current stock (see paragraph 1.3iii in Chapter 1). The present study included a national survey of elderly residents of specialised housing to examine how this resource is being used, including looking at the characteristics of those housed in schemes, and their attitudes towards this type of accommodation. The survey was also carried out to inform the design of the allocation model described in Chapter 8.

5.2   This chapter is divided into **four** sections: firstly, methodological issues and the sample design; secondly, the characteristics of elderly residents; thirdly, where they came from and aspects of their present home; and, finally, their receipt of health and social care services.

Research methodology and the survey sample

5.3   The survey was based on interviews with elderly people living in specialised housing schemes, comprising about 400 interviews in each of the nine DoE regions. The sample was based on residential schemes rather than individuals and an average of ten interviews were completed in each scheme. The survey was conducted between June and July 1992 and in total, 3,569 interviews were conducted in 361 schemes.

5.4   The sample of schemes was designed to be representative nationally and was stratified by type and tenure. As with the national survey of specialised housing, private sector schemes were not included. Almost three-quarters of interviews were conducted with elderly tenants of Category 2 or ordinary sheltered housing schemes, as this is the dominant form of specialised housing provision for elderly people, and two-thirds of respondents (before re-weighting) were local authority tenants. (More details are given about the sample profile in the individual report no. 8 on this survey – see Appendix 1)

5.5   In order to create sub-groups large enough for analysis and to simplify the presentation of findings, provision has been grouped into three main categories of specialised housing – Category 1/other specialised housing, Category 1.5/2 and Category 2.5 or very sheltered accommodation. The inclusion of residents of Category 1.5 schemes with those of Category 2 schemes is logical, given that both types of provision are meant to be catering for less active elderly people, for whom some form of warden support is essential. They simply differ in their approach to providing the necessary emergency support and cover.

5.6   The grouping of Category 1 and 'other specialised housing' is, however, slightly more problematic as 'other specialised housing' can range from granny annexes to schemes almost qualifying as nursing homes. Some caution must be exercised, therefore, in interpreting results relating to this latter pairing and comments to this effect are included at relevant points in the text.

Characteristics of residents

Age and sex

5.7   The age and gender profile of residents within specialised housing schemes is shown in Table 5.1. Residents are generally older than elderly people in mainstream, ordinary housing in the community. The majority are aged between 75 and 84 years old, and one in five are aged 85 or over. In contrast, the majority of elderly people outside schemes are aged 65-74 and less than a tenth are aged 85 or over. As might be expected, women outnumber men in schemes: the scale of the difference is, however, interesting.

Table 5.1 Age and gender profile of elderly residents of specialised housing: by category of accommodation and recent entrants

	All Residents			
	All residents	**Category of accommodation**		
Col%s		**1/Other**	**1.5/2**	**2.5**
Age of respondent:				
Up to 65	4	5	4	4
65-74	28	36	28	20
75-84	48	39	50	48
85+	20	20	18	28
Base	3,569	368	2,747	454
Gender:				
Male	23	27	23	21
Female	77	73	77	79
Base	3,569	368	2,747	454
	Recent Entrants (i.e. resident for less than 5 years)			
	All recent entrants	**Category of accommodation**		
Col%s		**1/Other**	**1.5/2**	**2.5**
Age of respondent:				
Up to 65	6	6	6	4
65-74	32	39	33	21
75-84	46	42	47	48
85+	16	14	14	27
Base	1,943	177	1,452	314
Gender:				
Male	26	28	27	23
Female	74	72	73	77
Base	1,943	177	1,452	314

Whereas elderly women outnumber elderly men by a ratio of approximately 3:2 in private households outside specialised housing, inside schemes the ratio is even greater – 3:1. The ratio of elderly women to men in these age groups, moreover, rises with each increase in age. These trends are, more or less, the same for recent entrants (those who had lived in the sampled schemes for less than five years), except that this sub-group has a lower proportion of elderly aged 85 or over and more aged 65-74.

5.8   Table 5.1 also shows the age distribution of residents within type of specialised housing scheme. It is clear that the age profile of residents increases in line with the level of frailty or dependency each type of scheme is meant to be catering for. Thus, very sheltered or Category 2.5 schemes which offer high levels of care support have the greatest proportion of residents aged 85 or over. It is surprising, nevertheless, that a fifth of residents of Category 1/other specialised housing schemes are aged 85 or over. This is probably partly linked to the wide spectrum of schemes included under the heading of 'other specialised housing'.

Household type

5.9   The majority (82%) live in single person households, with one in six (18%) living with one other person (Table 5.2 in Appendix 3). The older the respondent, the more likely she or he is to live on her or his own: 94% of elderly people aged 85 and over live as a single person household, compared with 62% of respondents aged up to 65. Residents living in Abbeyfield/almshouses, and those living in Category 2.5 schemes are also more likely to live alone (94% and 89% respectively). In terms of dependency, those classed in Category A/B on the Clackmannan scale (fully independent or with mild mental impairment) are more likely to live with another person (25% versus 18% on average).

5.10   Approximately one in six (16%) of respondents live with their spouse or partner, two-thirds (67%) are widowed, six per cent are divorced or separated, and a further nine per cent are single.

5.11   Turning to residents who have moved to the scheme within the last five years, household composition follows a similar pattern to the total sample, with the majority (80%) living on their own, and one in five (20%) living in two-person households. These more recent residents, however, are more likely to live with their spouse or partner (19% versus 16% of the total sample).

Receipt of state benefits

5.12   Table 5.3 shows levels of receipt of selected state benefits by elderly residents of specialised housing schemes. The higher the dependency score, the more likely respondents are to draw one or more of these allowances, excluding

Table 5.3 Receipt of state benefits by elderly residents of specialised housing: by level of dependency, age of respondent and household type

Row%s	None of these¹	Attendance allow.	Mobility allow.	Severe dis. allow.	Invalid care allow.	Housing benefit	Income support	Base
All residents	84	12	4	1	*	70	34	3,569
Age of respondent:								
Up to 65	61	20	23	10	3	66	39	141
65-74	82	11	8	1	*	70	24	994
75-84	87	12	1	*	*	72	36	1,724
85+	84	13	*	*	*	66	41	705
Household type:								
Single adult 65-74	86	8	7	1	0	76	29	722
Single adult 75+	88	10	1	*	*	71	40	2,134
2 adults: at at least 1 aged 65-74 none 75+	74	18	12	1	1	52	7	207
2+ adults: at least 1 aged 75+	68	30	4	1	1	61	19	388
Level of dependency:								
A/B	95	4	1	*	*	67	27	1,274
C	92	6	2	1	*	72	38	606
D	75	19	6	1	*	72	37	1,169
E/F	98	0	2	2	0	72	27	30
G	58	34	11	4	2	70	42	359

¹ This percentage figure does not include those who said they did not know if they received these benefits. Thus, only 15% of all households claimed to receive at least one of these benefits as 1% were not sure or did not know.

Note * – Less than 0.5%.

income support and housing benefit: two in five residents classed as in Category G on the Clackmannan dependency scale (39%) receive at least one state allowance, compared with just 2% of those classed as 'fully independent' (Category A/B). One in eight resident households receive income from attendance allowance, most frequently at the lower rate (6%). This is a significantly higher proportion of households in receipt than amongst all elderly people in the community, and this difference is evident across all levels of dependency (see Table 4.5 in Appendix 3). It is perhaps, not surprising, however, given that residents will have come to the attention of statutory and voluntary agencies in being rehoused and may well have had their benefit entitlements checked at that time.

5.13 Around a third of resident households receive income support (Table 5.3). Very elderly respondents aged 85 or over and those with a high level of dependency are more likely than average to receive it (41% and 42% respectively). Seven in ten residents receive housing benefit: half (51%) have part of their rent paid, and almost a fifth (19%) have all of their rent paid through housing benefit. Residents aged 65-74 and living alone are most likely to be in receipt (76%), and are also most likely to have all their rent paid by their local authority or local social security office (57% versus 51% overall). Residents living in Abbeyfield and almshouse society schemes are least likely to receive housing benefit (21% versus 70% on average).

Health

5.14 Just over one in two residents say they are registered as disabled or have long-term illnesses or disabilities which handicap or prevent them from doing things for themselves (Table 5.4 in Appendix 3). This is nearly twice the rate of registration or prevalence of long-term illnesses or disabilities found amongst all elderly people in the community (see Chapter 4). Registration varies with the level of dependency or physical/mental frailty of residents – 46% of elderly residents in the highest dependency grouping are registered compared with only 18% of those in the lowest dependency groupings. It is also linked to the type of specialised housing occupied and the landlord. Residents of Category 2.5 accommodation and local authority schemes in general are more likely to be registered than average (Table 5.4 in Appendix 3).

5.15 Respondents' perceptions of their health, moreover, follow exactly the same pattern, except that here age is also a factor (Table 5.4 in Appendix 3). Over a third (35%) of those aged 85 or over say they suffer from a long- term illness or disability compared with just over a quarter (26%) of those aged between 65 and 74 years old. Table 5.4 in Appendix 3 also shows that a small percentage of those who state that they are registered as disabled or have long-term illnesses and disabilities are permanently confined to a bed or chair.

5.16 Respondents were also shown a list of six long-term health problems, and asked to say which, if any, they experienced. The most common long-term

---

[14] See, however, footnote 10.

health problem is painful joints, mentioned by nearly two-thirds of elderly people (64%), particularly those aged 85 and over and residents living in Category 2.5 schemes (70% and 72% respectively). Other problems are mentioned to a lesser extent: a quarter of residents (26%) experience pain in the chest on effort; 7% have problems associated with a stroke; 6% have sugar diabetes; and 5% have leg ulcers. A quarter of residents (24%) say they have none of the health problems listed. Results are very similar among those who have moved to their present home within the last five years.

Dependency levels

5.17   As with the main survey of elderly people in the community, two measures of dependency were operated in this survey – the Clackmannan/Townsend and Leeds scales of dependency. The use of the Leeds scale in this context has the added advantage of providing a basis for comparison with previous surveys of sheltered housing residents.

5.18   Table 5.5 shows the distribution of elderly residents across the Clackmannan/Townsend measure by length of residence, age of respondent, type and tenure of scheme. Clearly, the resident population of specialised housing schemes is much more dependent or frail than elderly people as a whole within private households (see Table 4.8 and paragraph 4.22). It also appears, however, that a high proportion of recent entrants to both ordinary sheltered (41%) and very sheltered (22%) housing have no physical or mental frailty, despite the fact that the former was designed for less active elderly people and the latter is provided specifically for frail elderly people.

Table 5.5 Dependency profile of elderly residents of specialised housing: by recent entrants, age of respondent, tenure and category of accommodation (Clackmannan scale of dependency)

Row%s	A/B	C	D	E/F	G	Base[1]
All residents	36	17	33	1	10	3,569
All recent entrants	39	16	32	1	9	1,939
Age of respondent:						
Up to 65	49	8	20	5	12	141
65-74	54	11	22	1	8	994
75-84	33	20	33	1	10	1,724
85+	13	20	51	*	13	705
Category of accommodation:						
1/Other	48	16	25	1	8	368
1.5/2	37	17	32	1	10	2,747
2.5	19	16	47	1	14	454
Tenure of scheme:						
Local authority	34	17	34	1	11	2,602
Housing association	42	17	27	1	9	887
Abbeyfield/ Almshouse	31	19	42	0	3	80

[1]   The % figures in cols 2-6 do not add up to 100% because 107 or 3% residents could not be allocated to a Clackmannan dependency grouping due to missing information on questionnaire returns.

Note * – Less than 0.5%.

Within tenure, moreover, housing association ordinary and very sheltered schemes have higher proportions of tenants with no dependency than equivalent local authority and Abbeyfield/almshouse society schemes. This is particularly so for recent entrants (46% compared with 36% and 31% respectively). This is perhaps not surprising, however, with regard to Abbeyfield/almshouse society schemes as these providers do specifically aim to provide housing for older elderly people who are more likely to have higher levels of physical/mental frailty. It should also be pointed out that local housing authorities have the potential to significantly influence the selection of new tenants in housing association schemes through nomination agreements, and this may partly account for this finding.

5.19   There are several possible explanations for these high proportions of residents with no physical or mental dependency. The survey may have contained a respondent bias towards low dependency partners/spouses of high dependency elderly people, but almost three- quarters (74%) of those surveyed with no dependency were single elderly people, which is only slightly lower than the proportion of single elderly people in the sample as a whole (80%). Many of these people may be the remaining low dependency spouses/partners of high dependency elderly people who died shortly after entering the scheme. As will be shown later on, however, within the section on respondents' previous homes (see paragraph 5.27), this is extremely unlikely given that the death of a partner after entry to a scheme could only apply to roughly one in six recent entrant households.

5.20   Elderly people with no physical or mental dependency may have been encouraged to enter schemes in anticipation of their gradual deterioration, but, if this were the answer, there would be a more even distribution across the dependency groupings. This is not the case and, as is shown below, there is an increasing polarisation of elderly residents into the low/nil dependency and high dependency groupings.

5.21   Other possibilities might be that providers are still operating policies of mixing 'fit' and 'frail' residents; places are being offered to elderly people who are lonely or suffering from social isolation and those who feel the need for security, particularly elderly women; providers are using sheltered housing as a means of reducing under-occupation in their stock; and, elderly residents in high dependency groupings are now not able to move into residential care or long-stay hospitals as freely as before. All of these may be part of the answer but, given the cost and scarcity of subsidised specialised housing resources for elderly people, it raises **three** issues: firstly, do low or nil dependency people need to be re-housed in ordinary or very sheltered housing or could they be re-housed in less costly ordinary, smaller mainstream housing or Category 1 accommodation? Similarly, if their need is for greater security could this not have been met in other ways e.g. through changes to the physical security of their home and linking it to an alarm system offering mobile warden support. Secondly, could their social needs have been met through other means, such as day centres and voluntary groups? Thirdly, why are policies of a 'balanced' community still being pursued when research has consistently shown that 'fit' tenants do not provide significant amounts of care support for 'frail' tenants or contribute more schemes activities or make greater use of communal facilities (Middleton, 1987, Clapham and Munro, 1988, Tinker, 1989).

5.22   Level of dependency does, nevertheless, vary significantly by type of specialised housing. Very sheltered or Category 2.5 accommodation has twice as many elderly residents in the highest dependency groupings than Category 1/other specialised housing. There is also a clear relationship between the age of the respondent and the Clackmannan score: the older an elderly resident is the more likely he or she is to fall into higher dependency groupings than to be classified as 'fully independent'. For example, whilst over half (51%) of residents aged 85 or over are classified as belonging to Clackmannan group D, only just over a fifth (22%) of those aged 65-74 are placed in the same group.

5.23   Compared to earlier studies, the proportion of residents in ordinary and very sheltered housing schemes with no dependency appears to be increasing as does the proportion of residents with a high level of dependency. This polarisation in the profile of dependency amongst residents is more pronounced for local authorities and Abbeyfield/Almshouse tenants than it is for housing association tenants, and for recent entrants than for the sample as a whole. This might suggest that, as places become vacant, landlords are finding it easier to fill them with able-bodied as opposed to frail elderly people who need better housing (see paragraph 5.28) rather than supported housing specifically. It also conflicts with the widely-held belief that sheltered housing tenants, as a whole, are becoming more dependent and placing an increasing burden upon wardens (Table 5.6). (Temple, 1980, Tinker, 1989)

Table 5.6 Dependency profile of elderly residents of specialised housing compared with earlier studies: by category of accommodation (Leeds scale of dependency)

Row %s	0	1–3	4–7	8–12	Base
Ordinary Sheltered Housing:					
Current study	40	15	19	28	2,747
Previous nat. study[1]	30	29	28	12	608
Very Sheltered Housing:					
Current study	24	11	22	44	454
Previous nat. study[2]	15	20	27	38	1,011

[1] Butler, Oldman and Greve, 1978

[2] Tinker/Department of the Environment, 1989

Previous home

5.24   Respondents who had lived in their present home for less than five years were asked a set of questions about the accommodation that they had lived in immediately prior to moving. Questions covered the type of property, tenure, household composition and whether respondents had wanted to move or would have preferred to remain in their previous accommodation.

Type of accommodation and household type

5.25   Around two in five recent entrants had moved from a house and a similar proportion had moved from a flat/maisonette (42% and 39% respectively). One in eight (12%) had moved to specialised housing from a bungalow. The proportion re-housed from flats/ maisonettes is significantly higher than the proportion of the elderly population as a whole in this type of accommodation (20%), and the proportions from houses and bungalows are significantly lower (54% and 25% respectively).

5.26   Elderly residents most likely to have moved from a house to a scheme are those now living in Category 1/other schemes (64%); and those living with another person where both are less than 75 years old (57%). By region, respondents in London and the South East are most likely to have lived in a flat/maisonette (67% and 48% respectively); those in Northern region to have lived in a bungalow (23%), and those in North West, West and East Midlands to have lived in a house prior to moving (53%, 51% and 51% respectively). This finding for London and the South East is interesting as these regions contain areas of the greatest housing stress, and yet they do not seem to be re-housing elderly people who are likely to be significantly under- occupying their homes. A higher proportion of elderly households in London, however, do live in flats/maisonettes than the rest of the country (see paragraph 4.25) and this may restrict the scope for significant gains through releasing under-occupied accommodation.

5.27   Just over half of these respondents (56%) were living on their own in the previous home, and a third (34%) were living with their spouse/partner. In 5% of cases, the respondent's daughter or son and/or daughter or son-in-law was

Table 5.8a Former tenure of recent entrants: by present tenure and region

Row%s	Owner-occupier	Council rented	Housing association	Private rented	Base
All recent entrants	20	52	4	18	1,782[1]
Present tenure:					
Local authority	16	60	2	16	1,339
Housing association	32	29	11	21	401
Abbeyfield/ Almshouses	45	8	14	20	45
DoE Region:					
South-East	25	45	4	20	238
South-West	20	45	2	21	177
London	7	43	10	34	154
Eastern	14	61	4	15	219
West Mids	36	46	2	11	188
East Mids	21	54	5	14	166
North West	33	39	4	15	246
Yorks & Humberside	10	65	3	16	236
Northern	17	68	3	10	161

[1]All those living in schemes for less than five years, excluding those formerly living in residential/nursing home/hospital accommodation.

living in the household. Table 5.7 in Appendix 3 compares this previous household type profile with the current household type profile of recent entrants. It shows that the proportion of elderly people living alone has increased by 20% and the proportion of elderly couples living in schemes has gone down by 16%. This is significant because it counters the argument that most of those in schemes with nil or low dependencies are partners/spouses of high dependency elderly people who died some time after entering the scheme. This argument could only apply to approximately 16% recent entrants which is well below the percentage of all recent entrants (39%) that are 'fully independent'.

Tenure

5.28   Over four-fifths (83%) of recent entrants had moved into specialised housing from ordinary, mainstream housing in the community (Table 5.8a). Of these, just over half had moved from council properties, a fifth had been owner-occupiers and a similar proportion had lived in privately rented accommodation. This proportion of recent entrants from the private rented sector (18%) is approximately four times greater than the proportion of elderly people in this tenure within the community as a whole (5%). This finding is significant because some of the worst housing conditions are faced by elderly people in the private rented sector. It shows that public sector landlords are, to some extent, addressing this problem through re-housing elderly tenants rather than encouraging landlords to carry out necessary repairs. Most of those currently renting specialised housing from the council (60%) were council tenants immediately prior to moving. Abbeyfield/almshouse societies and housing associations had the highest proportions of former owner-occupiers (45% and 32% respectively) and local authorities the lowest (16%).

5.29   Former tenure of recent entrants also varies noticeably by region: residents in the West Midlands and the North West are most likely to have been owner-occupiers (36% and 33% respectively compared with 20% on average), with notably few Londoners having moved from their own homes (seven per cent). Residents in the Northern, Yorkshire and Humberside and Eastern regions are more likely to have lived in council property (68%, 65% and 61% respectively). In London, twice as many residents as average have moved into specialised housing from privately rented accommodation (34% versus 18% on average). One reason why such a high proportion of residents of specialised housing schemes in London moved from private landlords is because the region has the highest proportion of elderly people living in that form of tenure.

5.30   The remaining sixth of recent entrants (17%) moved from other specialised housing or long-term care in hospitals and residential homes (Table 5.8b). Compared to earlier studies, a growing number of recent entrants to specialised housing for elderly people are coming from a residential care or nursing home, whether run by a local authority, private or voluntary organisation. For very sheltered housing, there has been a four-fold increase (from 3% to 11%) over the last five years. Community care will probably increase this trend.

Col%s	Cat 1/Other	Cat 1.5/2	Cat 2.5	Previous National study of Cat 2.5[1]
Local authority residential care home or DHA nursing home	1	5	8	
Private or vol. org. residential care or nursing home	1	2	3	3
Hospital	0	*	0	2
Sheltered housing	7	9	9	11
Base	177	1,452	314	1,014

Table 5.8b Recent entrants moving from sheltered housing, residential care and hospitals: by Category of accommodation

[1]   Tinker/Department of the Environment, 1989.
Note   * – Less than 0.5%.

Attitude towards moving

5.31   Residents living in the scheme for less than five years were asked whether they would have preferred to stay in their previous home, or whether they had wanted to move. Three-quarters (75%) said they wanted to move, one in six (16%) would have preferred to stay where they were living, and a further one in fourteen (seven per cent) said they did not mind. 16% is a slightly lower proportion than previous studies have found. For example, the Leeds sheltered housing study found that nearly a quarter (22%) of sheltered housing tenants would have preferred to remain at home (Butler, Oldman and Greve, 1983).

5.32   Those who were more likely to have preferred to stay where they were included those now living in Category 1/other schemes and those living in the West Midlands (22% each). Residents living in the Northern region were more likely than average to have wanted to move (83% versus 75% on average).

Present home

Length of residence

5.33   Just over half of elderly people living in specialised housing (54%) have lived in their present home for less than five years, with 46% having lived there for five years or more. One in eight residents (12%) have moved to their present home within the last year. Those most likely to have moved in the last five years include younger respondents aged up to 65 (79%), those living in Category 2.5 schemes (69%), and those with two adults in the household where both are aged below 75 years old (71%). Very elderly people aged 85 and over are most likely to have lived in their present home for five years or more (56%); residents in Category 1/other schemes are also more likely to have lived there for five years or more (52%) (Table 5.9 in Appendix 3).

Type of accommodation

5.34   All respondents were asked a series of factual questions about their present home, relating specifically to the type of accommodation they occupy, the floor level, number of bedrooms and any facilities they share.

5.35   The majority of residents in specialised housing (63%) live in a flat or maisonette in a block. Of these, approximately three in five (62%) have access to a lift, and two in five (38%) do not – 41% of this latter group, moreover, do not live on the ground floor. Around one in five residents (18%) occupy a bedsit (ten per cent with access to a lift and eight percent without); the same proportion (18%) live in a bungalow. Very few respondents – less than half of one per cent – occupy a house or other form of accommodation. Residents who have moved within the last five years are slightly more likely to live in flats or maisonettes (66% versus 63% on average), and correspondingly less likely to live in a bungalow (15% versus 18% on average). Flats/maisonettes with a lift are the type of accommodation most likely to be provided in Category 2.5 schemes (69% versus 39% on average) (Table 5.10 in Appendix 3).

Shared facilities

5.36   Very small numbers of residents in specialised housing either share or lack basic facilities: one percent do not have a kitchen, and less than one half of one per cent do not have a wash hand basin, toilet or fixed bathroom/shower room. Residents lacking a kitchen tend to live in Abbeyfield/almshouses (36%), where bedsits are the most common type of accommodation.

5.37   In terms of sharing these facilities, less than half of one per cent share a kitchen, one per cent share a wash hand basin, two per cent share a toilet, and eight per cent share a fixed bathroom/shower room. Sharing is most common in Abbeyfield /almshouses where 10% of residents share a kitchen 27% share a wash hand basin, 62% share a toilet and 69% share a bathroom/shower room (Table 5.11 in Appendix 3).

Satisfaction with home

5.38   By a substantial majority (94%), residents in specialised housing express satisfaction with their present home; seven in ten (72%) say they are very satisfied. Dissatisfaction is low at three per cent. Results for residents who have moved within the last five years show the same pattern (Table 5.12 in Appendix 3).

5.39   Satisfaction correlates with age; those up to 65 years old are less likely to be positive about their homes than those aged 85 an over (65% versus 77% very satisfied respectively). Other residents who are slightly less likely to be positive about their home include housing association tenants (68% very satisfied, although 94% are satisfied overall), those who live in Category 1/other schemes (67%), and the highly dependent (Clackmannan category G), two-thirds of whom (65%) are very satisfied, while six per cent express dissatisfaction. Table 5.13 looks at housing association providers in more detail and shows that slightly lower levels of satisfaction in these schemes are not because the housing association sample contains more respondents aged up to 65, although it does contain fewer aged 85 or over. In fact, the local authority sample had slightly higher proportions of Category 1/other residents and highly dependent (Clackmannan G) people. Overall, however, the tendency for younger elderly people, those living in Category 1/other specialised housing schemes and the highly dependent to have lower satisfaction levels is accentuated within the housing association sample.

Table 5.13 Satisfaction with home amongst housing association tenants: by age of respondent, category of accommodation and level of dependency					
Row%s	Very satisfied	Fairly satisfied	Fairly dissatisfied	Very dissatisfied	Base
All residents	68	26	2	1	887
Age of respondent:					
Up to 65	63	26	2	4	34
65-74	66	26	2	2	259
75-84	69	26	2	1	444
85+	76	20	1	1	148
Category of accommodation:					
1/Other	63	31	4	1	58
1.5/2	69	25	2	2	737
2.5	79	16	0	1	91
Level of dependency:					
A/B	71	23	2	2	368
C	70	26	1	1	147
D	70	27	2	0	243
E/F	67	11	0	11	7
G	59	31	2	4	83

Desire to move

5.40   One in twenty elderly residents (5%) say they expect to move from their present home within the next 12 months, with just two per cent saying they are very likely to.

5.41   There is little difference in results across sub-groups: residents aged up to 65 are most likely to say they will want to move: one in eight (12%) say they are very or fairly likely to compared with five per cent of residents aged 65 or over. Respondents living in Category 1/other schemes and those living in London are also relatively more likely to want to move (9%) (Table 5.14 in Appendix 3).

Table 5.15 Receipt of social and health care services: by age of respondent, level of dependency and category of accommodation

Col%s	All residents	Up to 65	65-74	75-84	85+
Doctor	38	25	29	40	50
District nurse	21	10	13	22	32
Health visitor	4	2	2	4	4
Physiotherapist	2	2	1	2	3
Occupational therapist	1	4	1	*	1
Private nursing help	*	0	*	*	1
None of these	52				
Home help/home care aide	34	17	20	34	55
Chiropodist	22	8	13	21	38
Social worker	7	9	7	8	6
Private domestic help	6	5	3	6	10
Voluntary worker	1	1	1	1	2
Mobility officer for the blind	1	2	*	1	1
None of these	52				
Meals on wheels	11	2	6	12	20
Laundry service	3	1	2	3	6
Incontinence service	2	0	1	2	2
Night sitting service	*	0	*	0	*
None of these	85				
Base	3,569	141	994	1,724	705

Table 5.15 cont.

Col%s	1/Other	1.5/2	2.5
Doctor	33	37	52
District nurse	13	21	32
Health visitor	2	4	5
Physiotherapist	3	1	3
Occupational therapist	1	1	1
Private nursing help	0	*	*
Home help/home care aide	20	34	44
Chiropodist	14	20	39
Social worker	6	7	10
Private domestic help	8	5	7
Voluntary worker	2	1	1
Mobility officer for the blind	1	1	1
Meals on wheels	7	12	11
Laundry service	3	3	7
Incontinence service	2	2	1
Night sitting service	*	*	0
Base	368	2,747	454

Receipt of health and social care services

5.42 Receipt of social and health care services by residents of specialised housing schemes appears to be well-targeted with the very elderly aged 85 and over, those with high levels of physical and/or mental dependency and those in very sheltered housing schemes more likely to receive visits than other residents (Table 5.15).

5.43   Residents of specialised housing, however, also appear to be more likely to be in receipt of services at all levels of dependency than elderly people in the community (Table 5.15, see also Table 4.24 in Appendix 3). For example, whilst almost three-fifths (57%) of single elderly residents in Clackmannan group D interviewed in the survey say they have received visits from a home help/home care aide in the last six months, only 40% of the equivalent group of elderly people within the community have received visits from a home help/home care aide over the same time period. For those in receipt of health and social care services, there is, however, no difference in the frequency with which these services are delivered to elderly people in either setting.

5.44   Two possible explanations for this are that wardens or managers of sheltered housing are good advocates for their residents and also services will specifically organise themselves to meet the needs of residents in sheltered housing schemes e.g. by attaching two or three home care workers to a scheme. It is not, however, because informal care is making up for the shortfall in provision for elderly in the community. Table 5.16 shows that only two-fifths of the single elderly people in Clackmannan group D living in the community but not in receipt of visits from a local authority home help/home care aide, received any informal care support.

Table 5.15 cont.

Col%s	A/B	C	D	E/F	G
Doctor	19	41	55	19	60
District nurse	8	18	33	4	40
Health visitor	2	4	5	2	7
Physiotherapist	1	1	3	0	4
Occupational therapist*	*	0	1	2	3
Private nursing help	*	0	1	0	2
None of these	75	50	33	79	28
Home help/home care aide	9	37	56	7	54
Chiropodist	7	24	35	10	34
Social worker	3	9	9	0	15
Private domestic help	2	6	8	0	11
Voluntary worker	1	1	2	0	2
Mobility officer for the blind	*	1	1	0	3
None of these	82	45	28	83	27
Meals on wheels	3	10	20	3	18
Laundry service	*	3	5	0	9
Incontinence service	0	*	3	0	7
Night sitting service	0	0	0	5	1
None of these	96	88	74	92	73
Base	1,274	606	1,169	30	359

Note * – less than 0.5%

Table 5.16 Single elderly people in Clackmannan grouping D in mainstream or non-specialised housing in the community: receipt of visits from a home help/home care aide by receipt of informal care

Col%s/Row%s	Receipt of informal care		
Receipt of home help	Yes	No	Base
Yes	**41**	**38**	**40**
	45	55	100
No	**59**	**62**	**60**
	42	58	100
Base	452	593	1,045

118

6 A national survey of informal carers to elderly people

Introduction

6.1   For many elderly people, their ability to remain in their current homes is not only dependent on house adaptations and formal health and social care services, but also relies, to a large extent, on the informal care support they receive from spouses and partners, relatives or friends. It was important for this study, therefore, to look at informal care as part of the support package to enable an elderly person to stay at home. The survey of informal carers was also conducted to provide data for the exercise looking at the costs of maintaining an elderly person at home and to inform the design of the allocation model described in Chapter 8.

6.2   This Chapter is divided into five sections: firstly, a brief description of the informal carers sample and survey design; secondly, the characteristics of informal carers to elderly people; thirdly, the care and support they provide to dependants; fourthly, the contributions made by informal carers to housing costs; and, finally, receipt of care and support services by dependants of informal carers.

Research methodology and the survey sample

6.3   Information about receipt of informal care support was collected as part of a dependency form filled in with 4,123 elderly respondents included in the main survey described in Chapter 4. The dependency form measured respondents' ability to perform mobility, self-care and domestic tasks e.g. heavy shopping, getting in and out of bed and washing/bathing, and the help they received from others with these functions (see paragraph 1.26 of Chapter 1). Thus, the scope and nature of tasks coming under the heading of informal care in this study was more restricted than definitions of informal care used in other studies (General Household Survey 1985 OPCS/HMSO,1986, Green, 1988). This was a deliberate decision recognising that maintaining frail elderly people at home can very often involve much more than odd jobs around the dependant's house and garden or helping with paperwork or financial matters.

6.4   The survey included carers who did not live in the same household as their dependant (non-resident carers), and those who lived in the same household (resident carers), and this basic division informs most of the analysis of findings presented in the chapter and in the detailed individual report (no. 9 – see Appendix 1) on this element of the study. The names of informal carers as well as addresses for non-resident carers were recorded on the dependency forms completed with elderly dependants and this provided the basis of the sample for this survey. Where there was more than one person providing informal care, the elderly dependants were asked to identify which person provided the most care. A total of 832 interviews were conducted (545 with external carers and 287 with internal carers) between April and June 1992. This represents just over two-fifths (43%) of all the informal carers (using the definition given above) in the main survey sample of 9,000 elderly households. This data was then re-weighted on the basis of the incidence of resident and non-resident carers as identified via the dependency form. Before looking at the findings in detail, it should also be noted that the Leeds dependency scale is used in this chapter to compare the physical and/or mental frailty of dependants of informal carers.

Characteristics of informal carers to elderly people

Age and sex

6.5   Three-quarters of carers are women, and a quarter are men (Table 6.1). Across type of carer, women are more likely than average to be external carers (84%), and men to be internal carers (39%). Within gender, however, the differences are more pronounced: seven in ten men are resident carers compared with four in ten women. Men who are carers are also almost twice as likely to be aged 65 or over (63%) than women carers (36%). Differences between resident and non-resident carers are also clearly defined by age, with resident carers tending to be elderly (70% of them are aged 65 and over) and non-resident carers more likely to be younger (82% are under 65 years old). In fact, non- resident carers are particularly likely to be aged 45-64 (62%). Unlike gender, there are no major variations to this profile within age group.

6.6   The majority of resident carers (74%) look after their spouse/partner, with most of the remainder providing care for a father or mother (and/or father or mother-in-law). Three in five non-resident carers (61%) are looking after their father or mother (and/or father or mother-in-law). Around one in five non-resident carers (22%) are not related to the person they care for.

Table 6.1 Age and gender profile of carers by type of carer			
Col%s	**All carers**	**Resident carers**	**Non-resident carers**
Gender:			
Male	27	39	16
Female	73	61	84
Age:			
18-44	12	4	20
45-64	45	27	62
65-74	25	39	12
75+	18	31	6
Base	832	411	421

Health and disability

6.7 Five per cent of informal carers are registered as disabled, and a further 13% are disabled but not registered, having a long-term illness, health problem or handicap which limits their daily activities. As might be expected, resident carers are twice as likely as non-resident carers to have some level of disability. Disability is also correlated with age: 6% of carers aged 18-44 are disabled, compared with 22% of those aged 65- 74 and 33% of those aged 75+ (Table 6.2 in Appendix 3).

Length of time as a carer

6.8 Two in five carers (40%) have been looking after their dependant for up to five years, three in ten for between five and ten years and a similar proportion for ten years or more. There is little difference in this profile according to whether the carer is resident or non-resident. There are some variations, however, in the average numbers of hours per week provided in care support. Not surprisingly, those who have been looking after their dependant for up to five years are more likely to be putting in under five hours per week than twenty or more hours, and those carers of twenty or more years standing are more likely to be providing twenty or more hours (Table 6.3 in Appendix 3). Younger carers aged under 45 are also less likely to have provided care for ten years or more (20% versus 31% across the same as a whole).

Level of dependency of dependant

6.9 There is no real difference in the levels of dependency or disability amongst elderly people being cared for by resident or non-resident carers (Table 6.4). Two in five dependants of resident carers fall into the highest dependency grouping and exactly the same proportion of dependants of non-resident carers are in this group. There is also very little difference at medium and low dependency levels and in the proportions of dependants who are classified as `fully independent'. Two clear differences emerge, however, in the time carers spend looking after their dependant. Firstly, the amount of time spent in providing care differs considerably by the level of dependency of the dependant – half of those caring for a person with a Leeds dependency score of 8-12 spend 20 or more hours a week providing care, compared with at most one in five carers spending 20 or more hours looking after people with lower levels of dependency (Leeds dependency score of 7 or less). Secondly, at all levels of dependency, resident carers are providing, on average, considerably more time in care support to their dependants than non-resident carers (Tables 6.14 and 6.15). As will be explored in later sections of this chapter, there are two possible explanations for this: firstly, that resident carers provide much more time in support with domestic and practical tasks such as clothes washing, heavy housework, preparing and cooking meals, odd jobs in the house, paperwork and so on, simply because they are part of the same household as their dependant; and, secondly, that resident carers are not receiving as much formal health and

Table 6.4 Level of dependency of dependant (Leeds scale of dependency): by type of carer and number of hours per week provided in all care support

Col%s	All carers	Resident	Non-resident
0	22	25	19
1-3	13	11	15
4-7	24	23	25
8-12	41	41	42
Base	832	411	421

Row%s	0	1-3	4-7	8-12	Base
Under 5 hrs	21	19	28	31	205
6-19 hrs	24	11	27	38	289
20+ hrs	20	11	19	50	327

social care support as dependants of non-resident carers. It should be pointed out, nevertheless, that the estimates of time offered in care support in this paragraph and subsequent paragraphs come from respondents themselves and, therefore, some caution must be exercised in interpreting the findings, as perceptions may not always be reliable.

Care and support provided to dependants

Domestic care

6.10   All but three per cent of informal carers help their dependants with domestic tasks. Two-thirds of carers (67%) provide help with four or more tasks: 83% of resident carers, compared with 50% of non- resident carers. Carers are most likely to help their dependants with the light and heavy shopping (76% and 74% respectively). Around three in five help with the light and heavy housework (65% and 58% respectively), and with washing the clothes (62%). Just over half help prepare and cook hot meals, make the bed and iron the clothes (54%, 53% and 52% respectively). Resident carers are generally more likely to provide help with domestic tasks than non-resident carers. The main exception to this is heavy shopping, which both resident and non- resident are roughly equally likely to do (76% and 73% respectively). In line with this, the likelihood of helping with each of these tasks increases according to the number of hours per week that respondents provide care. Although, once again, shopping is the exception to this general pattern, with those who provide less than five hours' care more likely to help with the shopping than with other tasks. Female carers are more likely than male carers to do the washing and the ironing: 68% of women versus 46% of men wash the clothes; 60% of women versus 31% of men do the ironing. Lastly, dependants with a higher dependency score are more likely than average to receive help with ironing (61%), washing the clothes (70%), making the bed (62%), and preparing and cooking hot meals (65%) (Table 6.5 in Appendix 3).

6.11   Making the bed and preparing and cooking hot meals are everyday tasks for seven in ten carers (70% and 69% respectively). Just over half (55%) also do some light housework every day. Tasks performed at least once a week but not every day, include heavy and light shopping (84% and 72% respectively), ironing (81%), washing the clothes (77%), and heavy housework (63%). In terms of the number of hours spent on these tasks per week, three in ten carers (31%) spend up to four hours, around one in five spend five to nine or 10-19 hours (18% each), with a further three in ten (31%) helping out for at least 20 hours a week. Resident carers spend more time on domestic tasks than non-resident carers: three-quarters (76%) spend ten or more hours on these tasks each week, compared with 22% of non-resident carers. Carers looking after a person with a high level of dependency are also likely to spend more hours helping with domestic tasks: 58% of those caring for a person with a dependency score of 8-12 spend ten or more hours on domestic tasks, compared with 49% on average. There is no difference by gender in the time spent helping with domestic tasks (Table 6.6 in Appendix 3).

Col%s	Resident carers	Non-resident carers
Table 6.7 Number of hours spent performing domestic care tasks each week for high dependency (8–12 on the Leeds scale) elderly people (unweighted): by type of carer		
0-4 hrs	4	30
5-9 hrs	2	26
10-19 hrs	19	24
20-29 hrs	11	11
30+ hrs	64	10
Base	115	224

6.12   It is important to note, moreover, that the gap between resident and non-resident carers is significantly greater than for average time spent by type of carer in providing help with mobility (paragraphs 6.13 – 6.15) and personal care tasks (paragraphs 6.16 – 6.18). As such, it accounts for much of the extra time spent by resident carers in providing support to elderly dependents at all levels of dependency. In fact, resident carers are approximately four times more likely to be providing over 20 hours in domestic support each week to their high dependency dependants than non-resident carers (Table 6.7).

Help with getting around

6.13   Informal carers are less likely to help their dependants move around, whether inside or outside their home, than they are to help with domestic tasks: half of carers say they do not help with any of the six mobility tasks listed. This is, however, not unexpected as not all of the elderly dependants of the carers sampled suffered from mobility problems. Getting around outside on a level surface and getting in and out of a chair are the types of help most likely to be provided, by 28% and 25% of carers respectively. One in six carers help their dependants to get up and down stairs and in and out of bed (17% and 16% respectively), and 11% provide help with getting around inside on a level surface and travelling by bus. Overall, resident carers are slightly more likely to provide help with getting around, particularly with getting in and out of a chair (32% versus 17%) or bed (24% versus 8%). Respondents caring for a person with a high Leeds dependency score of 8-12 are also more likely than average to help with each of the tasks listed, with the exception of travelling by bus (Table 6.8).

6.14   Daily tasks for informal carers include helping their dependant to get in and out of bed or a chair and to move around inside on a level surface (71%, 61% and 58% respectively help with these tasks). Around two in five carers (43%) also help their dependants to get up and down stairs once a day or more. Of the two other mobility tasks, help with getting around outside on a level surface tends to be given at least once a week but not every day (60%). The frequency with which carers provide help with travelling by bus is less clearly defined: around two in five (37%) provide help at least once a week, one in five (21%) helps at least once a month, and a further two in five (41%) help less often than once a month.

Table 6.8 Mobility care tasks: by type of carer and level of dependency of dependant

Col%s	All carers	Resident	Non-resident	0	1-7	8-12
Getting around outside	28	29	27	23	21	38
Getting in/out of a chair	25	32	17	19	14	38
Getting up/down stairs	17	20	15	15	14	21
Getting in/out of bed	16	24	8	10	5	29
Getting around inside	11	13	9	8	4	17
Travelling by bus	11	13	8	12	11	9
None of these	50	46	54	57	61	37
Base	832	411	421	180	308	344

6.15 In contrast to the time spent helping with domestic tasks, carers tend to spend less time per week helping their dependant with mobility problems. Two-thirds of carers (65%) spend between one and four hours each week providing this sort of help, and 24% spend five hours or more. Once again, resident carers tend to spend more time helping than non-resident carers, although the gap between them is smaller than for domestic tasks. Time spent is also related to dependency, with carers of highly dependent people more likely to spend five or more hours each week helping them move around (31% versus 24% on average). Table 6.9 puts time spent in helping with mobility problems together with dependency levels and shows that the gap between the amount of time being spent in this activity by resident and non-resident carers for high dependency elderly people is smaller than the equivalent gap for domestic tasks (Table 6.7).

Table 6.9 Number of hours spent performing mobility tasks each week for high dependency (8-12 on the Leeds scale) elderly people (unweighted): by type of carer

Col%s	Resident carers	Non-resident carers
0-1 hrs	51	78
2-4 hrs	19	14
5-9 hrs	13	6
10+ hrs	17	3
Base	115	224

Table 6.10 Personal care tasks: by type of carer, gender of carer and level of dependency of dependant

Col%s	All carers	Resident	Non-resident	Male	Female	0	1-7	8-12
Putting on socks/shoes	25	37	14	27	25	17	16	39
Washing hair	25	25	25	8	31	20	17	34
Washing hands/face	6	10	3	6	6	5	2	10
Washing all over/ shower	25	36	14	22	26	17	13	40
Getting dressed	17	26	9	19	17	10	7	31
Getting undressed	15	24	7	17	15	7	7	27
Feeding	2	4	1	4	2	2	*	4
Cutting toenails	21	28	13	18	22	22	16	24
None of these	48	36	59	52	47	55	61	33
Base	832	411	421	227	605	180	308	344

Note * – Less than 0.5%.

Personal care

6.16   As with mobility tasks, around half of respondents (51%) help dependants with looking after themselves: 64% of resident carers provide such help, compared with 41% of non-resident carers. A quarter of carers help dependants to put on their socks and shoes, wash their hair and wash all over or shower (25% each). One in five (21%) provides help with cutting toenails, and slightly fewer help dependants to get dressed or undressed (17% and 15% respectively). Relatively few ever help their dependant with washing their hands and face or with feeding (6% and 2% respectively). Hair washing is the one task that resident and non-resident carers are equally likely to help the dependant with (25% each). Again, carers looking after highly dependent people with a Leeds score of 8-12 are more likely to provide help with each of these personal care tasks, particularly washing all over or showering (40% versus 25% on average). By gender, men and women are equally likely to help with personal care tasks, with the exception of hair washing (31% of women versus 8% of men) (Table 6.10).

6.17   Help with feeding, undressing and dressing, washing hands and face, and putting on socks and shoes is provided most regularly: daily by around two-thirds of carers for each of these tasks; help with washing all over or showering, and hair washing tends to be given at least once a week by around three-quarters (76% and 73% respectively); and help with cutting toenails is given least frequently: two-thirds (68%) provide help at least once a month, and a further 14% less often.

6.18   Just under half of informal carers spend an hour each week on personal care, a quarter spend two to four hours, an eighth spend five to nine hours and a tenth spend ten or more hours. Unlike help with domestic tasks and getting around, the amount of time spent on personal care does not vary significantly according to the level of dependency of the person being cared for. There is also little difference by gender in time spent providing personal care. In common with domestic tasks and mobility problems, however, resident carers offer more time in care support to their dependants than non-resident carers. The gap between types of carers in the amount of time provided in helping the most dependent with self-care tasks is, nevertheless, considerably less than the equivalent gap for domestic support. (Table 6.11).

Table 6.11 Number of hours spent performing personal care tasks each week for high dependency (8-12 on the Leeds scale) elderly people (unweighted): by type of carer

Col%s	Resident carers	Non-resident carers
0-1 hrs	47	80
2-4 hrs	23	14
5-9 hrs	16	5
10+ hrs	13	1
Base	115	224

Table 6.12 Practical care tasks: by type of carer, gender of carer and level of dependency of dependant

Col%s	All carers	Resident	Non-resident	Male	Female	0	1-7	8-12
Odd jobs in house	67	69	65	83	60	67	63	70
Odd jobs in garden	54	67	42	73	47	63	52	52
Nursing help at times of illness	55	67	45	54	56	56	46	64
Arranging for or doing repairs	48	51	45	62	42	49	44	51
Helping with paper-work or financial matters	63	61	64	67	61	63	54	70
None of these	10	8	13	6	12	10	15	7
Base	832	411	421	227	605	180	308	344

Practical tasks

6.19   Nine in ten carers (90%) help their dependant by doing practical tasks, most frequently odd jobs in the house and paperwork or financial matters (67% and 63% respectively). Around half provide nursing help at times of sickness, do odd jobs in the garden or repairs (55%, 54% and 48% respectively). While resident and non-resident carers are equally likely to help with odd jobs in the house, paperwork or financial matters and repairs, resident carers are more likely to provide nursing help in times of sickness and to help out in the garden. The type of practical help undertaken varies by gender: men are more likely than women to do odd jobs in the house (83% versus 60%), in the garden (73% versus 47%), and repairs (62% versus 42%). Carers looking after a highly dependent person are more likely to provide nursing help in times of sickness (64%), and help with paperwork or financial matters (70%) (Table 6.12).

6.20   Given the nature of the tasks, as might be expected, relatively few carers carry out practical tasks on a daily basis. Nursing help in times of sickness is an exception, provided at least once a day by two in five carers (38%). These carers are more likely to be resident, and to be looking after a highly dependent person with a Leeds score of 8-12 (56% and 50% respectively). Nursing help is also one of the practical forms of help which is least frequently given (43%) provide nursing help less often than once a month. Tasks more likely to be undertaken on a weekly basis include odd jobs in the garden, help with paperwork or financial matters, and odd jobs in the house (52%, 40% and 36% respectively). Arranging for, or doing, necessary repairs happens on a more sporadic basis, with a third (34%) of carers helping at least once a month, and just over half (54%) saying less often.

6.21   Around three in ten carers spend either an hour, or two to four hours, on these tasks (30% and 28% respectively), with 16% spending five to nine hours, and 19% spending ten or more hours each week. Resident carers are notably more likely than non-resident carers to spend five or more hours on practical tasks (54% versus 15% respectively). Men are significantly more likely than women to spend time on practical tasks (49% versus 29% respectively spend five or more hours) as are those aged 75+ (44%). Here the difference in the amount of time spent by resident and non-resident carers in these practical tasks for highly dependent elderly people is greater than the corresponding difference for mobility and personal care tasks, but equivalent to domestic tasks (Table 6.13).

Table 6.13 Number of hours spent performing practical tasks each week for high dependency (8-12 on the Leeds scale) elderly people (unweighted): by type of carer		
Col%s	Resident carers	Non-resident carers
0-1 hrs	25	60
2-4 hrs	22	29
5-9 hrs	21	7
10+ hrs	33	4
Base	115	224

Overall time spent in providing care

6.22   On average, around two in five informal carers (37%) provide up to nine hours help each week, and three in five (62%) help for ten hours or more. Resident carers spend considerably more time than non- resident carers providing help. Eighty-six per cent of resident carers spend ten hours or more, with half of them (51%) spending 30 hours or more. This compares with 38% of non-resident carers providing ten or more hours of care per week, and seven per cent of them spending 30 hours or more. By gender, three in four men (73%) spend ten or more hours a week looking after their dependant, compared with 58% of women. This is probably due to the fact that men are much more likely to be resident carers than women and resident carers provided more time in care support. Differences also emerge clearly by age, with two in five carers aged 65+ (40%) providing 30 hours or more of care per week, reflecting the fact that internal carers tend to be elderly themselves. Younger carers aged under 45 are more likely to spend a few hours each week providing care (51% spend up to nine hours per week). Similarly, by household type, three in five single adults (external carers) spend up to nine hours per week (57%), while the majority of carers in three adults households (78%) spend ten hours or more (42% spend 30 hours or more each week). The amount of time spent also varies significantly by the dependant's level of dependency (Table 6.14), although, rather perversely, those dependants with a Leeds dependency scale score of 0 receive, on average, more time in care support than those with Leeds dependency scale scores of 1-7. Perhaps more importantly, however, the total amount of time being offered by different types of carers to high dependency elderly people differs dramatically. While almost two-thirds of resident carers (64%) looking after an elderly person with a Leeds dependency score of 8-12 spend 30 hours or more each week providing support, only a tenth (10%) of non- resident carers do likewise (Table 6.15). This may account for the finding for those with a Leeds dependency scale score of 1-7: this group contains more non-resident carers (54%) than resident carers (46%), and the opposite is true for dependants with a Leeds dependency score of 0, where resident carers (56%) outnumber non-resident carers (44%).

Table 6.15 Overall time spent in providing care support each week for high dependency (8-12 on the Leeds scale) elderly people (unweighted): by type of carer		
Col%s	Resident carers	Non-resident carers
0-4 hrs	4	30
5-9 hrs	2	26
10-19 hrs	19	24
20-29 hrs	11	11
30+ hrs	64	10
Base	115	224

Table 6.14 Overall time spent in providing care support each week: by type of carer, gender of carer, age of carer, household type of carer and level of dependency of dependant

Col%s	All carers	Resident	Non-resident	Male	Female	18-44	45-64	65-74	75+	Single adult	2 adults: at least 1 aged 65+	2 adults: both aged 18-64	3+ adults	0	1-7	8-12
Up to 5 hrs	19	5	34	13	22	25	22	15	15	39	42	32	10	18	26	14
5-9 hrs	18	8	27	12	19	26	23	10	8	18	33	29	12	19	21	14
10-19hrs	23	22	23	27	21	21	22	24	21	24	14	22	24	26	20	22
20-29hrs	10	13	8	7	12	13	9	11	12	4	8	9	12	9	10	11
30+hrs	29	51	7	39	25	12	23	40	40	13	3	7	42	28	21	36
Base	832	411	421	227	605	100	372	210	150	65	62	180	525	180	308	344

Attitude to level of care provided

6.23   Three-quarters of carers (77%) think they help their dependant a great deal or a fair amount. While a majority of both resident and non- resident carers say they provide at least a fair amount of care (84% and 70% respectively), resident carers are more likely to say they provide a great deal (48%), and non-resident carers to say they provide a fair amount (47%). One in five carers (22%) say they only help a little, with non-resident carers more likely to give this answer (29%). There is a clear relationship with the amount of time that respondents spend providing care: half of those spending up to five hours per week (54%) say they help a little or not much at all; at the other end of the scale, 95% of those providing 20 or more hours of care (more likely to be resident carers) say they help a great deal/fair amount.

6.24   Most carers feel that they are helping their dependant as much as they can (62%). This is more frequently stated by resident than non- resident carers (68% versus 56% respectively), by respondents who are spending more 20 hours or more providing care (76%), and those looking after a highly dependent person (73%). Around one in five (18%) say that the person they care for does not need any more help from them, and one in ten (11%) say they would like to help more, particularly non-resident carers. Few carers say they do too much or that they do not want to help any more than they do (2% each) and there was no difference by type of carer (Table 6.16).

Contributions to housing costs

6.25   One part of this survey aimed at assessing the financial contribution made by both resident and non-resident carers to dependants' housing costs; this covers, for example, rent or mortgage payments, re-decoration or repairs and household items. Resident carers who were the spouse or partner of the person they care for were excluded from this part of the survey (Table 6.17 in Appendix 3).

6.26   Four per cent of carers contribute to their dependant's rent or mortgage. Contributors are more likely to be resident than non-resident carers (14% versus 2% respectively). Payments are equally likely to be made on a weekly or monthly basis (both 39%), although internal carers tend to contribute weekly, and external carers monthly (59% and 52% respectively). Similarly, four per cent of carers make a contribution to community charge payments, and, once again, these carers are more likely to be resident than non-resident (13% versus 1% respectively). The frequency of contributions is most likely to be once a month (63%). A greater proportion of carers contribute towards the repair and maintenance or re-decoration of their dependant's home than they do towards the rent/mortgage or community charge (14%). Resident carers are almost three times more likely to contribute than non-resident carers (29% versus 11%). Contributors are also more likely to be spending at least 20 hours per week providing care (25%).

6.27   All carers making a contribution were asked to give the amount of their last payment towards repairs, maintenance or redecoration. Contributions tend

Table 6.16 Attitude to level of care provided: by type of carer and number of hours per week provided in all care support

Col%s	All carers	Resident	Non-resident	Under 5 hrs	6-19 hrs	20+ hrs
A great deal	35	48	23	6	23	65
A fair amount	42	36	47	39	57	30
A little	17	10	23	40	15	2
Not much at all	5	5	6	14	3	2
Base	832	411	421	205	289	327

to fall into two categories: 45% of respondents have contributed up to £100, and 27% have contributed £300 or more. Resident carers are more likely to make larger contributions of £300 or more (39% compared with 19% of external carers).

6.28   Very few carers (three per cent) have made a contribution towards the cost of adaptations to their dependant's home in the last twelve months. Once again, resident carers are slightly more likely than average to make a contribution (seven per cent, compared with three per cent on average).

6.29   As well as assessing the amount of care they think they offer their dependant, respondents were asked for their views on the amount of financial help they provide. One in eight (12%) say they provide a great deal or a fair amount, with the majority of carers (58%) saying their contribution is a little or not much at all. Results vary by type of carer: two in five resident carers (40%) say they provide at least a fair amount, compared with six per cent of non-resident carers; the majority of non- resident carers (66%) say they provide at most a little financial help. In each case, however, around three in ten feel unable to make an assessment. Men carers living in households containing three or more adults, and those spending at least 20 hours providing care are more likely than others to say they provide a great deal or a fair amount of financial help (23%, 22% and 26% respectively). Carers in two adult households where both adults are under the age of 65 are more likely to say they provide a little or not much at all (70%). Four in five non- resident carers who currently make a contribution to housing costs (79%) say they provide a little or not much financial help at all.

6.30   When asked whether they thought their financial contribution was sufficient, around two in five carers (38%) say that their dependant does not need any more financial help from them, 15% say that he or she would not accept any more help, and a further 13% say they are giving as much financial help as they can. Six per cent would like to give more help, and one per cent do not want to give any more help. No carers say they give too much.

6.31   Resident carers and those providing at least 20 hours of care – two overlapping groups – are most likely to say they giving as much help as they can (32% and 24% respectively). Non-resident carers are most likely to say their dependant doesn't need any more financial help (40%). Non-resident carers contributing to their dependant's housing costs are more likely than average to say their dependant will not accept any more financial help (28%).

Receipt of health and social care services

6.32   For almost all of the sixteen health and social care services covered by the survey, a significantly higher proportion of non-resident carers say their dependants have received visits in the six months prior to the survey than resident carers (Table 6.18). This may be partly due to the fact that health and social care services tend to be targeted on elderly people living alone as opposed to elderly couples and others (see paragraphs 4.59 – 4.60 in Chapter 4). Once elderly people receive services, however, there is no real difference in the frequency with which services are provided to elderly people being cared for by resident and non-resident carer.

Table 6.18 Health and social services received by dependant of carer: by type of carer

Col%s	Type of carer		
	All carers	Resident carers	Non-resident carers
District Nurse	28	22	34
Health Visitors	10	7	14
Physiotherapist	3	4	2
Occupational therapist	2	3	1
Doctor	49	39	58
Private nursing help	1	1	1
None	37	45	29
Social worker	12	8	15
Mobility officer for the blind	1	1	1
Chiropodist	24	18	30
Home help/ home care aide	25	12	38
Private domestic help	7	8	6
Voluntary worker	4	3	4
None	50	62	37
Meals on Wheels	9	3	14
Laundry	2	*	3
Incontinence service	2	1	3
None	87	94	81
Base	832	411	421

Note * – less than 0.5%

6.33   Finally, Table 6.19 shows the level of demand amongst informal carers for these health and social care services. Carers most frequently mentioned the chiropodist (21%), doctor (13%), home help (8%), health visitor (7%) and district or community nurse (7%). Non-resident carers are more likely to mention each of these services, as are carers who look after a highly dependent person (although home visits from the doctor are equally likely to be requested by carers looking after people with nil dependency).

Table 6.19 Health and social services requested by carer for dependant: by type of carer and level of dependency of dependant

Col%s	Type of carer			Dependency Level		
	All carers	Resident	Non-resident	0	1-7	8-12
District Nurse	7	5	10	6	7	9
Health Visitors	7	3	12	4	7	10
Physiotherapist	5	3	7	3	4	7
Occupational therapist	1	1	1	*	*	2
Doctor	13	8	21	17	8	17
Private nursing help	1	*	1	*	1	1
None	79	86	68	77	86	70
Social worker	5	5	6	4	5	6
Mobility officer for the blind	2	1	3	2	2	2
Chiropodist	21	17	25	22	14	27
Home help/ home care aide	8	3	15	7	7	11
Private domestic help	1	1	2	1	1	2
Voluntary worker	2	2	3	2	1	4
None	67	75	62	65	72	64
Meals on Wheels	3	*	6	3	3	3
Laundry	3	2	3	3	2	3
Incontinence service	2	1	2	*	1	3
None	91	96	87	92	94	88
Base	832	411	421	180	308	344

7 A national survey of non-elderly disabled adults

7.1   As was stated in the introduction to Chapter 4, the most important element of any study of housing needs is a survey of the characteristics, circumstances and aspirations of the group being examined. This study, therefore, included an interview survey with a national sample of private households containing non-elderly disabled adults. This Chapter describes the main findings from this survey and is divided into five sections: the research methodology and survey sample; the characteristics of non-elderly disabled people and their households; their housing circumstances; their housing aspirations; and, their receipt of health and social care services.

7.2   Exactly the same information was collected for non-elderly disabled adults[15] as for elderly people, the only difference being that, whilst the latter data is regionally representative, the former is only nationally representative. It can, nevertheless, be used in the same way as the data on elderly people to allocate households to housing options appropriate to their assessed needs.

Research methodology and the survey sample

7.3   The survey was based on 850 interviews with non-elderly disabled adults and was conducted concurrently with the survey of elderly people in the community, using the same sampling and screening procedures. One implication of this is that the survey findings under- estimate the incidence of non-elderly disabled adults living with a person/people aged 75+. Where interviews were conducted with these types of households, the vast majority would have been with the elderly person(s) rather than the non-elderly disabled adult. The survey was carried out between October 1991 and April 1992. A total of 33,877 addresses were screened for non-elderly disabled adults, with 11% identified as containing a potential non-elderly disabled respondent. A decision was made when designing the survey that the definition of disability used to identify potential respondents would be based, as closely as possible, on the approach taken by the Office of Population Censuses and Surveys in the surveys of disability in Great Britain (OPCS/HMSO, 1988). Thus the contact sheet used at screened addresses was broadly modelled upon the postal screening questionnaire used in the OPCS studies and, if a potential respondent was not registered as disabled, blind or partially sighted with the local social services then they were asked if they had difficulty with any of the following due to a long-term health problem or disability: walking on level ground, steps and stairs, bending or straightening, falling or keeping balance, gripping or turning things, reading newspaper print even **with** glasses, hearing someone

---

[15] All those aged 16–64.

talking/deafness, breathlessness /wheezing/coughing, severe pain or irritation, poor bladder control, fits/convulsions (in past two years) and getting confused/disorientated. The contact sheet and other more detailed aspects of the methodology can be found in the individual report no. 10 on this element of the study (see Appendix 1).

7.4   Those people responding positively to at least one of these were included in the study and, as such, this was the threshold used to define disability for this survey. This is a relatively low threshold of disability, but it was considered important to obtain data about people across a wide range of levels of disability. There will, nevertheless, still be some people with disabilities below this threshold who have not been included in the sample. Of those identified as disabled, 40% were registered as disabled and 60% had at least one long-term health problems or disability.

The characteristics of non-elderly disabled adults and their households

Age and sex

7.5   Table 7.1 shows the age and gender profile of non-elderly disabled adults. A slight majority are aged between 50 and 64 years old (56%). 13% are aged between 16 and 29 years old and 32% are aged between 30 and 49 years old. Overall, slightly more non-elderly disabled adults are women than men. Within the 16-29 age group, however, women out number men by approximately two to one.

Table 7.1 Age and gender profile of non-elderly disabled adults				
Col%s/ Row%s	16-29	30-49	50-64	All
Male	34	47	48	46
	9	32	59	100
Female	66	53	52	54
	15	31	54	100
Base	107	268	475	850
	13	32	56	100

Marital status

7.6   Three in five non-elderly disabled people are married (61%), with a further 3% living as married. One in six (16%) are single, 11% are divorced or separated and 8% are widowed. As may be expected, young people aged under 29 are more likely to be single than any other age group.

Household type

7.7   The majority of disabled adults aged 16-64 (83%) live with one or more other people. Two in five (37%) live in two adult households, which is over twice the rate for the population as a whole (16% of households in the General Household Survey 1991, OPCS/HMSO, 1993) and almost one in two (45%)

live as part of a larger household of three or more people. Finally, one in six live on their own (17%), which is also a higher rate than for the population as a whole (10% – GHS 1991).

Table 7.2 Household type profile of non-elderly disabled adults: by age of respondent				
Row%s	Single adult	2+ adults no children	Children in household	Base
Age of respondent				
16-29	4	22	74	148
30-49	10	21	69	476
50-64	23	61	16	226

7.8   The older the disabled person, the more likely he or she is to live alone: 4% of those aged 16-29 live on their own, compared with 23% of those aged 50-64. Younger disabled people generally tend to live in households of three or more people (78% of those aged 16-29 and 67% of those aged 30-49), respondents aged 50-64 more frequently living with one other person (54%). Two in three disabled people aged 16-64 live with their spouse/partner (64%), two in five have their daughter(s) /son(s)/in law living with them and, in 8% of cases, non-elderly disabled people live with their mother and father. Almost all of this last group are young people aged between 16 and 29 years old (Table 7.2).

Employment, pensions, income and savings and state benefits

7.9   Just over half of non-elderly disabled adults class themselves as sick or disabled (55%), one in five are employed (13% – full time and 7% – part time), and a further one in five (22%) are engaged in full-time housework. Those aged between 30 and 49 years old are most likely to be in employment (33%).

7.10   A high proportion of non-elderly disabled people have lower weekly incomes than the population as a whole (at the time of the survey) (Table 7.3 in Appendix 3). For example, whereas just over one in ten households containing non-elderly disabled people have a weekly household income of under £50, only 2% of the population as a whole fall into this category (General Household Survey 1991, OPCS/HMSO 1993). Similarly, whilst over a half (59%) of non-elderly disabled adults have incomes below £150 per week, this only applies to one-third (32%) of the population as a whole.

7.11   Respondents aged 50-64 (18%) are more likely than average to have an income of less than £50 per week. Younger respondents aged 16-29 are more likely to fall into the next income bracket of £50 to £99.99 (39%), as are adults living on their own and those classed in the `other' tenure category i.e. privately rented and living with parents/relatives (55% and 39% respectively). Disabled adults aged 30- 49, respondents with children in the household and owner-occupiers are the most likely to have higher incomes of at least £150 per week (60%, 55% and 51% respectively).

7.12   One in two non-elderly disabled adults say they and/or their spouse or partner have no savings and investments (Table 7.4 in Appendix 3). Owner-occupiers, disabled people with a weekly income of up to £50, older respondents aged 50-64 and those living with at least one other adult but no children, are most likely to have savings or investments (67%, 61%, 57% and 57% respectively). Around half (48%) have saved or invested up to £5,000, and a third (32%) have £5,000 or more saved. Rather surprisingly, those with the lowest weekly incomes are just as likely as those with the highest weekly incomes to have savings of £16,000 or more. As the vast majority of those on low weekly incomes in the sample are aged 50-64, these savings may represent a lump sum on early retirement or a settlement following long-term sickness or industrial injury. One in five respondents (19%) are unable or unwilling to indicate the extent of their savings.

7.13   Over a third of the households surveyed containing non-elderly disabled adults have at least one person receiving an invalidity pension (37%) (Table 7.5 in Appendix 3). This seems to be a higher proportion of the non-elderly disabled adult population than was found in the OPCS studies of disability (27%) (see Report 2 – The Financial Circumstances of disabled adults living in private households, OPCS/HMSO, 1988). Men are more likely to draw this pension than women (52% of men versus 25% of women) as are middle-aged and older respondents, council or housing association tenants, those with weekly incomes up to £150 and those with a high level of dependency or disability (45% and 52% respectively).

7.14   Fifteen per cent of households benefit from occupational pensions, and 12% receive a state retirement pension. Relatively small proportions have income from the other pensions listed: 3% receive a widow's state pension, and 1% a private pension or war disablement pension.

7.15   Table 7.6 in Appendix 3 shows the state benefits or allowances received by households containing non-elderly adults. The benefit most frequently received is mobility allowance by one in five disabled people (23%). This is, once again, a higher proportion than was found for this group in the OPCS surveys of disability – 13%. Those with medium to high levels of dependency or disability are most likely to draw this benefit. 21% of disabled people receive child benefit, 9% draw an attendance allowance and the same proportion receive the severe disablement allowance; these are also most likely to be drawn by disabled people with a high dependency score.

7.16   One in five disabled adults and/or their spouse/partner (21%) receive income support. Respondents aged 16-29 and council or housing association tenants are more likely than average to receive income support (38% and 34% respectively). Seven in ten of those who rent their homes (69%) receive housing benefit: 29% have all of their rent paid, and 40% have part of their rent paid through housing benefit. Disabled people with children in the household are most likely to have all their rent paid by the local authority or local social security office (43%). Overall, respondents with a weekly income of £50-£99.99 and disabled people living on their own are more likely than average to be recipients (86% and 80% respectively versus 69% on average). This is not surprising, however, as these groups contained the highest proportions of renters (public or private) and the lowest levels of owner-occupation (see paragraphs 7.29 – 7.30).

Health

7.17   As with the main survey of elderly people in the community, non-elderly disabled adults were asked a series of questions about their state of health, some of which were based on respondents' own overall assessments and others on specific measures of performance in carrying out mobility, self-care and domestic tasks.

7.18   Over three-quarters of respondents said they were registered as disabled, blind or partially-sighted with the local social services or had long-term illnesses or disabilities which handicapped or prevented them from doing things for themselves (77%). Three per cent of respondents who are registered or have a long-term illness or disability are bed- or chair-fast. While there is little difference across sub-groups, the bed and chairfast are more likely to be living in property in the `other' tenure category (8%) which includes disabled adults living with relatives or friends.

7.19   Respondents were asked in greater detail about their health problems and disabilities. They were first shown a list of 12 difficulties due to long-term health problems (Table 7.7 in Appendix 3) and then, a list of six specific illnesses and disabilities.

7.20   Just over half of disabled adults (55%) say they have difficulty with steps or stairs. Around two in five have difficulty bending or straightening (44%), experience severe pain or irritation (42%), and breathlessness, wheezing or coughing (41%). Other problems mentioned less frequently include difficulties walking on level ground (31%), falling or keeping balance (29%), and gripping or turning things (28%). Generally, the higher respondents' dependency and the older they are, the more likely they are to suffer from these problems, except for breathlessness, wheezing or coughing, for which there is no clear difference across dependency levels or by age. For most of these difficulties, moreover, a higher proportion of non-elderly disabled adults suffer from them than elderly disabled people (see Table 4.7 in Appendix 3). The main exceptions being falling or keeping balance and hearing someone talk/deafness. An explanation for this might be the generally higher level of dependency amongst the non-elderly disabled adult survey sample in comparison with the elderly survey sample (see paragraph 7.24 below).

7.21   The most common long-term illness is painful joints, mentioned by half of respondents (52%), most frequently by those aged 50-64 (59%), and those with a high dependency level. A quarter of disabled adults (24%) refer to pain in the chest on effort and a third of disabled people (32%) have none of these long-term illnesses.

Table 7.8 The Dependency profile of non-elderly disabled people: by age and household type

Row%s	Clackmannan dependency					Leeds dependency				
	A/B	C	D	F/G	Base[1]	0	1-3	4-7	8-12	Base
All households	43	6	31	20	839	53	12	17	18	850
Age of respondent:										
16-24	57	2	25	18	61	70	6	14	11	63
25-44	48	6	27	19	219	58	12	14	16	223
45-64	39	7	33	20	559	48	13	19	20	564
Household type:										
Single adult	51	12	24	12	147	62	15	14	9	148
2+ adults no children	38	6	34	22	468	46	12	19	23	476
Children in household	46	4	30	20	224	60	10	15	15	226

[1] 11 of the respondents could not be classified on the more complex Clackmannan scale because of missing data on their dependency forms. This applies to the base figures for Clackmannan dependency used in other tables.

Dependency levels

7.22   As in the main survey of elderly people in the community (see Chapter 4), two measures of dependency were produced from the questions asked of non-elderly disabled adults, and Table 7.8 shows the distribution across these two scales by the age and household type of the respondent.

7.23   It is clear from both measures that there are substantial numbers of disabled adults who have no physical/mental dependency. It would seem, therefore, that their disability is not causing them problems in performing basic domestic, mobility and self-care tasks. The two measures differ, however, in the proportion of the sample classified as fully independent and with medium levels of dependency. For the reasons given in the introductory chapter, it is suggested that the Clackmannan /Townsend scale is probably the more internally consistent of the two measures.

7.24   Dependency correlates, to some extent, with **age**: older respondents are more likely to be physically and/or mentally dependent than younger non-elderly disabled adults. There are, however, roughly equal proportions of non-elderly disabled adults in the highest dependency groupings within each age group; and **household type**: a lower proportion of single adults fall into the highest dependency groups than any other household type. In comparison with the elderly population (see Table 4.8), at almost all levels of dependency, a higher proportion of non-elderly disabled adults experience difficulties or are unable to perform basic domestic, mobility and self-care tasks.

Type of property

7.25   Two-thirds of non-elderly disabled people (66%) live in a house, nearly four times as many as live in a bungalow or flat (17% and 16% respectively) (Table 7.9) and this distribution is, more or less, the same as for the population as a whole (English House Condition Survey 1991, DoE/HMSO, 1993).

Table 7.9 Housing occupied by non-elderly disabled people: by household type and tenure				
Row%s	House	Bungalow	Flat/ maisonette	Base
All households	66	17	16	850
EHCS 1991	69	9	22	19,725
Household type:				
Single adult	40	11	48	148
2+ adults, no children	68	22	10	476
Children in household	79	11	9	226
Tenure:				
Owner-occupier	72	21	6	417
LA/HA rented	57	13	30	310
Other	69	13	14	123

7.26   The type of accommodation occupied by non-elderly disabled adults varies most noticeably by their household type and their tenure. Respondents living as part of households with two or more adults, and especially those with children, are most likely to live in a house (68% and 79% respectively), whereas single adults are most likely to live in a flat or maisonette (48%). By tenure, seven in ten owner-occupiers (72%) live in a house, compared with 57% of council and housing association tenants. Conversely, three in ten council and housing association tenants live in a flat or maisonette, compared with just six per cent of o er-occupiers.

Age of property and length of residence

7.27   Slightly fewer non-elderly disabled adults live in property built before 1919 and more live in housing built in the two decades after the Second World War than the population as a whole (EHCS 1991, 1993) (Table 7.10 in Appendix 3). Council or housing association tenants are more likely to live in housing built in the immediate post-war era than any other non-elderly disabled group and this partly explains the distribution of the sample across these construction periods: as will be shown in the next section, non-elderly disabled adults are more likely than any other group in the population, except lone parents, to rent from a local authority and almost two-fifths of the local authority stock was built in the immediate post-war period (39% – EHCS 1991).

7.28   A majority of seven in ten non-elderly disabled adults have lived in their present home for five or more years – just over half having lived there for ten or more years – and three in ten had moved in the last five years. (Table 7.11 in Appendix 3). Those least likely to have moved in the last five years are respondents aged 50-64 (20%) and those living with one other person but no children (22%).

Table 7.12 Tenure of dwellings occupied by non-elderly disabled people: by age of respondent, household type and household weekly income

Row%s	Owner-occupier	LA/HA rented	Other	Base
All households	49	36	14	850
GHS 1991	67	27	6	9,922
Age of respondent:				
16-29	20	24	57	107
30-49	53	35	12	268
50-64	53	40	6	475
Household type:				
Single adult	32	55	14	148
GHS 1991	58	28	14	984
2+ adults no children	55	31	13	476
Children in household	48	35	17	226
Household weekly income:				
Up to £50	52	35	13	91
£50-£99	25	49	26	183
£100-£150	50	40	10	220
£150+	60	28	12	356

Source: General Household Survey 1991, HMSO/OPCS 1993.

Tenure

7.29   So far the profile of housing occupied by non-elderly disabled adults has not differed significantly form housing occupied by the population as a whole. This changes for tenure: around half of non- elderly disabled adults live in property that they either own outright or for which they pay a mortgage (Table 7.12), and a third rent their accommodation from a local authority. As such, they are less likely to owner-occupy than the population as a whole and more likely to rent from a local authority or to live with friends and relatives.

7.30   As may be expected, tenure varies by age and household type, with younger respondents aged 16-29 less likely than average to be owner- occupiers and more likely to live with relatives and friends. In fact, as a group, they are considerably more likely to be living with friends and relatives (49%) than people of the same age within the population as a whole. Single non-elderly disabled adults are also less likely to be owner-occupiers and more likely to rent from the council or housing association. In comparison with their equivalent group in the population, approximately twice as many rent their homes from local authorities and half as many owner-occupy. Lastly, tenure varies with income levels, a higher proportion of non-elderly disabled households with a weekly income of at least £150 own their home and fewer rent than any other group in the sample. Those with incomes of between £50 and £99 per week at the time of the survey, are also more likely than any other group to rent from a local authority.

Amenities and shared facilities

7.31   Very small numbers of non-elderly disabled adults either share or lack basic household facilities in their accommodation. One per cent share a kitchen, fixed bathroom/shower room, wash-hand basin, inside toilet or hot water supply. No non-elderly disabled adult households lack a kitchen and less than half of one per cent do not have a bathroom/shower room, wash hand basin, inside toilet or hot water supply.

House size

7.32   Two-thirds of non-elderly disabled adults live in housing with three or more bedrooms, one in four have two bedrooms and one in nine, one. In terms of tenure and household type, council and housing association tenants are most likely to live in one and two-bed housing (49%), as are those living alone (70%). Owner-occupiers and, not surprisingly, households with children are more likely than average to have three or more bedrooms (75% and 87% respectively).

House condition

7.33   Almost two in three non-elderly disabled adults (excluding those living with relatives or friends) had paid for repairs and improvements to their homes in the 12 months prior to the survey. Owner-occupiers, households with a weekly income of at least £150 and those with children are most likely to have paid for repairs. In contrast, those living alone and in private rented property or living with friends/relatives are the least likely to have carried out improvements to their homes. Around a quarter of these households had paid £1,000 or more for repairs (Table 7.13 in Appendix 3) and these tended, once again, to be owner-occupiers and those with a weekly income of £150 or more (39% and 32% respectively).

7.34   Just over a half of non-elderly disabled adults say their home needs repairs or improvements to make it easier for them to live there (Table 7.14a in Appendix 3). These tend to be council/housing association tenants. External windows are most frequently cited as needing attention (21%), followed by the heating system and damp/condensation (13%) and 12% respectively). Those with higher dependency levels are most likely to mention the need for repairs and improvements to their bathrooms and shower rooms, while council and housing association tenants more frequently mention their heating system. When asked what types of help and advice about repairs and improvements it would be helpful to have, one in six non-elderly disabled people mention help with raising finance and approximately one in ten refer to each of the following: support and reassurance while the work is being carried out; technical and legal advice; financial advice and help with the organisation and supervision of builders (Table 7.14b in Appendix 3). This suggests that there is more interest in making use of advice and support services provided by organisations such as home improvement agencies amongst non-elderly disabled adults than amongst elderly people (see paragraph 4.44 in Chapter 4).

144

Table 7.15 Adaptations in homes occupied by non-elderly disabled adults: by household type, level of dependency, tenure and household weekly income

Col%s	All households Base = 850	Row%s	Presence of adaptations	1-mentioned	2+ mentioned	Base
Ramps outside	4	**Tenure:**				
Additional handrails outside	7	Owner-occupier	33	19	14	417
Ramps inside	1	LA/HA rented	39	18	21	310
Additional hand rails inside	12	Other	25	11	14	123
Any doors altered for better access	3	**Household type:**				
Any other alterations for better access	1					
Stairlift	2	Single adult aged 16-64	33	17	16	148
Specially designed or adapted kitchen	2	2+ adults no children	37	18	19	476
Specially designed or adapted bath/shower	9	Children in household	28	17	12	226
Relocated bath	1					
Relocated shower	2					
Specially designed or adapted toilet	3	**Level of dependency:**				
Relocated toilet	2	A/B	19			359
Hoist	1	C	43			54
Electrical modifications	5	D	41			264
Door entry phone	3	F/G	52			162
Extra locks/safety gates	5	**Household weekly income:**				
Warden/emergency alarm system	4	Up to £50	48	22	26	91
Additional heating	3	£50-£99	26	15	11	183
Other	5	£100-£149	32	19	14	220
None of these	66	£150+	36	17	19	356

Adaptations and alterations

7.35   A third of non-elderly disabled people (34%) have adaptations in their homes to make it easier for them to live there (Table 7.15). The most frequently fitted adaptations are handrails (both inside and outside) and a specially designed or adapted bath or shower. Adaptations appear to be targeted[16] upon the most severely disabled and dependent. Low income households within the non-elderly disabled adult population also seem more likely to have had adaptations made to their homes than medium and high-income households containing non-elderly disabled adults. Least likely to have had adaptations and improvements to their homes are non-elderly disabled people with children, private renters and those living with relatives or friends. Local authority and housing association tenants are no more likely to have had adaptations than owner-occupiers.

7.36   Slightly more non-elderly disabled people say they need some or additional adaptations and alterations than elderly people (Table 7.16, see also Table 4.18 in Appendix 3). The most frequently requested adaptation is a specially-designed or adapted bathroom or shower room, especially by those in the highest dependency grouping. In fact, not surprisingly, the more severely disabled respondents are, the more likely they are to state that they needed adaptations. For example, whilst almost three- fifths of those in the highest dependency groupings say they require adaptations, only a fifth of those classified as `fully independent' identify similar needs. Council and housing association tenants are also more likely than owner-occupiers, private renters and those living with friends or relatives to say they need adaptations or alterations to their homes.

Satisfaction with home

7.37   A majority of four in five (83%) non-elderly disabled adults are very or fairly satisfied with their present homes: one in two are very satisfied. One in nine (11%), however, express dissatisfaction with 4% saying they are very dissatisfied. Most likely to be satisfied are owner- occupiers (90%) and two adult households (87%). Disabled people aged 30-49 and council or housing association tenants are least likely to be satisfied overall. In all these sub-groups, one in six (17%) respondents are dissatisfied with their present homes.

Housing aspirations

7.38   It is important within any assessment of the housing needs of a particular group to find out what they themselves want by way of accommodation. As was explained in the Chapter on the survey of elderly people, this study did not ask about particular housing options, but framed questions around the specific features of different forms of provision, so that respondents' combined answers would indicate their preferences (see paragraphs 8.18-8.19 in Chapter 8).

---

[16]   See footnote 12 in Chapter 4.

Table 7.16 Adaptations needed by non-elderly disabled adults: by level of dependency, household type and tenure

Col%s	All households Base = 850
Ramps outside	2
Additional handrails outside	3
Ramps inside	1
Additional hand rails inside	5
Any doors altered for better access	2
Any other alterations for better access	1
Stairlift	5
Specially designed or adapted kitchen	3
Specially designed or adapted bath/shower	9
Relocated bath	1
Relocated shower	3
Specially designed or adapted toilet	2
Relocated toilet	4
Hoist	1
Electrical modifications	4
Door entry phone	4
Extra locks/safety gates	5
Warden/emergency alarm system	2
Additional heating	6
Other	4
None of these	64

Row%s	Need for adaptations	1-mentioned	2+ mentioned	Base
Tenure:				
Owner-occupier	30	17	12	417
LA/HA rented	46	25	21	310
Other	31	18	12	123
Level of dependency:				
A/B	20			359
C	35			54
D	49			264
F/G	58			162
Household type:				
Single adult aged 16-64	32	18	13	148
2+ adults, no children	39	21	17	476
Children in household	33	20	13	226

Housing preferences

7.39   Respondents were first shown a list of six broad housing options, and asked which they thought would best suit them (and other disabled/non-disabled members of their household, where appropriate) at present (Table 7.17). A majority of over seven in ten non-elderly disabled adults say that their current home is the type of accommodation that best suits them at present: just under a half say they would keep their home exactly as it is at the moment, and nearly a quarter say their home would require repairs and adaptations to make it easier for them to live there. This is a lower overall proportion of households wishing to remain at home than amongst the sample of elderly people, but a higher proportion of households requiring adaptations (see Table 4.19). There might be for several reasons for these two trends: firstly, non-elderly adults may have a greater willingness to move, secondly, they may be more aware of the possibilities for adapting their homes and less concerned about the disruption caused by the building process, thirdly, there may be groups within the non-elderly disabled population that are particularly keen to move and, finally, it may be because a higher proportion of the non- elderly sample were classified as disabled at almost all levels of dependency than the elderly sample (see Table 7.8) and therefore, are more likely to require adaptations. Having said that, Table 7.17 shows that owner-occupiers and those aged 50-64 are most likely to say their present home exactly as it is provides the most suitable type of accommodation for them at present. Council or housing association tenants and those in the medium to high dependency groups are, moreover, more likely than average to opt for repairs and adaptations to their present home.

7.40   Turning to the group that expressed a desire to move to alternative accommodation – almost three in ten non-elderly disabled adults – there is some evidence of pent-up demand from one group of respondents. Those aged 16-29 are particularly keen to move. In fact, they are almost twice as likely to want to move as those aged 50-64. This is not surprising, nevertheless, as the slight majority (54%) were living with their parents at the time of the survey. Apart from this, however, there is no relationship between desire to move to alternative accommodation and household type, level of dependency or current tenure.

Preferred type of property

7.41   Of those who said they wished to move, just over half would prefer to live in a bungalow, almost twice as many as would prefer to live in a house. Approximately, one in ten would choose to live in a flat or maisonette (Table 7.18). Amongst those most likely to prefer a bungalow are respondents aged 50-64 and two-adult households. Those preferring a house include young disabled adults (57%) and households with children (61%). A flat or maisonette in a purpose-built block is more popular amongst private renters/those living with relatives and friends and those aged 16-29.

Table 7.17 Housing aspirations of non-elderly disabled adults: by tenure, age of respondent and level of dependency

Row%s	Present home as it is	Present home with repairs/adaptations	Other accomm: same size	Other accomm: smaller	Other accomm: larger	Move to live with friends/rels	Base
All households	47	23	9	8	11	1	850
Age of respondents:							
16-29	31	21	10	7	24	5	107
30-49	46	21	7	7	18	1	268
50-64	52	24	9	9	4	*	475
Tenure:							
Owner-occupier	55	18	7	9	11	0	417
LA/HA rented	40	30	12	7	10	1	310
Other	40	20	7	11	15	5	123
Level of dependency:							
A/B	55	15	9	9	11	1	359
C	54	26	4	6	11	0	54
D	47	28	9	8	8	*	264
F/G	36	30	12	7	14	1	162

Note * – Less than 0.5%.

Table 7.18 Preferred type of property: by tenure, household type, current accommodation and gender

Col%s	All households	Age of respondent			Household type			Tenure		
		16-29	30-49	50-64	Single adult 16-64	2+ adults no children	Children in household	Owner-occupier	LA/HA rented	Other
House	29	57	39	9	15	13	61	32	29	17
Bungalow	55	18	48	75	54	73	28	58	57	44
Purpose-built flat	10	19	7	10	15	10	8	5	9	29
Converted flat	1	2	1	1	5	1	0	1	1	2
Other	2	3	1	3	5	2	0	2	1	3
Base	243	45	88	110	45	121	78	114	89	40

7.42   Respondents were also asked a number of other questions about their preferred type of property including tenure, number of bedrooms, special design features such as easy access for wheelchairs, floor level and willingness to share facilities (Table 7.19 in Appendix 3).

7.43   Roughly one in two would want to own their home and two-fifths would prefer to rent. Current owner-occupiers are most likely to want to own their own home (81%), and council or housing association tenants are most likely to want to rent (74%). Other groups which tend to want to own their property, include those with a weekly income of £150 or more, those with children and respondents aged 30-49 (67%, 66% and 64% respectively).

7.44   One in six respondents (16%) would prefer a property with one bedroom, this view is expressed most frequently by disabled people living on their own (53%). Almost half (45%) would seriously consider accommodation with two bedrooms, particularly respondents aged 50- 64 years old and two adult households (62% and 61% respectively). Two in five (39%) would prefer three or more bedrooms, especially households with children (76%).

7.45   Only a third of respondents (35%) would prefer to live in housing specifically designed for easy access, and a slightly greater proportion (44%) say they would not. Respondents with a medium or high dependency level are more likely than average to opt for housing with adaptations for easy access (38% of those with medium dependency levels and 56% of those with high levels of dependency).

7.46   Lastly, approximately one in five of those respondents who would consider moving to a flat or maisonette would be prepared to share the toilet or bathroom (21% each – i.e. six respondents) and 17% (i.e. five respondents) would consider sharing the kitchen. All these respondents would consider moving to a flat/maisonette with an entrance on the ground floor, and half (51%) would move to one with an entrance on the first floor with no access to a lift. However, they are more likely to consider a flat or maisonette on the first or second (or higher) floor if they have access to a lift (66% and 58% respectively).

Help and support needed

7.47   Respondents were shown a list of five broad types of help and asked whether they or other members of their household needed any of these types of support to enable them to remain in their present home or to live in alternative accommodation. Those wishing to stay at home express less demand for any of these types of help and support in their new home than those wishing to move to alternative accommodation (Table 7.20). Just over one in five of those wishing to remain at home select one or more of the forms of support compared with one in three of those wanting alternative accommodation. Help with household chores is the type of support most frequently mentioned by both groups, with one in eight (12%) of those seeking alternative accommodation also saying they

Table 7.20 Help and support needed by those wishing to stay at home: by level of dependency

Row%s	Wish to receive at least one of these	Help with household chores	Help with self-care e.g. bathing	Help getting about outside	Help getting about indoors (inc. getting in and out of bed/chair)	Being able to call a warden	Base
All households	22	15	3	5	3	4	594
Level of dependency:							
A/B	7						251
C	28						43
D	27						197
F/G	31						108

Table 7.20 continued. Help and support needed by those wishing to move: by level of dependency

Row%s	Wish to receive at least one of these	Help with household chores	Help with self-care e.g. bathing	Help getting about	Help getting about indoors (inc. getting in and out of bed/chair)	Being able to call a warden	Base
All households	34	18	4	7	3	12	243
Level of dependency:							
A/B	14						104
C	18						11
D	52						65
F/G	56						52

would like to be able to call upon a warden in emergencies. Within both groups, respondents with medium and high levels of dependency are more likely to say they need each type of help and support than those who are fully independent or have low levels of dependency.

Desire to move

7.48   Almost one in five (18%) non-elderly disabled adults say they are very or fairly likely to want to move within 12 months of the survey. This compares with 8% of elderly households in the main survey. Younger people aged 16-29 are most likely to want to move (38%, including 28% saying they are very likely to move), while older respondents aged 50-64 are among the least likely to want to move (13%). By tenure, disabled people classed as `other' (i.e. mainly private renters and those who live with relatives and friends) are more inclined to want to move than owner-occupiers or council and housing association tenants (30% versus 15% and 20% respectively). Disabled people with a zero or low dependency score are more likely to want to move than those of medium to high levels of frailty.

Receipt of health and social care services

Care and support services received

7.49   Care and support services for non-elderly disabled adults seem to be well targeted – respondents with higher dependency scores are more likely to receive home visits than those with low or medium levels of dependency. For any given level of dependency, however, non-elderly disabled adults are generally less likely to receive visits from health and social care services than elderly people. This is despite the finding that there are a greater proportion of disabled adults at all levels of dependency than elderly people. One explanation for this might be the much greater incidence of single adult households amongst the elderly population than amongst the non-elderly disabled population (17%); social and health care services tending to be targeted on single adults (Table 7.21, see also Table 4.24 in Appendix 3).

Care and support services requested by non-elderly disabled adults

7.50   Latent demand for care and support services amongst the non- elderly disabled population is quite low, although slightly higher than amongst elderly people (Table 7.22). The most frequently requested services, amongst those not in receipt, are a physiotherapist (5%), a doctor (4%), a chiropodist (6%) and a social worker (5%). Disabled adults with a high level of dependency are most likely to request care and support services generally and, in particular, the chiropodist, physiotherapist, the doctor and social worker/welfare officer.

Table 7.21 Health and social services received by non-elderly disabled people: by level of dependency

		Clackmannan Dependency Level		
Col%s	A/B	C	D	F/G
District Nurse	4	12	11	17
Health Visitors	4	4	3	2
Physiotherapist	0	0	2	1
Occupational therapist	0	4	3	7
Doctor	9	17	27	28
Private nursing help	0	0	0	1
None	85	79	66	62
Social worker	3	6	9	11
Mobility officer for the blind	0	0	0	1
Chiropodist	1	2	4	3
Home help/home care aide	1	4	3	10
Private domestic help	2	4	4	3
Voluntary worker	1	4	2	4
None	92	84	82	71
Meals on wheels	0	0	1	2
Laundry	0	0	1	1
Incontinence service	0	0	1	3
None	99	100	98	89
Base	359	54	264	162

Table 7.22 Health and social services requested by non-elderly disabled people: by level of dependency

		Clackmannan Dependency Level		
Col%s	A/B	C	D	F/G
District Nurse	1	2	2	3
Health Visitors	1	0	3	4
Physiotherapist	2	2	5	10
Occupational therapist	1	2	1	4
Doctor	1	4	5	6
Private nursing help	0	0	0	0
None	83	74	59	49
Social worker	2	4	6	7
Mobility officer for the blind	1	2	2	1
Chiropodist	1	11	6	13
Home help/home care aide	1	4	5	3
Private domestic help	0	0	1	0
Voluntary worker	0	2	0	4
None	89	65	64	54
Meals on wheels	0	0	1	1
Laundry	0	2	0	1
Incontinence service	0	0	1	0
None	100	98	98	97
Base	359	54	264	162

154

8 The allocation model and estimates of need

8.1   In order to produce estimates of their need for subsidised housing and housing with care provision, this study collected information about the housing circumstances, aspirations and physical/mental frailty of elderly and disabled people. In this Chapter, a model is described which uses the data obtained from the surveys of 9,000 elderly households and 850 households containing non-elderly disabled adults to produce these estimates of need. It looks at estimates by different types of households and age groups within the elderly and disabled populations and it examines potential indicators of need that emerge.

8.2   Before describing the allocation model, however, it is important to consider some issues and underlying principles in the process of estimating the housing needs of elderly and disabled people. There are limits to the range and depth of information that can be collected in an interview survey which preclude detailed individual assessments. It is, nevertheless, possible to produce estimates, for planning purposes, of need for subsidised housing and housing with care provision based on the allocation of groups of households with broad characteristics and aspirations in common.

Housing and housing with care

8.3   Housing is only one element in the package of services required by many frail elderly and disabled people to enable them to remain at home. Some will need care support from home care aides, district nurses and occupational therapists as well as the installation of adaptations in their homes. Problems arise when it is recognised that there is some scope for substitution between housing and care inputs to maintaining an elderly or disabled person at home. The study did not attempt to address this issue as it would require research based upon a case-by-case analysis of allocations to individuals and their households far beyond the scope of this exercise. When allocations to staying at home options involving a combination of housing and care support are described in this report, therefore, these simply refer to the necessity to have both types of input, and not to the relative contribution of each form of provision.

An expensive resource

8.4   As was shown in Chapter 3, specialised housing for elderly people can be an expensive approach to meeting housing needs. And, whilst costs information was not collected on housing options for disabled people, it is likely that the same is true for wheelchair and mobility housing/housing adapted for disabled people. It is important, therefore, that optimum use is made of this resource and it is only available to those elderly and disabled households that both 'need' and 'want' a place in specialised housing. As the research has shown, this has not always been the case for elderly people, a high proportion of tenants in sheltered housing schemes have no physical or mental frailty and this raises doubts about their need to be in accommodation with warden support. The research has also shown that a significant proportion would have preferred to remain in their previous homes rather than moving to sheltered housing. In view of this, the present model requires elderly and disabled households to not only have an assessed need for specialised housing but also to want to move into accommodation with warden and care support before allocating households to this option.

Risk, choice and independence

8.5   It is clear that choice can often be limited by a lack of awareness of the full range of options available. The same form of housing provision can also be perceived in completely different ways and preferences can be indicated without the full implications of a choice being considered. In order to avoid these potential difficulties, this study asked a series of questions covering preferences on a number of different aspects of each housing option. The preferred option of each household interviewed was estimated on the basis of their combined response to these questions and not on questions which prejudged respondents knowledge about specific forms of provision.

8.6   Measuring individual and household preferences about the housing and care inputs they need to continue living in private households in the community is also fraught with other difficulties. There will inevitably be some people whose objective circumstances suggest they need support, but whose wish is simply to be left alone. For example, as will be discussed later, there were some elderly people in the survey who were highly dependent and did not wish to move to alternative, more appropriate, accommodation. They were, however, equally unwilling to have adaptations made to their homes or to receive domiciliary care support. This highlights the tensions that can sometimes exist between respecting individuals' wishes and the desire to intervene to avoid undue risk of injury or improve quality of life. In fact, it could be argued that independent living is as much about allowing elderly and disabled people to make their own choices, as it is to ensure that they are given the right level of support to enable them to lead ordinary lives. In these cases, this study took the view that unless there were good reasons to the contrary (e.g. they suffered from fairly extreme mental or emotional disorders) their preferences would influence the allocation model.

8.7 There will also be some people who want to receive more care support and have more adaptations installed than their level of physical/mental disability or dependency would warrant. In the allocation model, this is dealt with for adaptations by setting a maximum level of receipt for each category of dependency, taking into account current adaptations, if any, in the home. Households stating they needed more adaptations than was broadly appropriate for their levels of dependency are allocated only part of what they feel they require. Similarly, if households already have sufficient adaptations to cover their requirements, they are allocated to the `no change' grouping.

8.8 Finally, there are some elderly people who currently receive more than the present survey indicates they need. Whilst this allocation model identifies such households and places them in the 'no change' category, it does not attempt to re-distribute care and specialised housing resources within the sample.

Designing the model

8.9 The initial structure and broad principles underlying the design of the allocation model were worked out at a seminar held in the summer of 1992. Some twenty-five leading, housing, medical and social services practitioners and academics were invited to a one-day needs assessment seminar. The aim of the day was to identify and discuss needs assessment criteria which could be used to develop a model allocating elderly and disabled people to a range of housing and housing with care options on the basis of data collected through the main interview surveys (see Chapters 4 and 7). The day progressed through debating the broad principles of needs assessment to detailed discussion of the individual criteria for allocating households to each of eleven different housing and housing with care options. (Two further options were added after the seminar – a move to live with relatives/friends and a move to mobility housing/housing adapted for disabled people.) As part of this discussion, 40 anonymised case studies were selected from the interview surveys, each case study covering details of household type, age and gender; current receipt of health and social care support and installation of aids and adaptations; housing circumstances: floor level and repairs; financial circumstances; housing aspirations and health/level of dependency. Participants in the seminar were asked to allocate these case studies to specific options (or to a range of options, where appropriate) and to discuss their reasons for doing so.

Principles underlying and practical constraints upon the model

8.10 Three broad principles underpin the allocation model as follows:

i. Wherever possible, a household's housing aspirations should be met, provided that the respondent within the household has the cognitive ability to make reasoned judgements;

ii. The physical/mental disability and dependency of the respondent and other household members needs to be taken into account when determining the most appropriate allocation to housing and housing with care options. A 'fully independent' elderly person may live with a highly dependent elderly person. If the judgement about the household's needs is based purely upon the 'fit' elderly person then this would lead to inadequate provision for the household as a whole. Equally, if the judgement is based on the 'frail' elderly person, this would not take account of the ability of other household members to provide informal care support. Throughout the model, the emphasis is upon household needs with regard to aspirations, requirement for and current use of adaptations and domiciliary care support and financial circumstances. Some caution should be exercised here, however, as all information about the needs, level of physical/mental disability, receipt of health and social care services and financial situation of other household members was collected from the main respondent (see paragraph 1.12 of Chapter 1);

iii. Resources are finite. There is, therefore, a need to find an equitable method of allocating services between elderly households of different means. This broad principle is important because some elderly and disabled people will not be eligible for subsidised housing provision, although they may remain eligible for non means- tested provision of health and social care services.

8.11   There are also some practical constraints upon the model as follows:

i. If information on a specific topic was not collected in the interview surveys and no proxy questions can be used, then it is not possible to reflect it as a criterion of need in the allocation model. For instance, whether individual properties can be adapted successfully depends upon a number of factors including:

a. the space available to install the required adaptations;

b. planning constraints on structural alterations; and,

c. if the person is living in rented accommodation, whether the landlord would allow such alterations to be made.

This detailed information is not available from the survey. It is unlikely, however, that data on these topics would significantly affect regional differences in need for specific types of provision as they would only be relevant in a small number of cases. Information on topics b. and c., moreover, could not be known beforehand or predicted anyway.

ii. The estimates of need it produces are based upon a static as opposed to a dynamic assessment of need. Thus, the estimates cannot reflect any changes in the circumstances of respondents or their households following the surveys e.g. as result of a dramatic breakdown of a care arrangement. The size of the sample, however, is probably sufficient to provide a reliable snapshot of households that have just experienced such events.

Definitions

8.12   The model allocates elderly households to one of eleven housing or housing with care options and households containing non-elderly disabled adults to one of two options. The more restricted range of options for non-elderly disabled adults takes account of the following:

- non-elderly disabled adults tend to be rehoused into two main forms of specialised accommodation – wheelchair and mobility housing/housing adapted for disabled people. Elderly households, in contrast, can be rehoused into four forms of specialised housing- Categories 1 ,1.5, 2 and 2.5 sheltered accommodation (see paragraphs 2.4 – 2.5, Chapter 2);

- as the introductory chapter pointed out (see paragraph 1.26), the study was originally set up to examine the housing needs of elderly people and the survey of non-elderly disabled adults was added at a later stage. As a result, the allocation model was designed primarily with the aim of producing estimates of need for elderly households and would require several significant changes, outside the scope of the present exercise, to produce similar estimates for non-elderly disabled adults covering the full range of staying at home and non- specialised housing options described below.

8.13   Turning to the housing and housing with care options themselves, these are described below:

Housing and housing with care options for elderly people

No change: remain in present accommodation. This does not always mean that a particular elderly household does not qualify for aids and adaptations or health and social care services. It does mean, however, that if these are currently provided then no additional support is required;

Stay at Home 1 (SAH 1): remain in existing accommodation, but only provide subsidised new/additional aids and adaptations to help the elderly household with normal day to day functions, where necessary;

Stay at Home 2 (SAH 2): remain in existing accommodation, but provide the elderly household with both subsidised aids and adaptations and new/additional health and social care services such as nursing visits, home helps, meals on wheels, where necessary;

Stay at Home 3 (SAH 3): remain in existing accommodation, but provide only new/additional health and social care services, where necessary;

Move to smaller or same size ordinary/mainstream accommodation: involves a move to non-specialised accommodation requiring no subsidised provision of additional aids and adaptations or health and social care services;

Move to friends/relatives: self-explanatory, although if additional health and social care services are required, these would be provided through informal as well as formal carers. As no information was collected on houses occupied by relatives in the national survey of elderly people, it has to be assumed that the new property would (if appropriate) already have the required aids and adaptations in situ;

Category 1: contains specially-designed units of accommodation for more active elderly people. Communal facilities such as a common room, a laundry room or a guest room may be also provided, although these are optional;

Category 1.5: is broadly similar to Category 1 accommodation but it has an alarm system and (resident or non-resident) warden support. It does not provide any communal facilities;

Category 2 or ordinary sheltered housing: are schemes with units of accommodation for less active elderly people. They must have a resident or non-resident warden and a system for calling him or her. Communal facilities such as a common room, a laundry room or a guest room must also be provided;

Category 2.5 or very sheltered housing: these are also known as extra-care schemes. They are for frail elderly people and provide a greater level of care than Category 2 accommodation. They may, for example, provide meals, extra wardens, care assistants and additional communal facilities such as special bathrooms, sluice rooms etc.;

Housing and housing with care options for non-elderly disabled adults

Mobility housing/housing adapted for disabled people: accommodation designed to cater for those who can walk and can cope with steps and stairs but with difficulty. This type of accommodation would normally have widened doorways and a toilet on the ground floor;

Wheelchair housing: accommodation specifically designed to cater for those who are wheelchair bound or regularly use a wheelchair to get about inside and outside their accommodation;

Residential care/nursing home: a form of accommodation where the elderly person would normally require 24 hour support or nursing care.

The allocation model

Designing the model from the seminar

8.14   Following the seminar, detailed work on designing the allocation model took the form of identifying questions on the survey questionnaires and databases that matched the assessment or selection criteria outlined at the seminar. This covered both the broad underlying principles of the model and the detailed criteria for individual options. Following early testing of the model, it also required the incorporation of other rules of eligibility to draw out criteria not described in sufficient detail in early versions of the model. For example, early versions of the model sought to estimate the numbers of households eligible for subsidised provision of repairs and adaptations to their homes through house renovation grants by applying eligibility for income support as a means test. This significantly underestimates the number of households that would be eligible for grant. Later versions of the model, therefore, incorporated a test of resources developed for use with the English House Conditions Survey to identify all households eligible to receive a grant contribution towards the costs of their repairs and adaptations, irrespective of the size of the grant or the percentage of the full cost of works. Further versions of the model also went through sensitivity analyses to identify whether some variables had an impact upon the final allocation out of proportion to their relative importance. These analyses suggested that no single criterion or combination of one or two variables was unduly influencing the outcome of a run of the model. Further details of the design of the model, stages in its development and results from early versions are given in the individual reports 11 and 12 (see Appendix 1) on this element of the programme of research. Appendix 4, however, shows a sample of the rules governing the allocation of households to housing and housing with care options.

Basic components of the model

8.15   The allocation model has approximately twenty basic needs assessment criteria. Twelve relate to the potential allocation of households to any housing and housing with care option and eight cover specific selection criteria for specialised housing and care. Each component part of the model combines data from several questions on the database. For example, the test of eligibility to receive a grant contribution towards the cost of necessary repairs and adaptations looks at data on household type, age, level of disability, provision of informal care and the presence of children in the household of which the elderly person is the head of household.

All housing and housing with care options

8.16   The allocation model puts all the approximately 9,000 elderly covered in the main interview survey through a first filter consisting of twelve general factors or topics. No households go through all of the questions or topics, but by far the majority, are taken through at least five. The questions or topics are as follows:

i. Do the elderly people in the household have a cognitive level sufficient to make reasoned judgements?;

ii. If one or more of the elderly people in the household do suffer from cognitive disorders, is help from other household members or formal health and social care services sufficient?;

iii. Do the elderly people in the household want to move?;

iv. Do they want to move to relatives or friends?;

v. Are any elderly people in the household physically dependent? If so, who has the highest level of dependency?;

vi. Is the current level of aids and adaptations in their present home sufficient for their needs?;

vii. Is the current level of receipt of health and social care services sufficient for their needs?;

viii. Could the elderly household realise over £40,000 on the sale of their home?;

ix. Is the household eligible for receipt of renovation and disabled facilities grant contributions towards the costs of repairs and adaptations to their home?;

x. Do household savings exceed £8,000?;

xi. Is the total cost of required aids and adaptations and repairs less than the notional maximum set for the household's overall dependency level?;

xii. Does the elderly person with the highest dependency level in the household receive informal care?

8.17   A full description of how responses to these twelve topics or questions are combined is given in Appendix 4 of the individual report (no 11) on this element of the study. Some examples, however, are as follows:

> *A single elderly person:* He or she can make reasoned judgements and wants to move. He or she does not want to move to relatives or friends and is physically fully independent. As an owner-occupier, less than £40,000 will be realised on the sale of his or her own home – this person would enter the test for specialised housing (see paragraph 8.18 below);

> *An elderly couple:* They can make reasoned judgements and do not want to move. They wish to remain in their present home but with necessary repairs and adaptations to make it easier to live there. Both are dependent, although one is slightly more frail than the other, and little informal care support is capable of being provided. Aids and adaptations in the household are not sufficient for their needs nor is current formal health and social services care support. They are eligible for a disabled

facilities grant towards the cost of their repairs and adaptations and their savings do not exceed £8,000 – this household would be allocated to staying at home 2 (see earlier 'Definitions' section of this Chapter);

An elderly couple: They can make reasoned judgements and do not want to move. They wish to remain in their present home exactly as it is without any additional repairs or adaptations or health and social care support. Both are dependent elderly people in receipt of some informal care from relatives – this household would be allocated to the `no change' option (see earlier `definitions' section of this chapter).

Specialised housing and housing with care options

8.18   Those elderly households eligible for specialised housing and the 850 households containing non-elderly disabled adults are put through a second filter. For elderly and disabled households to be allocated to one of the specialised housing and care options, eight basic issues were examined as follows:

    i. The size of the accommodation they wish to occupy;

    ii. Whether they are currently occupying a ground-floor property;

    iii. Whether their accommodation is in a poor state or repair;

    iv. If they want care and support help from a warden/alarm system, with household chores, with self-care tasks or mobility tasks;

    v. Their dependency level and that of their household members, including mental health;

    vi. Their type of household and potential for experiencing social isolation;

    vii. Their regular use of aids to overcome mobility problems; and,

    viii. Their desire to live in accommodation specially designed for easy access.

8.19 These eight basic issues were combined in different ways for the seven specialised housing options, although none of the options incorporated all eight aspects of need. In summary, elderly households were allocated to:

Category 1 – if the household Clackmannan dependency is C, similar or smaller-sized accommodation is desired and:

- the household is not living in ground floor accommodation; or,

- the household is living in ground floor accommodation but the buiding is in a poor state of repair;

Category 1.5 – if all the above criteria are met and the household has an expressed requirement for a warden/ alarm system;

Category 2 – as Category 1, but the elderly person is in Clackmannan grouping C or D, living alone and has no relatives or friends living close by;

Category 2.5 – as Category 1, and if the household Clackmannan score is D, E or F and the elderly people require help in bathing/washing/dressing or help with walking/getting upstairs/getting in or out of bed and a warden/alarm system;

Mobility housing/housing adapted for disabled people – as Category 1, and if the household Clackmannan score is C, and the household want to live in accommodation specially-designed for easy access, for example, by someone using a wheelchair;

Wheelchair – as Category 1, and if the household Clackmannan score is G (Critical Interval – functional, see Appendix 2), a member of the household is bed- or chair-fast or uses a wheelchair to help them perform mobility or domestic tasks and wants to live in accommodation specially-designed for easy access, for example, by someone using a wheelchair;

Residential care/nursing home – if the household Clackmannan score was F or G, a household member is bedridden and/or had severe mental impairment.

8.20   Lastly, it should be pointed out that all those elderly households not meeting these selection criteria are fed back into the allocation model. They are then put through a third filter which tests for staying at home and other non-specialised options involving aids and adaptations and necessary repairs. It should also be noted that the model allocates elderly households in the 8,901 sample known to be living in Category 2 and 2.5 accommodation and eligible under the rules set out above to these two forms of specialised housing rather than to the 'no change' grouping. This accounts for the inclusion of Clackmannan Group D elderly households in Category 2 housing. These are elderly people who are currently resident in ordinary sheltered housing who do not wish to move. In contrast, Clackmannan Group D households in Category 2 housing that do wish to move are placed in Category 2.5 accommodation.

Unallocated households

8.21   Inevitably, there were some households that either did not complete the questionnaire because they failed the mental state filter (see paragraph 1.27 in Chapter 1) or could not be allocated because of missing data on crucial topics for the model. This applied to 491 households in the full sample of 8,901 elderly households (6%). Most missing values occurred over the level of savings and key elements in the dependency scores of the respondent and other household members. There were no unallocated households in the non-elderly disabled adults sample.

Estimates of need for housing and housing with care options

National and Regional estimates of need

8.22 This section of the chapter looks at the estimates of need produced by the final version of the allocation model when applied to the main elderly in the community sample of approximately 9,000 households and the non-elderly disabled adults sample of 850 households. Due to the size of the latter sample only national estimates can be produced and, for reasons given in paragraph 8.12 above, these are restricted to need for wheelchair or mobility housing/housing adapted for disabled people.

8.23 Table 8.1 shows the national estimates of need produced by the model when applied to these two national and regional samples. (All tables use weighted figures). The majority – two in three – of elderly households interviewed in the main survey are allocated to the 'no change' category by the model. In other words, they are allocated to mainstream or ordinary housing with no additional subsidised provision of aids and adaptations or health and social care support.

Table 8.1 National estimates of need by elderly and non-elderly disabled people for subsidised housing and housing with care provision

Col%s	
No change	66
Staying at home 1	2.9
Staying at home 2	3.2
Staying at home 3	14.1
A move to ordinary, mainstream accom.	2.5
Living with friends/relatives	0.8
Category 1 accommodation	0.5
Category 1.5 accommodation	0.2
Category 2 accommodation	2.4
Category 2.5 accommodation	1.3
A move to residential/nursing care	0.7
Unallocated	5.5
Base	8901
Wheelchair housing	2.0
Mobility/housing adapted for disabled people	3.4
Base	850

8.24   The main reasons for this are that a large proportion of the sample (45%) do not want to move and are not physically or mentally impaired. This reflects, to some extent, the finding reported in Chapter 4 that the majority (69%) of those elderly people interviewed in the main survey say they wish to live in their 'present home exactly as it is at the moment'. Roughly one in eight (12%) elderly households, moreover, who are physically or mildly mentally impaired, do not want to move and state that they have sufficient aids and adaptations for their needs. This group is described in greater detail in paragraphs 8.38 – 8.39 below. Lastly, approximately one in eleven (9%) of the sample are allocated to the 'no change' grouping mainly because they fail the means-tests for renovation and disabled facilities grants and/or a place in subsidised specialised housing.

8.25   Only a small proportion of the elderly sample (6%) are allocated to staying at home options involving the provision of both aids and adaptations repairs and domiciliary care support. This is probably due to a number of factors. For example, the application of the means-test to the provision of grants for adaptations and repairs identified many households with weekly incomes or savings above the current limits for eligibility. It may also be due to fears some elderly people have about the upheaval created by building works in their homes. This may be behind the finding reported in Chapter 4 that only 15% of elderly households wanted adaptations to enable them to remain at home. One other factor might be that many elderly households have already obtained sufficient adaptations for their needs. The main interview survey indicated that almost two-fifths of elderly households in the sample already have adaptations and that they are reasonably well targeted on those in most need. On the other hand, the survey also showed that demand for additional or any adaptations is low and this figure would, therefore, probably rise slightly if elderly peoples' wishes are not taken into account and adaptations are allocated purely on the basis of physical abilities and disabilities.

8.26   One in seven elderly households (14%) of the total elderly sample are allocated to staying at home options involving the provision of health and social care services only. As was shown in the main survey of elderly people, this does not necessarily mean that these households are demanding a wide range or significant amount of additional health and social care provision. In fact, most elderly people seem to only want visits from a chiropodist (see para 4.61). The higher proportion of elderly households allocated to this staying at home option in comparison with staying at home options involving repairs and adaptations, moreover, is because health services are provided free of charge and, whilst social care services can be charged for, this is normally done on a non-means tested basis, such as a flat rate charge for meals.

8.27   Roughly one in twelve (8%) elderly households are assessed as needing a place in alternative housing or care options, ranging from smaller or same size ordinary/mainstream housing to residential/nursing care homes. Overall, the low proportion of households allocated to these options by the model is a reflection of the fact that relatively few elderly people – 14% – wish to move to alternative accommodation. These options can be grouped into three categories:

non-specialised accommodation (smaller or same size, ordinary/mainstream housing and a move to friends or relatives); specialised accommodation (Categories 1, 1.5, 2 and 2.5 housing); and, residential care.

8.28   The sub-group of households allocated to smaller or same size ordinary/ mainstream housing are split 3:1 in favour of smaller accommodation, although this ratio is only 2:1 amongst local authority tenants. Overall, they are slightly more likely to be currently occupying larger accommodation than the elderly sample as a whole. For example, whereas 47% of this sub-group occupies three-bedroom properties, this applies to only 39% of households overall. Similarly, they are slightly more likely to contain single-person households – 50% versus 45%. This does not mean, however, that there are significantly higher levels of under-occupation amongst this sub-group than amongst the full sample. In fact, while 33% of the full sample of approximately 9,000 elderly households are under-occupying their properties by two or more bedrooms above the bedroom standard (see Appendix 5), 35% of this sub-group are under-occupying to the same extent.

8.29   Within this general picture, nevertheless, there is one interesting variation. Just over twice as many local authority tenant households (37%) within the sub-group allocated to smaller or same-size ordinary/mainstream housing are under-occupying by two or more above the bedroom standard than local authority tenant households within the sample as a whole (18%). In fact, overall, 71% of the local authority tenant households within this sub-group are occupying more bedrooms than allowed by the Bedroom Standard. Given that approximately two in every three of these households wish to move to smaller accommodation, this produces a grossed-up national estimate of roughly 50,000 under-occupying elderly households in the local authority sector that might be re-housed to release larger accommodation. This does not take into account, however, local level variations in the availability of suitable alternative acommodation and the housing demands of elderly pople in a particular locality. The actual process of releasing this under-occupied property, therefore, should not be over-simplified.

8.30   Within specialised housing options, ordinary and very sheltered housing (Categories 2 and 2.5) are more in need than specially-designed accommodation without warden support and Category 1.5 accommodation. Estimates of need for Category 2 and Category 2.5 housing do, however, include households in the sample known to be already living in these types of accommodation, that would continue to be eligible under the rules in the allocation model. Lastly, less than one per cent of the households in the elderly sample are allocated to a place in residential care.

8.31   Turning to the sample of households containing non-elderly disabled adults, the allocation model would suggest that 2% of this group nationally have a need for wheelchair housing and just over 3% have a need for mobility housing/housing adapted for disabled people (Table 8.1). These figures are, once again, quite low, but reflect the relatively small proportion of the sample that wished to move from their current accommodation or used a wheelchair on a regular basis.

Table 8.2 National estimates of need by elderly people for subsidised housing and housing with care provision: by tenure, age of respondent, household type and level of dependency

Col%s	Tenure			Age of respondent			Household type				Level of dependency						
	Owner-occupier	LA rented	HA rented	65-74	75+	85+	Single adult aged 75+	Single adult aged 65-74	2 adults at least 1 aged 65-74 none 75+	2 adults at least 1 aged 75+	A	B	C	D	E	F	G
No change in current circumstances	76.6	52.2	50.3	75.2	54.4	36.3	51.4	71.5	78.4	61.4	94.6	92.1	43.1	35.2	0	36.5	26.7
Staying at home 1	2.2	3.6	4.7	2.7	3.1	3.1	2.8	2.4	3.0	3.5	0.1	0.4	6.9	6.6	0	5.0	5.3
Staying at home 2	2.5	4.3	4.5	1.8	4.8	6.3	5.2	2.9	1.2	4.1	0	0	6.6	6.9	13.1	9.3	7.2
Staying at home 3	11.4	18.7	21.7	8.0	22.0	36.2	25.3	9.5	6.6	16.8	0.1	0.1	26.7	33.9	86.9	30.3	40.8
A move to ordinary, mainstream	0.8	4.5	2.8	3.3	1.6	1.0	1.6	4.3	2.7	1.5	4.6	6.4	0	0	0	0	0
Living with friends/relatives	0.4	0.3	0.2	0.5	1.2	2.2	0.6	0.5	0.1	0.6	0.5	0.4	0.7	1.1	0	1.6	1.2
Category 1 accommodation	0	1.1	1.0	0.6	0.4	0.2	0.3	0.7	0.6	0.4	0	0	5.2	0	0	0	0
Category 1.5 accommodation	0	0.2	1.2	0.1	0.2	0.1	0.3	0.2	0	0.2	0	0	1.5	0	0	0	0
Category 2 accommodation	0.8	4.9	6.6	1.9	3.0	2.8	3.3	2.0	1.8	2.9	0	0	5.8	7.2	0	0	0
Category 2.5 accommodation	0.1	2.9	2.2	1.0	1.6	1.6	1.5	1.1	1.4	1.3	0	0	0	3.7	0	5.3	0
A move to residential/nursing care	0.1	1.6	0.8	0.6	0.8	1.3	0.9	1.0	0.3	0.7	0	0.1	0	0	0	4.1	14.6
Base[1]	4,948	2,619	378	4,973	3,910	744	2,253	1,794	2,346	1,685	4,093	623	867	2,247	6	569	201

[1] All these base figures include 'unallocated' households.

8.32   Table 8.2 looks at the estimates of need amongst the elderly households by age of respondent, household type, tenure and dependency level. There is a clear relationship between the age of the respondent and their eventual allocation by the model. Three-quarters of those aged between 65 and 74 years old are allocated to the 'no change' category compared with just over a third of those aged 85 or over. Those aged 75-84 and 85 or over, are also between two and five times more likely to be assessed as having a need for staying at home options involving adaptations, repairs and domiciliary care support than elderly people aged 65-74. The picture is reversed, however, for a move to a smaller or same size ordinary/mainstream accommodation with younger elderly people being slightly more likely to be allocated to this option. For ordinary sheltered housing there is only a slight difference by age group.

8.33   There are also clear differences by household type for some of the options. For example, single adult households where the elderly person is aged 75 or over, are more likely than any other group to be allocated to staying at home options: one in three of these households are allocated to staying at home options compared with one in ten two- adult households, where at least one is aged 65-74. Single elderly people aged 75 or over are also least likely to be allocated to the 'no change' group and two- adult households, where at least one is aged 65-74, most likely to be allocated to this option. Finally, younger single elderly adults are almost twice as likely to want to move into smaller or same size ordinary/mainstream housing than the sample as a whole.

8.34   Elderly households in Clackmannan groups A and B are almost exclusively allocated to the 'no change' grouping (Table 8.2). The only other option provided in the allocation model for these groups being a move to smaller or same-size ordinary /mainstream housing. Staying at home options 2 and 3 involving health and social care services are also related to dependency – the more dependent elderly households are the more likely they are to be allocated to these options. For example, whereas 48% of those in the Clackmannan G grouping are allocated to either staying at home option 2 or 3, this applies to only 33% of households in the Clackmannan C grouping.

8.35   Lastly, allocation outcomes for elderly households vary significantly by tenure. Owner-occupiers are much more likely than local authority and housing association tenants to be allocated to the 'no change' category and less likely to be allocated to options involving additional adaptations and health and social care support and moves to ordinary and very sheltered housing. These differences, however, are largely accounted for by variations in the age, household type and dependency profile of owner-occupiers in comparison with renters. Owner-occupiers, as a group, are more likely to be 'fully independent' aged 65-74 and in two-person households than renters (see paragraphs 4.27-4.30 in Chapter 4). A slightly higher proportion of local authority tenants are assessed as having a need for smaller or same size ordinary/mainstream housing and housing association tenants are more likely to be allocated a place in Category 2 accommodation.

8.36   Table 8.3 in Appendix 3 shows the regional estimates of need produced by the allocation model. There are few significant regional differences in the allocation outcomes for elderly households. Overall, a slightly higher proportion of elderly households in northern regions -West Midlands, East Midlands, North-West, Yorkshire and Humberside and Northern – have an assessed need for a move to alternative accommodation. The proportion of households being allocated to staying at home options is also slightly lower than average in the South- East and South-West regions and slightly higher than average in West Midlands and Yorkshire and Humberside regions. Part of the explanation for this is the higher than average proportion of elderly households with no dependency in the South-East and South-West regions, and the marginally lower number of low-income households in the South-East, resulting in a greater rate of means-testing failure for renovation grants (Table 8.3 in Appendix 3).

8.37   Some other individual figures in Table 8.3 stand out. The relatively high proportion of households in London, Yorkshire and Humberside and Northern regions with an assessed need for smaller mainstream/ordinary housing and the comparatively high proportions requiring a place in very sheltered housing in East Midlands, Yorkshire and Humberside and Northern. All three of these regions have higher than average numbers of elderly households assessed as requiring a move.

Further analysis of a sub-group

8.38   Tables 8.4 – 8.11 in Appendix 3 show the characteristics of a sub- group of households allocated to the `no change' option that are clearly dependent but still do not want any or additional aids and adaptations and/or health and social care support. This sub-group of households has a higher dependency profile than the sample as a whole (Table 8.4). It has fewer single elderly households aged 65-74 and more two- and three plus adult households (Table 8.5) and has an older age profile, being more likely to contain household members aged 75 or over (Table 8.6). There are few differences with regard to housing type and tenure (Tables 8.7 and 8.8). Tables 8.9, 8.10 and 8.11, however, show the main distinguishing characteristics of this sub-group. Overall, they are marginally less likely to be in receipt of informal care than the full sample and significantly less likely, at all levels of dependency, to be receiving equivalent amounts of formal health and social care support and aids and adaptations. For instance, whereas elderly households in the Clackmannan D group in the full sample received health and care support costing approximately £470 per person per annum, the equivalent amount for elderly households in the Clackmannan D group in the sub-sample is £181 per person per annum.

8.39   Clearly, therefore, this sub-group is not refusing additional help and support from a position of strength. Households in this group are already receiving less than most dependent elderly households in the sample as a whole. In fact, their objective circumstances would suggest they are a prime target for additional provision. The allocation model, nevertheless, places importance upon the wishes individuals and this sub-group appears simply to want to be left alone. This is re- inforced by this sub-groups' response to a question asked in the main survey of elderly people in the community about sources of advice and support with the process of installing adaptations or conducting repairs to properties. Table 8.12 in Appendix 3 shows that this sub-group was less interested overall in obtaining advice and support than the sample of approximately 9,000 elderly households as a whole. It also shows that this applies to all the various forms of advice and support, including financial advice, help with the organisation of repairs and adaptations and general support and reassurance.

Indicators of need

8.40   Apart from estimates of housing need, the allocation model was also used to examine possible simple indicators of, or proxies for, need for subsidised housing and housing with care provision amongst elderly people. A full description of the attempts to produce indicators of need is given in the individual report no. 12 (see Appendix 1) on this element of the study.

8.41   Two basic approaches were considered. Firstly, a model-based or top-down approach was investigated. This involved identifying the handful of variables which were the main characteristics of all elderly households determining their allocation by the model. The results of this exercise suggested that there were ten key `drivers' of the model ranked in terms of their contribution to explaining allocation outcomes:

1. Clackmannan dependency level
2. Desire to move
3. Sufficiency of current help
4. Desire to move to relatives or friends
5. Cognitive sufficiency
6. Sufficiency of aids and adaptations
7. Requirement for 24 hour care
8. Age of household members
9. Current ground floor accommodation
10. Number of people living in the household

8.42   Clackmannan dependency level explains most of the variation in allocation to housing options and the number of people in the household has the least explanatory power. Overall, these ten independent variables account for 73% of allocations to housing options. In other words, almost three-quarters of elderly households were allocated on these factors alone. Having said that, data on all of these factors must be present in any database to even consider operating a simplified version of the allocation model and some, such as dependency level and sufficiency of current help are based on several component questions. Further work was carried out, therefore, to find potential proxies for these variables. For example, sufficiency of current help might be addressed by looking at the number of health and social care services already received, the presence of long-term illnesses and disabilities and the availability and receipt of informal care. The explanatory power of proxies, however, is inevitably weaker than the main variables they replace and the exercise indicated no satisfactory reduced set of indicator variables.

8.43   Secondly, a bottom-up approach was considered. This sought to focus upon the households allocated to options and to see if they had clear characteristics in common, most of which were not overtly taken into account by the model. Nineteen characteristics were examined – household type, income level, receipt of certain key state benefits, dwelling type occupied, tenure, age of housing occupied, number of bedrooms, presence and number of adaptations, lack of amenities, basic level of dependency, registration as disabled, inability to perform selected physical acts, selected health problems, the presence of long- term illnesses or disabilities, number of health and social care services received, receipt of a private pension, savings and investments, ages of household members and, finally, number of people living in the household. If households allocated to options had clearly discernible features in comparison with the rest of the sample, then it could be argued that they should be the target group for that housing and housing with care option.

8.44   Unfortunately, whilst there were differences in the profiles of elderly households allocated to options in terms of their current housing, household type, age, income level and other traits, taken together, the differences were not large enough to discriminate significantly between groups. In many ways this is not surprising. Given the complexity of the allocation model and the demonstrably weak links between the main model variables and proxy variables discussed above, some of the limitations of this approach were apparent from the start.

8.45   The conclusion must be, therefore, that the estimates of need or prevalence rates described in this Chapter are the best available method for quantifying demand, and that simple and reliable indicators of need for particular forms of provision cannot be produced.

9 Conclusions

Introduction

9.1   This report has examined the housing needs of elderly and disabled people from a number of different angles. It has looked at the existing stock of specialised housing for elderly and non-elderly disabled people and its use, in order to compare estimates of housing needs with current provision. It has considered the relative cost-effectiveness of a range of housing and housing with care options for elderly people, in order to place the assessment of housing needs within a financial framework. It has evaluated the burden placed on informal carers by some options intended to enable elderly people to remain in their current homes, and it has looked in detail at the housing, social and health characteristics and circumstances of elderly and non-elderly disabled people.

9.2   This final Chapter draws out some more general conclusions about the findings from the study and how they relate to previous research, summarises key aspects of elderly and disabled peoples' housing needs and the changing profiles of need amongst elderly households and discusses possible new patterns of provision.

Previous studies

9.3   The findings of the present study confirm many of the main results from other smaller-scale surveys of elderly peoples' housing needs and circumstances. Some examples are:

- the opportunity to remain in their current home with suitable aids and adaptations and health and social care support is the preferred option of most elderly people;

- staying at home options for elderly people are generally less expensive than specialised housing solutions to their needs;

- specialised housing contains high proportions of elderly residents with no apparent physical need for the level of care and emergency support offered.

Staying at home

9.4   Several studies conducted in the mid-eighties on elderly peoples' housing and care aspirations, showed that the vast majority wish to remain in their present homes and can be enabled to do so (Tinker, 1984, Wheeler, 1985, Challis and Davies, 1986, Smith 1986, Salvage 1986) through adaptations and domiciliary care support. As one response, the Government made funding available under the 'Assisted Agencies Initiative' to stimulate the growth of home improvement agencies, which help elderly and disabled people with the process of carrying out repairs, improvements or adaptations to their homes. Several research studies have looked at the effectiveness of these agencies and confirmed that they provide a responsive and valuable service, for which demand is high (Leather and Mackintosh, 1990a, b, 1993a, b). Staying at home options are also obviously in line with care in the community policies. Other studies have also shown that a substantial proportion of residents in specialised housing schemes would have preferred to remain in their previous home, with repairs and improvements to make it suitable for them to live there (Butler, Oldman and Greve, 1983, Tinker 1984, 1989).

Cost of housing and housing with care options

9.5   The high cost of specialised housing for elderly people and other special needs groups has been highlighted by many studies (Tinker, 1984, 1989, Clapham and Munro, 1988, Goldsmiths' College, 1993). This study, in common with others, has shown that not only is specialised accommodation such as very sheltered housing expensive, it is more costly than maintaining elderly people at home with domiciliary care support and house adaptations. It has also confirmed, amongst other things, that one of the major influences on the revenue costs of specialised housing for elderly people is the expenditure required to employ permanent care staff in schemes instead of making greater use of visiting domiciliary care staff (Tinker, 1989). This is, in fact, one of the main reasons why housing association schemes for elderly people were found to be more expensive on a per person per annum basis than equivalent local authority schemes.

Dependency levels amongst residents of specialised housing

9.6   Several pieces of research have identified a significant core of elderly residents in specialised housing schemes with no physical or mental dependency (Butler, Oldman and Greve, 1983, Tinker, 1984, 1989, Middleton, 1987, Clapham and Munro, 1988, Oldman, 1990). Whilst this study did not look at the use made of staff and communal facilities in schemes and the relative importance to residents of unique aspects of specialised accommodation, e.g. the warden and the alarm system, these other studies have found that this group tends to under use facilities and is less likely to value the care support features of specialised housing. It is debatable, therefore, whether it is an effective use of costly resources to provide specialised housing for this group of `fit' elderly residents, as opposed to offering them smaller ordinary/ mainstream housing or Category 1 accommodation. This study did, however, look at the use made by residents of visiting health and social care services and found a similar picture of possible over-provision for fit elderly people. Residents, including groups identified as fully independent, were receiving considerably more formal care support than elderly people in the community at all levels of dependency.

9.7   The study also contains findings which contrast with those of previous surveys. Some examples are:

- an increasing polarisation in dependency levels amongst residents of sheltered housing towards the extremes of high and low dependency;

- an increasing number of new entrants to sheltered housing from residential care.

Dependency levels

9.8   One enduring belief about sheltered housing, and often cited as a reason for the development of very sheltered housing, is that levels of dependency amongst residents are steadily increasing and placing an ever growing burden on wardens (Temple 1980, Butler, Oldman and Greve 1983, Oldman 1990). Indeed, as Oldman reports, both the Wagner report (1988) on residential care and the Griffiths report (1988) on community care call for the up-grading of sheltered housing facilities to cope with a growing demand from frail elderly people. This research has shown that the situation is more complex; although there is a growing core of high dependency residents in schemes, there is also an increasing proportion of residents with no physical or mental dependency. The former may be the result of Part III homes and long- stay hospital wards being steadily closed. The latter suggests, however, that wardens are still coping with the demands arising from a balanced community of 'fit' and 'frail' elderly people, as opposed to an increasingly uniform high dependency resident population.

New entrants to sheltered housing

9.9   Previous research has been doubtful about the basis of allocations of elderly people between residential care and sheltered housing. Several studies have suggested that a significant proportion of those entering residential care are more suitable for sheltered housing (Plank 1977, Bradshaw and Gibbs 1988, Neill et. al. 1988). Tinker's (1989) study of very sheltered housing also showed that only a very small proportion of residents had come from residential care and this cast doubt upon the role of extra-care housing in meeting in the needs of those considered unsuitable for Part III accommodation. The present study has found, however, that the numbers of new entrants to very sheltered housing coming from residential and nursing care homes has increased from 3% to 11%. This is probably partly attributable to the programme of closure of Part III or old peoples' homes operated by many local authorities.

Assessing elderly and disabled peoples' housing needs

9.10   Assessing the housing needs of any group of people is an extremely difficult and complex task. For example, there are several levels of assessment, ranging from the kind of assessment carried out by housing or care professionals in a series of meetings with their clients and other interested parties, to the kind of assessment required for planning provision at local, regional and national levels. For elderly and disabled people, there is a wide range of housing options and a potentially long list of things that need to be taken into account when assessing housing and housing with care needs. Having said that, this study provides several pointers to future housing needs analysis amongst the elderly and disabled populations including:

- the importance of looking separately at the needs of the over 75 year olds;

- the significance of peoples' aspirations as well as their objective needs;

- the recognition that some people will not want provision despite their objective circumstances;

- the particular needs of young disabled adults aged 16 – 29; and,

- the importance of assessing need for a combined package of housing and care inputs to enabling an elderly or disabled person to remain at home.

9.11   There is a growing awareness that it is necessary when looking at the housing needs of elderly people to view older elderly people aged 75 or over separately from elderly people aged between 65 and 74 years old. In this study, age has been shown to be a key variable in explaining many different profiles of elderly people such as the income distribution, household type, health and dependency, tenure, housing aspirations and receipt of aids and adaptations. Whilst it is not the only factor which explains many of these variations, it is, nevertheless, the most frequently occurring factor.

9.12   No single housing solution is suited to the housing needs of all elderly people and a range of alternative housing and care options should be considered by providers and elderly people themselves. Sheltered housing and other forms of specialised housing have a role to play. This research has shown, however, that they are a costly and limited resource and, when assessing elderly households that might require re-housing, to ensure cost-effective use of subsidised housing resources, they should be offered to physically/mentally dependent people who actually want it as well as need it. For those that do not want it other housing and housing with care solutions can be found, such as staying at home with aids and adaptations. An important message of this research, therefore, is that elderly and disabled peoples' housing and care **aspirations** are just as relevant as their objective **needs** when making assessments of housing requirements. These two important aspects of assessment should not be examined separately, as has often been the case in previous studies, but must be looked at together. The only qualification being that aspirations should be carefully measured to avoid some of the potential misunderstandings and pitfalls described in Chapter 8 (see paragraphs 8.5 – 8.8).

9.13   This study has clearly shown that within the elderly population there is a group of households which despite their objective circumstances, do not want any (or additional) subsidised housing and housing with care provision. This group of mainly physically dependent people simply want to remain in their existing home exactly as it is, even though, they may have difficulty coping with steps or stairs or it is in need of repair. Any assessment of elderly people, for planning purposes, needs to take account of this group and decisions have to be made on how to treat them within the analysis. For example, it is important to decide whether they are capable of making independent decisions and, if allowing them to remain in their present state, constitutes a risk to others as well as themselves. It is likely that each individual housing needs study will have to arrive at its own decision on how to treat this group.

9.14   The study has also identified a sub-group within the non-elderly disabled adult population with particular needs. Young disabled adults aged between 16 and 29 years old are especially keen to obtain alternative accommodation. This is not surprising as a high proportion of them are still living within their parents' homes and probably desire independence. Nevertheless, it may be a source of burden to their parents for them to continue to live at home and, because of the lack of suitable alternative accommodation, a problem of access to housing rather than willingness to move on the part of the young disabled people.

9.15   Housing for elderly and disabled people is often provided in conjunction with care support, as part of a package to deal with physical and/or mental frailties. Assessments of the housing needs of elderly and disabled people, cannot, therefore, avoid the necessity of looking at health and social care services received and required. It would also be difficult to conceive of a housing needs assessment that did not attempt to examine the relative costs of different options for elderly and disabled people at the same level of dependency.

9.16   Each of these points will be addressed in the Department's (forthcoming) guidance on assessing the needs of local elderly populations, including a description of the methods used to produce the estimates in Chapter 8.

Changing profiles of need

9.17   This research has also highlighted some new issues, especially in the changing nature or profile of needs amongst elderly people. The main issues appear to be as follows:

- the range of options available to elderly people is increasing with the growing significance of staying at home options and the development of different types of specialised housing, such as Category 1.5 and Category 2.5;

- the range of characteristics and circumstances of elderly people and their households that need to be taken into account in assessments of housing needs for planning purposes is also expanding; and,

- there seems to be some shift in emphasis towards higher care solutions and away from lower care housing solutions to elderly peoples' needs.

9.18   Previous studies have tended to concentrate on the need for specialised accommodation as the only distinctive housing option for elderly and disabled people. Thus, estimates of need have been produced for ordinary sheltered housing units and other forms of specialised accommodation. The range of elderly and disabled peoples' housing needs has expanded, however, to cover packages of aids and adaptations and domiciliary care support to remain at home. There is also a greater sophistication to the choices available to elderly people and their households in today's market with the growth of private sector sheltered housing, Categories 1.5 and 2.5 or very sheltered housing and the increasing possibility that people will be required to pay for their care through realising the equity tied up in their homes. Estimates of need have been produced for these new types of specialised housing and packages of adaptations and support in this study.

9.19   Previous studies have also tended to concentrate on a handful of characteristics such as whether an elderly person lived alone, had children living nearby and was dependent (Townsend and Wedderburn, 1970). This study, in common with more recent surveys of the housing needs of elderly and disabled people (Hart and Chalmers, 1990) has looked at a wider range of characteristics, including income and savings, current aids and adaptations, receipt of informal care, receipt of health and social care services, desire to move, aspects of present accommodation and severity of disability.

9.20   Partly, perhaps, because of the ageing elderly population, there seems to be an increased need for higher care solutions to housing needs. This research has identified a significant unmet need for very sheltered housing and a potential over-provision of ordinary sheltered housing. Some of the implications of this change will be discussed in the next section of this chapter.

9.21   Overall, however, this research has re-inforced the general message of housing research over the last decade that, from the viewpoint of cost-effectiveness and individuals' aspirations, housing solutions for elderly and disabled people with physical and/or mental difficulties should, first and foremost, start at home. They should look at the possibilities of adapting homes currently occupied by elderly and disabled people to their needs with the help and advice of relatives, where appropriate. Once it is clear that this is not what the elderly or disabled person wants, or it is not practicable, then specialised options should be considered.

Future patterns of provision?

9.22   This research has demonstrated that there is no longer the demand for traditional or ordinary sheltered housing that existed previously. Void levels within sheltered housing seem to be rising as providers find increasing difficulties letting units in schemes (Barelli, 1992). This is partly due to factors relating to the nature and location of the existing stock and partly due to the increasing ability of elderly people in low-medium dependency groups to remain at home. This presents problems to policy-makers and providers but also new opportunities. Several providers are currently examining the future of their difficult-to-let sheltered stock (Micallef, 1994) and this is the subject of several research studies (Age Concern Institute of Gerontology, 1994 NFHA, 1994).

One possibility is to upgrade a part of the stock to very sheltered or extra-care housing. This would help to address the unmet need for extra-care housing from frail elderly people in the community which was identified in this study, and the demand from transfers into the community from long-stay geriatric wards as a result of community care policies. Providers are also looking at the possibility of changing the design of units in schemes from bedsitters to self-contained one-bed flats to make them more attractive to potential tenants, and changing the use of dwellings from elderly people to single homeless people and other special needs groups, e.g. people with AIDS/HIV infection. There is, nevertheless, clearly a growing awareness of the need to re-evaluate the role of sheltered housing (NFHA/Anchor, 1991, NFHA, 1994).

9.23   In addition, this study has revealed a quite significant demand for smaller or same size/ordinary mainstream housing – as paragraph 8.28 showed the demand for smaller accommodation outnumbers the demand for accommodation of the same size by 3:1. Many of these elderly people will probably be vacating property they are under- occupying by one or two bedrooms above the bedroom standard and, in the social rented sector, this can be translated into accommodation for homeless families and families on general waiting lists. The research has also found significant numbers of residents in ordinary and very sheltered housing with no physical or mental frailty who might be offered other accommodation. Both of these findings have potential implications for Category 1 housing. This form of provision has often been seen as the Cinderella to ordinary or traditional sheltered housing: not as flexible or as capable of housing elderly people with physical needs. Category 1 is, nevertheless, particularly suitable for elderly people under-occupying their accommodation who are physically/mentally fit and may want to move. Within the subsidised specialised stock as a whole, moreover, it still represents a sizeable proportion of available units. It would also be a more cost-effective and appropriate option for elderly people who are currently being re-housed into ordinary sheltered housing who are physically fit but are suffering from social isolation and/or feelings or insecurity.

9.24   Looking at these two trends together suggests some interesting possibilities for the future pattern of specialised housing provision. There may be a divergence in provision with a substantial proportion of the current ordinary sheltered stock being upgraded to higher care housing or down-graded to specially-designed accommodation without any care support. Another scenario might be the cessation of new building for any forms of provision below very sheltered housing and a switch in the use of the current stock to accommodation for other special needs groups. Yet another possibility might be the development of a new form of specialised housing for elderly and disabled people which is more adaptable and sensitive to changing care needs and brings in support to individuals only when it is required. This would overcome some of the problems associated with large schemes containing elderly people with differing care and social needs, but all receiving the same costly staff inputs from wardens and others. Whatever the outcome, it is clear that the rationale for ordinary or Category 2 sheltered housing provision is being severely questioned not only because of internal inconsistencies, but also due to external pressures such as community care policies which might require specialised housing with extra-care support, and the future revenue funding of warden activities in local authority schemes through the Housing Revenue Account.

9.25 Turning to solutions involving elderly people remaining in adapted housing in the community rather than moving to specialised housing, there are also problems in pursuing these options. In particular, they create tensions with policies to reduce under- occupation. They may also lead to a small part of the owner-occupied stock steadily deteriorating in state of repair because dwellings are occupied by elderly people who do not want to have any repairs or adaptations made to their homes. There is also anecdotal evidence of growing concern amongst public sector providers about mainstream housing that has been heavily adapted in order to enable elderly and disabled people to continue living at home. As the level of adaptation increases, it becomes more and more difficult to re-convert or restore a property to general use and the adaptations are not easily transferable to another property, thus, they become an expensive investment for a limited lifetime usage. Many of these difficulties could be overcome by more effective methods of linking those who have a need for adapted properties with available and suitable accommodation in the general stock (Morris 1990). These are, nevertheless, potential side-effects or unintended consequences of policies directed at enabling elderly and disabled people to remain at home.

9.26 The general conclusion of this study is that the majority of elderly and disabled people have no assessed need for any form of subsidised specialised housing or other housing with care support to remain at home. Of those that do have an assessed need, most wish to remain at home and can be enabled to do so through adaptations and domiciliary care support. This is also the most cost-effective solution to their housing needs. There is, however, a small but significant minority of elderly and disabled people who both need and want a move to specialised accommodation. Current provision meets most of this demand but there are some shortfalls in units for those with high levels of dependency and disability and extra-care requirements. There is also evidence of over-provision of some types of specialised accommodation and it may be that part of this stock can be converted to other uses more in line with current needs.

Appendix 1 Reports on individual elements of the study

Twelve reports written by Ernst and Young and MORI on individual elements of the study are available as priced publications from the Department. For further details write to Room N7/12 Department of the Environment, 2 Marsham Street, London SW1P 3EB or telephone 071-276 3223. They are as follows:

Report 1 [Ernst and Young] - A National Study of the provision of Specialised Housing for Elderly People;

Report 2 [Ernst and Young] - The Cost of Specialised Housing;

Report 3 [Ernst and Young] - The Cost of Maintaining an Elderly Person at Home;

Report 4 [Ernst and Young] - Benchmark Study of the Costs of aids and adaptations;

Report 5 [Ernst and Young] - A Comparison of the Costs of Housing Options for Elderly People;

Report 6 [Ernst and Young] - Allocation Policies and Practices: Specialised Housing for Elderly People;

Report 7 [MORI] - A National and Regional survey of elderly people in the community;

Report 8 [MORI] - A National Survey of residents of specialised housing;

Report 9 [MORI] - A National Survey of Informal Carers;

Report 10 [MORI] - A National Survey of non-elderly disabled adults;

Report 11 [Ernst and Young] - The Allocation model;

Report 12 [Ernst and Young] - Indicators of Need.

Appendix 2 Dependency scales

1.   A range of questions was used in the interview surveys that would enable scores to be derived for the Leeds scale and for Clackmannan dependency categories. These are described in further detail below:

The Leeds Scale of Dependency [1]

This is a 12 point dependency score covering mobility, self-care and domestic activities. 1 point is scored for each activity with a positive response. The higher the score the higher the level of dependency. Thus a score of 0 equates to 'fully independent'. Scores may be combined to ranges giving dependencies of:

low	1 - 3
medium	4 - 7 and
high	8 - 12

Questions:

1.   Hospitalisation in the last 12 months.

2.   Walking aid.

3.   Cannot bathe without difficulty/help.

4.   Cannot get in and out of bed without difficulty/help.

5.   Cannot get up and down stairs/steps without difficulty/help.

6.   Cannot get around the house/flat without difficulty/help.

7.   Cannot get out of doors without difficulty/help.

8.   Cannot use public transport without difficulty/help.

9.   Unable to do all shopping without help.

10. Unable to do all housework without help.

11. Unable to do all preparing and cooking of meals without help.

12. Unable to do all washing of clothes without help.

---

[1] Butler, A., Oldman, C., Greve, J., *Sheltered Housing for the Elderly*, Allen and Unwin, 1983.

The Clackmannan/ Townsend Scale of Dependency

The Clackmannan dependency categories were developed by Bond and Carstairs for a study of elderly in the community using an interview survey in the Clackmannan area[2] Scotland. The components of dependency were broken down to functional and clinical criteria and these were further divided as follows:

functional - mobility incapacity, self-care incapacity, house care incapacity

clinical - incontinence, mental impairment

The reason for this basic division of the components of dependency is that incontinence and mental impairment can also result in the need for care and supervision. Scales for mobility, self care and house care have been developed based on inter-item correlations and these were subjected to a Guttman scaling analysis in order to develop cumulative, uni-dimensional scales for mobility, self care and house care. The resulting scales are shown in the table below. They are based on the assumption that they are hierarchical - thus having difficulty or being unable to perform an activity associated with 'failure' on all earlier items in the scale.

Mobility incapacity	Self care incapacity	House care incapacity
1. Difficulty travelling by bus. 2. Difficulty walking outside. 3. Unable to travel by bus. 4. Unable to walk outside. 5. Difficulty walking outside. 6. Unable to get up from chair. 7. Unable to walk inside.	1. Difficulty washing hair. 2. Unable to wash hair. 3. Unable to wash all over or bath. 4. Difficulty dressing. 5. Difficulty washing hands and face. 6. Unable to put on shoes or stockings. 7. Unable to dress. 8. Unable to wash hands and face.	1. Unable to do heavy shopping. 2. Difficulty washing clothes. 3. Difficulty ironing 4. Unable to wash clothes. 5. Difficulty preparing 7. Difficulty with light 8. Unable to prepare and cook meals. 9. Unable to make bed. 10. Unable to do light housework.
Coefficient of reproducibility 0.97	*Coefficient of reproducibility 0.99*	*Coefficient of reproducibility 0.96*
Coefficient of scalability 0.71	*Coefficient of scalability 0.69*	*Coefficient of scalability 0.62*

---

[2] Bond, J. and Carstairs, V. 1982. *Services for the Elderly*, Scottish Health Service Studies No. 42, Edinburgh: Scottish Home and Health Department.

The clinical components of dependency are assessed separately. Continence was classified in four categories:

- continent;

- occasional urinary incontinence (mainly stress incontinence and accidental loss occurring less than once a month);

- incontinence of urine; and

- incontinence of urine and faeces.

Mental state is assessed using questions which are intended to distinguish between organic and affective disorders.

The component of dependency also incorporates a time dimension. Long interval dependency refers to needs for help with tasks such as shopping, housework and laundry which may be performed daily or less often. This group is further sub-divided into those who were only mentally impaired and those who suffered functional incapacity. Short interval dependencies refer to those needs for help at regular intervals such as dressing, undressing or help with feeding and are sub-divided into those requiring night time help or not. Critical interval dependencies generate needs for help on demand at short and often unpredictable time intervals, requiring a helper to be constantly available. These dependencies are also further sub-divided as categories F and G shown in the table below.

Clackmannan Dependency Matrix

Dependency Categories	Components of Dependency				
	Mobility	**Self-care**	**House care**	**Incontinence**	**Mental**
A. Independent	No difficulty with any of the <u>scale</u> activities	No difficulty with any of the <u>scale</u> activities	No difficulty with any of the <u>scale</u> activities	None	No problems
B. Long interval – mental only	No difficulty with any of the <u>scale</u> activities	No difficulty with any of the <u>scale</u> activities	No difficulty with any of the <u>scale</u> activities	None	Mild organic disorder or mild affective disorder or psychoneurosis
C. Long interval – functional	Difficulty: – walking outside on level surface Unable: – travel by bus	Difficulty: – washing hair – dressing – washing hands and face Unable: – wash hair – wash or bath all over	Difficulty: – washing clothes – ironing clothes – preparing and cooking hot meal Unable: – do heavy shopping – wash clothes – iron clothes	Incontinent of urine	May have mild disorder
D. Short interval – no night help help	Difficulty: – walking inside on level surface Unable: – walk outside on level surface	Unable: – put on shoes and socks – dress – wash hands and face	Unable: – prepare and cook meals – make bed – do light housework	Not incontinent of faeces	Not severe
E. Short interval – night help required	As short interval	As short interval <u>and</u> night help required	As short interval	As short interval	As short interval
F. Critical interval – mental independent	As independent	As independent	As independent	None	Severe organic or functional disorder
OR with long interval functional	As long interval functional	As long interval functional	As long interval functional	As long interval functional	
G. Critical interval – functional	Unable: – get up from chair – walk inside Permanently or temporarily bedfast or chairfast	Any	Any	Incontinent of faeces	Any
OR	Short interval	Short interval	Short interval	Short interval	Severe

Note: At A and B, E and F, all of the conditions must be satisfied. At C and D one of the incapacities listed for mobility, self-care, house-care or incontinence must be present, and degree of mental impairment is a necessary condition. At G one of the mobility conditions must be satisfied or incontinence as stated. Source: Bond and Carstairs, 1982.

Appendix 3

Table 2.5 Units of subsidised specialised housing for elderly people by Category of accommodation and type of local authority (grossed-up figures)						
Col%s/ **Row%s**	**Category of accommodation**					
	1	**1.5**	**2**	**2.5**	**Other**	**Total**
London Boroughs	6,344 **5%** 11%	6,029 **4%** 11%	39,494 **12%** 69%	2,809 **19%** 5%	2,106 **10%** 4%	56,782 **9%** 100%
Metropolitan District Councils	34,258 **27%** 21%	43,707 **29%** 27%	75,600 **23%** 46%	2,513 **17%** 2%	5,872 **29%** 4%	161,950 **25%** 100%
District Councils	86,261 **68%** 20%	100,979 **67%** 24%	213,652 **65%** 51%	9,460 **64%** 2%	12,411 **61%** 3%	422,763 **66%** 100%
Base	126,863	150,715	328,746	14,782	20,389	641,494

Table 2.6 Units of subsidised specialised housing for disabled people by Category of accommodation and type of local authority (grossed-up figures)			
Col%s/ **Row%s**	**Wheelchair housing**	**Mobility housing/housing adapted for disabled people**	**Total**
London Boroughs	4,858 **18%** 46%	5,825 **9%** 54%	10,683 **12%** 100%
Metropolitan District Councils	8,533 **31%** 20%	34,827 **56%** 80%	43,360 **49%** 100%
District Councils	13,761 **51%** 39%	21,271 **34%** 61%	35,032 **39%** 100%
Base	27,152	61,923	89,075

Source: These figures are taken from HIP1 returns for 1.4.93. They exclude provision by 'other public sector' organisations and units owned and managed by local authorities outside their administrative boundaries.

Table 2.9 Units of subsidised specialised housing for elderly people by Category of accommodation and housing type within Type of provider (un-grossed figures)

Local Authorities

Row%s/Col%s	1	1.5	2	2.5	Other	Total
Bungalows	51,031	58,998	44,835	349	4,969	160,182
	32%	37%	28%	0	3%	100%
	54%	**57%**	**26%**	**7%**	**45%**	**42%**
Houses	2,863	1,394	800	1	54	5,112
	56%	27%	16%	0	1%	100%
	3%	**1%**	**1%**	**0**	**1%**	**1%**
Self-contained flats	40,151	43,151	113,916	4,566	5,501	207,285
	19%	21%	55%	2%	3%	100%
	43%	**42%**	**66%**	**91%**	**50%**	**54%**
Non self-contained flats	0	112	11,509	82	354	12,057
	0	1%	96%	1%	3%	100%
	0	**0**	**7%**	**2%**	**3%**	**3%**
Other	443	173	812	2	153	1,583
	28%	11%	51%	0	10%	100%
	1%	**0**	**1%**	**0**	**1%**	**0**
Shared rooms	0	0	0	2	68	70
	0	0	0	3%	97%	100%
	0	**0**	**0**	**0**	**15**	**0**

Housing Associations

	1	1.5	2	2.5	Other	Total
Bungalows	2,950	1,843	2,506	24	180	7,503
	39%	25%	33%	0	2%	100%
	16%	**16%**	**4%**	**0**	**6%**	**7%**
Houses	223	48	257	34	40	602
	37%	8%	43%	6%	7%	100%
	1%	**0**	**0**	**1%**	**1%**	**1%**
Self-contained flats	14,755	9,691	66,853	1,935	1,237	94,471
	16%	10%	71%	2%	1%	100%
	82%	**83%**	**94%**	**39%**	**41%**	**87%**
Non self-contained flats	0	56	1,857	2,418	1,333	5,664
	0	1%	33%	43%	24%	100%
	0	**1%**	**3%**	**49%**	**45%**	**5%**
Other	164	0	26	511	208	909
	18%	0	3%	56%	23%	100%
	1%	**0**	**0**	**10%**	**7%**	**1%**
Shared rooms	0	0	18	149	90	257
	0	0	7%	58%	35%	100%
	0	**0**	**0**	**3%**	**3%**	**0**

Table 2.11 Units of subsidised specialised housing for elderly people by Type of provider and size of units (un-grossed figures)

Col%s/ Row%s	Local Authority	Abbey-field	Housing Association	Alms-house	Total
Bedsits	42,088 **11%** 52%	5,091 **82%** 6%	29,847 **27%** 37%	4,464 **22%** 6%	81,672 **16%** 100%
1-Bed units	255,905 **66%** 77%	995 **16%** 0	63,716 **58%** 19%	13,238 **64%** 4%	333,854 **64%** 100%
2-bed units	84,596 **22%**	130 **2%**	15,438 **14%**	2,755 **13%**	102,919 **20%**
3-bed units	3,630 **1%** 93%	14 **0** 0	148 **0** 4%	119 **1%** 3%	3,911 **1%** 100%
Total	386,219	6,230	109,149	20,758	522,356

Table 2.12 Units of subsidised specialised housing for elderly people by Category of accommodation and size of units within Type of provider (un-grossed figures)

Local Authorities

Row%s Col%s	1	1.5	2	2.5	Other	Total
Bedsit	1,734 4% **2%**	2,420 6% **2%**	36,245 86% **21%**	980 2% **20%**	709 2% **6%**	42,088 100% **11%**
1 Bed	61,855 24% **66%**	67,291 26% **65%**	114,855 45% **67%**	3,756 2% **75%**	8,148 3% **74%**	255,905 100% **66%**
2 Bed	28,246 33% **30%**	33,485 40% **32%**	20,528 24% **12%**	261 0 **5%**	2,076 3% **19%**	84,596 100% **22%**
3+ Bed	2,653 73% **3%**	632 17% **1%**	244 7% **0**	3 0 **0**	98 3% **1%**	3,630 100% **1%**

Housing Associations

	1	1.5	2	2.5	Other	Total
Bedsit	1,885 6% **10%**	363 1% **3%**	23,250 78% **33%**	2,869 10% **58%**	1,480 5% **49%**	29,847 100% **27%**
1 Bed	13,566 21% **75%**	6,162 10% **53%**	41,072 65% **57%**	1,831 3% **37%**	1,085 2% **36%**	63,716 100% **58%**
2 Bed	2,601 17% **14%**	5,112 33% **44%**	7,084 46% **10%**	222 1% **5%**	419 3% **14%**	15,438 100% **14%**
3+ Bed	40 27% **0**	1 1% **0**	93 63% **0**	0 0 **0**	14 10% **1%**	148 100% **0**

Table 2.13 Units of subsidised specialised housing for elderly people by Category of accommodation and floor level (un-grossed figures)

Col%s/Row%s	Category of accommodation					Total
	1	1.5	2	2.5	Other	
Ground floor	37,829 **66%** 21%	33,874 **62%** 19%	95,217 **48%** 53%	5,050 **48%** 3%	8,898 **60%** 5%	180,868 **54%** 100%
1st-5th floor	19,213 **34%** 13%	19,618 **36%** 13%	100,993 **51%** 67%	5,463 **52%** 4%	5,780 **39%** 4%	151,067 **45%** 100%
6th floor and above	286 **0** 5%	1,579 **3%** 28%	3,612 **2%** 64%	57 **1%** 1%	117 **1%** 2%	5,651 **2%** 100%
Total	57,328	55,071	199,822	10,570	14,795	337,586

Table 2.14 Units of subsidised specialised housing for elderly people by Type of provider and alarm and warden support (un-grossed figures)

Col%s/Row%s	Local Authority	Abbeyfield	Housing Association	Total
Warden & alarm	276,002 **72%** 75%	5,551 **91%** 2%	88,113 **81%** 24%	369,666 **74%** 100
Alarm only	21,569 **6%** 81%	25 **0** 0	5,155 **5%** 19%	26,749 **5%** 100%
Warden only	5,170 **1%** 72%	526 **9%** 7%	1,524 **1%** 21%	7,220 **1%** 100%
No provision	79,222 **21%** 85%	2 **0** 0	13,799 **13%** 15%	93,023 **19%** 100%
Total	381,963	6,104	108,591	496,658

Table 2.15 Units of subsidised specialised housing for elderly people by Type of provider and alarm and warden support (un-grossed figures)

Col%s/Row%s	Local Authority	Abbeyfield	Housing Association	Total
Scheme-based	67,389 **24%** 51%	5,105 **94%** 4%	60,246 **69%** 45%	132,740 **36%** 100%
Centrally-based	207,970 **76%** 88%	310 **6%** 0	27,065 **31%** 12%	235,345 **64%** 100%
Total	275,359	5,415	87,311	368,085

Col%s/ Row%s	Local Authority	Abbey-field	Housing Association	Alms-house	Total
Bungalows	2,643 **38%** 80%	32 **7%** 1%	570 **10%** 17%	73 **14%** 2%	3,318 **25%** 100%
Houses	18 **0** 14%	0 **0** 0	58 **1%** 44%	55 **11%** 42%	131 **1%** 100%
Self contained flats	4,328 **62%** 45%	198 **42%** 2%	4,670 **84%** 49%	394 **78%** 4%	9,590 **71%** 100%
Non self contained flats	−48 **−1%** −12%	241 **52%** 61%	218 **4%** 55%	−15 **−3%** −4%	396 **3%** 100%
Other	0 **0** 0	−4 **−1%** −80%	11 **0** 220%	−2 **0** −40%	5 **0** 100%
Shared rooms	0 **0** 0	−4 **−1%** 100%	2 **0** −50%	−2 **0** 50%	−4 **0** 100%
Base	6,941	467	5,527	505	13,440

Table 2.19 Planned units of subsidised specialised housing for elderly people by Type of provider and housing type (un-grossed figures)

Table 3.2 and 3.3 Profile of subsidised specialised housing by Category of accommodation, Type of provider and size of units

Col%s	Category 1			Category 1.5				Category 2				Category 2.5		
	LA	HA	Alms	LA	HA	Abbyf	Alms	LA	HA	Abbyf	Alms	LA	HA	Abbyf
Housing type:														
Bungalows	47	11	29	74	0	0	11	17	3	14	0	2	0	0
Houses	1	1	22	1	0	0	0	0	0	0	0	0	0	0
Self-contained flats	47	87	49	25	100	100	21	75	94	32	48	98	71	30
Non self-contained flats	5	2	0	0	0	0	68	8	3	54	52	0	29	70
Size of units:														
1-Bed	73	73	94	77	83	100	95	89	92	100	100	97	100	95
2-Bed	26	27	4	23	17	0	5	11	8	0	0	3	0	5
3+ Bed	1	0	3	0	0	0	0	0	0	0	0	0	0	0
Total	100	100	100	100	100	100	100	100	100	100	100	100	100	100

Table 3.4 Age profile of local authority and housing association Category 2 accommodation (cumulative percentages)

Year when first built	Local authority schemes	Housing Association schemes
>1945	0.5%	0.6%
1946-1960	2.7%	0.6%
1961-1970	19.9%	3.8%
1971-1980	57.5%	48.8%
1981-1985	79.6%	75.6%
1986>	100%	100%

Table 3.7 Average number of full-time equivalent staff per 100 residents by Category of accommodation and Type of provider

	Category of accommodation			
Type of provider	Cat 1	Cat 1.5	Cat 2	Cat 2.5
Local authority	1.6	5.1	7	17.8
Housing association	8	4.6	10.4	45.1

Table 3.9 Costs of state benefits received by elderly residents of specialised housing (£ per person per annum): Category of accommodation by level of dependency

	Level of dependency					
	A	B	C	D	G	Total
Cat 1	2,833	2,775	3,003	3,146	3,697	3,007
Cat 2	2,831	2,836	2,998	3,261	3,657	3,007
Cat 2.5	2,886	2,795	2,890	3,289	3,814	3,195
Total	2,838	2,838	2,984	3,247	3,657	3,086

Table 3.10 Housing tenure and type by level of dependency (weighted data)

Col%s	Level of Dependency					
	A	B	C	D	F	G
Tenure:						
Owner-Occupier	65	60	41	46	49	47
Local authority	23	27	41	36	34	33
Housing association	3	4	7	5	12	4
Private rented	4	3	6	4	1	3
Friends/relatives	2	2	1	5	3	8
Housing Type:						
Detached	11	9	5	6	6	8
Semi-detached	28	27	24	23	22	25
Terraced	19	21	17	18	20	18
Bungalow	24	24	25	27	25	29
Flat	17	18	28	26	25	18
Base[1]	3,715	1,281	738	2,218	77	608

[1] 256 of the respondents could not be classified on the more complex Clackmannan scale because of missing data on their dependency forms. This applies to the base figures for Clackmannan scale because of missing data on their dependency forms. This applies to the baxe figures for Clackmannan dependency use in other tables. 8 respondents refused to state their age and 4 households could not be classified into these household types.

Table 3.11 Revenue Cost (£ per person per annum) by level of dependency

Col%s		Level of Dependency				
	A	B	C	D	F	G
Revenue costs	621	645	603	555	717	536

Table 3.13 Costs of informal care (£ per person per annum) by the type of carer and level of dependency of the dependant

	Level of Dependency		
	C	D	G
Resident carers	5,787	6,809	9,377
Non-resident carers	2,268	3,055	2,622

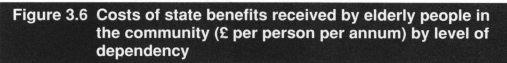

Figure 3.6 Costs of state benefits received by elderly people in the community (£ per person per annum) by level of dependency

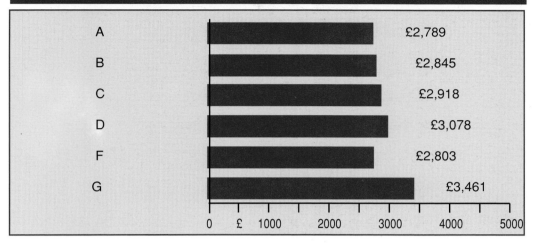

Table 3.14 Average gross resource costs (£ per person per annum) for all housing and housing with care options for elderly people by level of dependency

	Clackmannan Group A				Clackmannan Group B				Clackmannan Group C			
	SAH	Cat 1	Cat 2	Cat 2.5	SAH	Cat 1	Cat 2	Cat 2.5	SAH	Cat 1	Cat 2	Cat 2.5
Notional rent	3,642	4,289	4,843	5,379	3,686	4,289	4,843	5,379	3,665	4,289	4,843	5,379
Revenue costs	621	709	1,023	5,237	645	709	1,023	5,237	603	709	1,023	5,237
Health and social care	75	82	270	185	106	294	198	120	297	701	653	683
Gross resource costs	4,338	5,080	6,136	10,801	4,437	5,292	6,064	10,736	4,565	5,699	6,519	11,299
Informal care	0	0	0	0	1,000	0	0	0	2,803	0	0	0
State benefits	2,798	2,833	2,831	2,886	2,845	2,775	2,836	2,795	2,918	3,003	2,998	2,890
Total costs	7,136	7,913	8,967	13,687	8,282	8,067	8,900	13,531	10,286	8,702	9,517	14,189

Table 3.14 Average gross resource costs (£ per person per annum) for all housing and housing with care options for elderly people by level of dependency

	Clackmannan Group D				Clackmannan Group G				Total			
	SAH	Cat 1	Cat 2	Cat 2.5	SAH	Cat 1	Cat 2	Cat 2.5	SAH	Cat 1	Cat 2	Cat 2.5
Notional rent	3,302	4,289	4,843	5,379	3,080	4,289	4,843	5,379	3,512	4,289	4,843	5,379
Revenue costs	555	709	1,023	5,237	536	709	1,023	5,237	598	709	1,023	5,237
Health and social care	552	832	1,187	1,286	813	842	1,511	1,948	297	431	735	1,014
Gross resource costs	**4,409**	**5,830**	**7,053**	**11,902**	**4,429**	**5,840**	**7,377**	**12,564**	**4,407**	**5,429**	**6,601**	**11,630**
Informal care	4,509	0	0	0	5,500	0	0	0	4,324	0	0	0
State benefits	3,078	3,146	3,261	3,289	3,461	3,697	3,657	3,814	2,946	3,007	3,077	3,195
Total costs	11,996	8,976	10,314	15,191	13,390	9,537	11,034	16,378	11,677	8,436	9,618	14,825

Table 3.15 Percentage proportions of different cost elements in gross resource costs of subsidised specialised housing

Col%s	Category of accommodation			
	1	2	2.5	Other
Notional rent	79%	74%	46%	58%
Revenue costs	13%	16%	45%	39%
Health and social care costs	8%	11%	8%	3%

Table 3.17 Average gross resource cost (£ per person per annum) of subsidised specialised housing for elderly people: Type of provider by level of dependency

Clackmannan C	Local authority	Housing association	Abbeyfield Societies	Almshouse Societies
Notional rent	4,440	4,941	4,613	4,719
Revenue costs	1,019	1,296	4,069	1,071
Health and social care	729	491	305	723
Gross Resource costs	6,188	6,728	8,987	6,513
State benefits	2,984	2,984	2,984	2,984
Total costs	9,172	9,712	11,971	9,497
Clackmannan D/E				
Notional rent	4,440	4,941	4,613	4,719
Revenue costs	1,019	1,296	4,069	1,071
Health and social care	1,273	940	522	377
Gross Resource costs	6,732	7,177	9,204	6,167
State benefits	3,247	3,247	3,247	3,247
Total costs	9,979	10,424	12,451	9,414

Table 3.18 Average gross resource cost (£ per person per annum) subsidised specialised housing for elderly people: Category 2 accommodation by type of provider within level of dependency

Clackmannan C	Local authority	Housing association
Notional rent	4,565	5,052
Revenue costs	838	1,125
Health and social care	723	529
Gross Resource Cost	6,126	6,706

Table 3.19 Average gross resource costs (£ per person per annum) for maintaining an elderly person in the community by housing type

	Type of Housing						
	Detached	Semi-Detached	Terraced	Bungalow	Flat/ m'nette	Single adult	Elderly couple
Notional rent	6,555	3,248	3,047	3,904	2,661	4,073	2,712
Revenue costs	725	598	546	611	569	667	486
Health and social care	186	204	260	319	430	385	149
Gross Resource costs	7,466	4,050	3,853	4,834	3,660	5,125	3,347
Informal care	5,740	4,570	4,679	4,209	3,619	3,375	6,149
State benefits	2,885	2,913	2,927	2,965	2,985	3,019	2,826
Total costs	16,091	11,533	11,459	12,008	10,264	11,519	12,322

Table 4.3 Household weekly income of elderly people: by age of respondent, gender, household type and tenure

Row%s	Up to £54	£54-84	£85-115	£115+	Base
All households	18	33	20	29	8,901
Age of respondent:					
65-74	17	26	21	35	4,989
75-84	18	40	20	21	3,166
85+	27	43	15	14	746
Gender:					
Male	12	25	23	40	3,548
Female	23	38	18	21	5,353
Household type:					
Single adult aged 65-74	28	43	14	16	1,806
Single adult aged 75+	24	54	12	10	2,256
2 adults: at least 1 aged 65-74 none 75+	11	16	24	48	2,366
2 adults: at least 1 aged 75+	11	19	32	38	1,686
3 adults: at least 1 aged 65+	18	29	22	31	773
Tenure:					
Owner-Occupier	16	25	20	39	4,952
LA rented	21	43	21	15	2,620
HA rented	16	47	18	19	378
Private rented	17	45	16	22	423
Living with friends/rels	36	34	16	14	270

Table 4.4 Savings and investments of elderly people: by age, gender and household type

Row%s	Savings	Base	Up to £5,000 in savings	£5000+ in savings	Base[1]
All households	75	8,901	39	39	6,713
Age of respondent:					
65-74	76	4,989	35	44	3,798
75-84	75	3,166	44	33	2,384
85+	70	746	48	24	531
Gender:					
Male	77	3,548	34	45	2,765
Female	73	5,353	44	33	3,948
Household type:					
Single person households	73	4,062	47	33	2,999
2 or more person households	76	4,825	33	43	3,708

[1] This base figure includes all those who refused to state how much their savings or investments amounted to. This accounts for the percentages in the fourth and fifth column of this table not adding up to 100%.

Table 4.5 State benefits or allowances received by elderly people: by age, household type and level of dependency

Row%s	None of of these[1]	Attendance allow.	Mobility allow.	Severe dis. allow.	Invalid care allow.	Housing Benefit[2]	Income Support	Base
All households	90	6	3	1	*	68	12	8,901
Age of respondent:								
65-74	91	4	4	1	*	63	7	4,989
75-84	91	6	1	*	*	72	17	3,166
85+	81	14	1	1	1	73	22	746
Household type:								
Single adult aged 65-74	94	2	3	*	*	73	13	1,806
Single adult aged 75+	93	4	*	*	*	76	24	2,256
2 adults: at least 1 aged 65-74 none 75+	90	5	6	1	*	55	4	2,366
2 adults: at least 1 aged 75+	86	12	1	*	*	64	9	1,686
3 adults: at least 1 aged 65+	85	11	3	1	1	49	12	773
Level of dependency (Clackmannan grouping):								
A/B	98	1	1	1	*	62	8	4,996
C	97	3	3	*	*	73	21	738
D/E	89	11	6	1	*	72	17	2,226
F/G	79	21	7	1	1	72	18	685

[1] This percentage figure does not include those who said they did not know if they received these benefits. Thus, only 8% of all households claimed to receive at least one of these benefits as 2% were not sure or did not know.

[2] The base for the percentage figures in this column is all renting/shared ownership.

Note * – less than 0.5%.

Table 4.6 Registration as disabled or long-term illnesses and/or disabilities: by age of respondent, gender, household type and level of dependency

Row%s	Registered as disabled	Long-term illnesses	Bedfast/ Chairfast	Base
All households	10	20	3[1]	8,901
Age of respondent:				
65-74	10	16		4,989
75-84	10	24		3,166
85+	13	32		746
Gender:				
Male	12	18		3,548
Female	10	21		5,353
Household type:[2]				
Single adult aged 65-74	10	16		1,806
Single adult aged 75+	10	26		2,256
2 Adults: at least 1 aged 65-74 none75+	11	8		4,769
2 adults: at least 1 aged 75+	11	11		3,383
3+ adults; at least 1 aged 65+	10	6		2,734
Level of dependency:				
A/B	4	8		4,996
C	10	32		738
D/E	20	38		2,226
F/G	32	39		685

[1] This figure has not been broken down by age of respondent, gender, household type and level of dependency because of the small cell sizes involved. It was only asked of those who said they were registered as disabled or had long-term illnesses or disabilities.

[2] The base figures in this part of the table represent 'all household members' not simply respondents.

Table 4.7 Long-term illnesses or health problems suffered by elderly people: by age of elderly respondent

Col%s	All households	65-74	75-84	85+
Walking on level ground	13	9	14	30
Steps and stairs	30	23	35	55
Bending or straightening	23	18	26	39
Falling or keeping balance	20	13	25	43
Gripping or turning things	16	13	18	29
Reading newspaper print even with glasses	10	5	13	29
Hearing someone talking/ deafness	21	15	26	42
Breathlessness/wheezing/ coughing	24	22	27	29
Severe pain or irritation	12	10	14	19
Poor bladder control	11	9	13	20
Fits/convulsions (in past 2 years)	*	*	*	1
Getting confused/ disorientated	5	4	6	14
None of these	37	46	28	13
Base	8,901	4,989	3,166	746

Table 4.11 Age of dwellings occupied by elderly people: by tenure and region

Row%s	Pre-1919	Inter War War	Post War	Post 1964	Base
All households	18	21	26	30	8,901
Tenure					
Owner-occupier	22	24	26	26	4,952
LA rented	3	17	33	38	2,620
HA rented	18	8	7	61	378
Private rented	56	22	9	8	423
Living with friends/rels	21	25	24	22	270
DoE Region					
South-East	14	19	29	35	1,417
South-West	21	14	24	38	956
London	25	31	19	19	1,058
Eastern	14	15	31	35	1,017
W. Mids	15	19	31	28	1,008
E. Mids	14	22	30	29	752
N. West	22	28	21	27	1,236
Yorks & Humberside	19	21	21	32	957
Northern	14	21	32	24	500

Table 4.13 Lack of basic amenities in housing occupied by elderly people: by tenure, age of property, age of respondent and household type

Row%s	Type of basic amenities					
	Kitchen	Fixed bathroom/ shower room	Wash hand basin	Inside toilet	Hot water supply	Base
All households	*	1	1	1	*	8,901
Age of respondent:						
65-74	*	*	*	1	*	4,989
75-84	*	1	1	1	1	3,166
85+	*	2	1	2	1	746
Household type:						
Single adult aged 65-74	*	*	1	1	*	1,806
Single adult aged 75+	*	1	1	1	1	2,256
2 adults: at least 1 aged 65-74 none 75+	0	*	*	*	0	2,366
2 adults: at least 1 aged 75+	0	1	1	1	*	1,686
3 adults: at least 1 aged 65+	*	*	*	*	*	773
Tenure:						
Owner-occupier	*	*	*	1	*	4,952
Council rented	*	*	*	*	*	2,620
Housing association rented	*	*	*	*	*	378
Private rented	1	5	5	7	3	423
Living with friends/ rels	*	0	0	*	0	270
Age of property:						
Pre-1919	*	3	2	4	2	1,578
Inter-war	*	*	1	*	*	1,887
Post war 1945-64	0	0	*	*	*	2,309
Post 1964	*	0	0	0	0	2,675

Col%s	All households	Pre-1919	Inter-war	Post war 1945-64	Post 1964
Table 4.16a Need for repairs and improvements in housing occupied by elderly people: by age of property, tenure and housing aspirations					
External walls	5	8	7	4	2
External windows	13	14	15	16	10
Chimney stack	3	5	3	2	*
Roof	5	11	8	3	2
Drain pipes	3	5	4	3	2
Damp proofing	4	10	3	2	1
Damp/condensation	6	9	5	5	4
Electrics/wiring	5	8	5	7	3
Lighting	1	1	1	*	1
Plumbing	3	4	3	3	2
Bath/shower	6	7	6	7	6
Internal toilet	2	4	2	2	1
Wash basin	1	2	2	1	1
Hot water supply	1	2	1	1	1
Heating system	6	8	7	7	4
None of these	63	56	58	62	74
Base	8,901	1,578	1,887	2,309	2,675

Table 4.16a continued.

Col%s	Owner-occupier	Council tenant	Housing assoc. tenant	Private rented	Living with friends/ rels.
External walls	5	3	4	11	2
External windows	12	16	10	19	9
Chimney stack	3	2	1	4	1
Roof	6	3	2	10	6
Drain pipes	4	3	3	8	1
Damp proofing	3	3	4	15	2
Damp/condensation	4	8	5	15	3
Electrics/wiring	6	3	4	13	2
Lighting	*	*	2	2	0
Plumbing	3	3	3	7	2
Bath/shower	5	9	7	11	7
Internal toilet	2	2	1	8	2
Wash basin	1	1	1	5	1
Hot water supply	1	1	1	6	0
Heating system	4	8	8	11	6
None of these	66	60	72	47	70
Base	4,952	2,620	378	423	270

Table 4.16a continued

Col%s	Present home as it is	Present home: with adaptations and repairs	Other accomm: same size/ larger	Other accomm: smaller	Live with rels./friends
External walls	3	9	4	10	3
External windows	9	26	18	22	18
Chimney stack	2	5	2	5	1
Roof	3	10	5	12	1
Drain pipes	2	7	3	8.	3
Damp proofing	2	9	6	8	4
Damp/con- densation	3	14	8	9	4
Electrics/wiring	4	10	7	12	6
Lighting	*	1	1	2	2
Plumbing	2	6	6	5	1
Bath/shower	4	16	8	6	10
Internal toilet	1	7	4	3	6
Wash basin	1	3	1	2	0
Hot water supply	1	3	1	3	1
Heating system	3	15	10	13	9
None of these	74	32	54	43	58
Base	6,154	1,374	486	741	68

Table 4.16b Help and support needed with carrying out repairs: by age of respondent, tenure and household type

Row%s	Help and support with:						Base
	Org. of work	Raising finance	Technical/ legal advice	Support and reassurance	Financial advice	None of these	
All households	6	9	7	6	9	73	8,901
Age of respondent:							
65-74	7	10	8	6	9	69	4,989
75-84	6	8	6	5	7	77	3,166
85+	4	5	3	4	8	80	746
Household type:							
Single adult aged 65-74	7	9	8	7	10	69	1,806
Single adult aged 75+	5	7	4	4	8	78	2,256
2 adults: at least 1 aged 65-74 none 75+	8	10	10	6	10	68	2,366
2 adults: at least 1 aged 75+	6	7	6	5	7	76	1,686
3 adults: at least 1 aged 65+	5	10	6	6	6	74	773
Tenure:							
Owner-occupier	9	9	10	7	10	68	4,952
LA rented	3	9	2	2	8	79	2,620
HA rented	3	6	4	6	6	81	378
Private rented	3	7	6	5	7	78	423
Living with friends/rels	2	5	2	5	2	85	270

Table 4.18 Adaptations needed by elderly people: by tenure, level of dependency and housing aspirations

Col%s	All households Base=8.901
Ramps outside	1
Additional handrails outside	2
Ramps inside	*
Additional hand rails inside	5
Any doors altered for better access	*
Any other alterations for better access	*
Stairlift	3
Specially designed or adapted kitchen	1
Specially designed or adapted bath/shower	8
Relocated bath	1
Relocated shower	2
Specially designed or adapted toilet	1
Relocated toilet	3
Hoist	2
Electrical modifications	2
Door entry phone	2
Extra locks/safety gates	3
Warden/emergency alarm system	3
Additional heating	3
Other	3
None of these	70

Row%s	Need for adaptations	1-mentioned	2+ mentioned	Base
Tenure:				
Owner-occupier	24	16	7	4,952
Council rented	38	23	14	2,620
Housing association rented	39	22	16	378
Private rented	34	22	11	423
Living with relatives/friends	38	21	16	270
Level of dependency:				
A/B	18			4,996
C	41			738
D/E	45			2,226
F/G	56			685
Housing aspirations:				
Present home exactly as it is	19	14	4	6,154
Present home but with repairs and adaptations	71	36	35	1,374
Other accommodation: same size/larger	40	22	17	486
Other accommodation: smaller	36	21	15	741
Move to live with friends/relatives	35	21	13	68

Table 4.21 Preferred tenure, size, self-containment and wheelchair access of property: by tenure, household type, age of respondent and level of dependency

Col%s	All house holds	Household type					Tenure					Age of respondent			Level of dependency			
		Single adult 65-74	Single adult 75+	2 adults 1 aged 65-74 none 75+	2 adults 1 aged 75+	3+ adults 1 aged 65+	Owner-occupier	Council rented	Housing assoc. rented	Private rented	Living with friends/ rels	65-74	75-84	85+	A/B	C	D/E	F/G
A Preferred tenure																		
Own	47	45	32	55	49	53	73	7	10	12	50	51	40	32				
Rent	45	48	58	40	41	39	18	89	79	86	34	43	50	56				
B. No. of Bedrooms																		
1	26	39	51	13	14	12	17	38	42	41	35	22	34	42				
2	61	55	44	69	77	54	68	56	42	53	36	64	58	50				
3	9	3	2	14	8	29	12	3	4	7	17	11	6	4				
4+	1	0	*	2	1	5	1	1	0	0	13	1	*	2				
C. Wheelchair access																		
Yes	24	18	24	23	29	35	22	26	41	17	32	22	26	46	16	22	38	37
No	41	46	37	44	39	32	44	41	26	41	24	45	37	25				
Base A,B,C	1,226	284	234	392	219	97	704	352	44	75	24	785	390	51	654	110	305	122
D. Willing to share																		
Toilet	1	0	2	5	0	0	*	1	0	0	38	1	1	0				
Bathroom	3	2	3	5	0	8	1	2	0	4	56	3	3	0				
Kitchen	2	2	2	5	0	0	*	2	0	4	38	3	1	0				
Base	220	76	81	30	25	8	101	73	11	26	4	115	97	9				

Table 4.22 Help and support needed by those wishing to move: by housing aspirations, age, household type and level of dependency

Row%s	Wish to receive at least. one of these	Help with household chores	Help with self-care e.g. bathing	Help getting about outside	Help getting about indoors (inc. getting in and out of bed/chair)	Being able to call a warden	Base
All households	43	23	3	5	2	26	1,226
Age of respondent:							
65-74	36	17	2	3	1	21	785
75-84	53	31	5	7	4	33	390
85+	80	53	14	21	11	52	51
Housing aspirations:							
Other accomm: same size/larger	42	19	4	6	3	27	486
Other accomm: smaller	44	26	3	5	2	26	741
Household type:							
Single adult aged 65-74	43	24	1	4	2	27	284
Single adult aged 75+	64	37	4	9	4	43	234
2 Adults: at least 1 aged 65-74 none 75+	32	13	2	2	1	18	392
2 adults: at least 1 aged 75+	45	27	7	7	5	24	219
3+ adults: at least 1 aged 65+	35	19	4	5	1	25	97
Level of dependency:							
A/B	31						654
C	49						110
D/E	57						305
F/G	63						122

Table 4.22 Help and support needed by those wishing to stay at home: by housing aspirations, age, household type and level of dependency

Row%s	Wish to receive at least one of these	Help with household chores	Help with self-care e.g. bathing	Help getting about outside	Help getting about indoors (inc. getting in and out of bed/chair)	Being able to call a warden	Base
All households	25	19	4	4	2	9	7,528
Age of respondent:							
65-74	16	11	2	2	1	5	4,150
75-84	32	24	5	5	2	11	2,710
85+	53	42	13	14	5	19	669
Housing aspirations:							
Present home exactly as it is	22	16	3	3	1	7	6,154
Present home with repairs and adaptations	41	30	8	8	5	14	1,374
Household type:							
Single adult aged 65-74	24	18	2	3	1	9	1,499
Single adult aged 75+	43	34	6	8	3	17	1,975
2 Adults: at least 1 aged 65-74 none 75+	11	7	1	1	1	4	1,963
2 adults: at least 1 aged 65+	27	19	6	4	3	7	1,447
3+ adults at least 1 aged 65+	13	8	5	3	3	2	636
Level of dependency:							
A/B	12						4,310
C	36						622
D/E	45						1,885
F/G	45						550

Table 4.24 Health and social services received by elderly people: by level of dependency, age, tenure and household type

Col%s	Clackmannan Dependency Level			
	A/B	C	D/E	F/G
District Nurse	4	11	18	29
Health Visitors	1	3	5	7
Physiotherapist	*	*	2	3
Occupational therapist	*	*	2	3
Doctor	8	23	30	42
Private nursing help	0	*	1	1
None	89	69	58	48
Social worker	1	5	7	8
Mobility officer for the blind	0	*	1	1
Chiropodist	2	12	16	20
Home help/home care aide	2	15	24	19
Private domestic help	4	6	9	9
Voluntary worker	*	2	2	4
None	92	66	58	60
Meals on Wheels	1	3	8	6
Laundry	*	2	2	3
Incontinence service	0	*	1	3
None	99	95	89	90
Base	4,996	738	2,226	685

Table 4.24 continued

Col%s	Age of respondent		
	65-74	75-84	85+
District Nurse	5	14	25
Health Visitors	1	4	8
Physiotherapist	1	1	2
Occupational therapist	*	1	1
Doctor	11	22	38
Private nursing help	*	*	1
None	86	67	48
Social worker	2	5	8
Mobility officer for the blind	*	*	2
Chiropodist	4	10	25
Home help/home care aide	4	15	32
Private domestic help	4	7	11
Voluntary worker	1	1	4
None	88	70	44
Meals on Wheels	1	5	12
Laundry	1	2	3
Incontinence service	*	1	2
None	98	92	83
Base	4,989	3,166	746

213

Table 4.24 continued

Col%s	Tenure				
	Owner-occupier	Council rented	Housing association rented	Private rented	Living with friends/ relatives
District Nurse	8	13	14	8	19
Health Visitors	2	4	4	2	3
Physiotherapist	1	1	1	0	2
Occupational therapist	1	1	0	*	1
Doctor	14	21	22	17	27
Private nursing help	*	*	*	*	*
None	80	71	70	77	65
Social worker	3	5	5	3	5
Mobility officer for the blind	*	*	1	1	*
Chiropodist	6	9	10	7	12
Home help/home care aide	7	16	17	11	5
Private domestic help	8	1	3	3	3
Voluntary worker	1	1	1	2	1
None	81	74	73	79	77
Meals on wheels	2	5	5	3	1
Laundry	1	1	1	2	*
Incontinence service	*	1	1	1	2
None	96	93	93	94	96
Base	4,952	2,620	378	423	270

214

Table 4.24 continued

Col%s	Household type				
	Single adult 65-74	Single adult 75+	2 adults: at least one aged 65-74 none aged 75+	2 adults: at least one aged 75+	3 adults: at least one aged 65+
District Nurse	5	16	4	15	11
Health Visitors	2	6	1	3	2
Physiotherapist	*	1	1	1	1
Occupational therapist	1	1	*	1	1
Doctor	11	26	10	21	19
Private nursing help	*	*	*	*	*
None	85	61	87	70	77
Social worker	3	6	2	4	3
Mobility officer for the blind	0	1	0	*	*
Chiropodist	5	15	2	9	8
Home help/home care aide	8	25	2	8	2
Private domestic help	5	8	3	7	2
Voluntary worker	1	2	*	1	2
None	82	58	92	76	86
Meals on Wheels	2	9	*	2	1
Laundry	1	3	*	1	1
Incontinence service	*	1	*	1	1
None	97	87	99	95	97
Base	1,806	2,256	2,366	1,686	773

215

Table 4.25 Health and social services requested by elderly people: by level of dependency, age, tenure and household type

Col%s	Clackmannan Dependency Level			
	A/B	C	D/E	F/G
District Nurse	*	2	2	4
Health Visitors	*	2	2	5
Physiotherapist	*	1	3	5
Occupational therapist	*	1	1	2
Doctor	*	3	4	5
Private nursing help	0	*	1	1
None	88	64	54	42
Social worker	1	2	2	5
Mobility officer for the blind	*	*	1	3
Chiropodist	2	8	11	14
Home help/home care aide	1	5	4	7
Private domestic help	*	1	1	2
Voluntary worker	*	1	1	2
None	96	86	82	75
Meals on Wheels	*	1	1	1
Laundry	*	1	2	2
Incontinence service	0	*	1	3
None	99	98	97	95
Base	4,996	738	2,226	685

Table 4.25 continued

Col%s	Age of respondent		
	65-74	75-84	85+
District Nurse	1	2	4
Health Visitors	1	1	4
Physiotherapist	1	1	2
Occupational therapist	1	*	1
Doctor	1	3	6
Private nursing help	*	*	1
Social worker	1	2	4
Mobility for the blind	*	1	2
Chiropodist	4	8	15
Home help/home care aide	2	4	5
Private domestic help	*	1	1
Voluntary worker	*	1	2
Meals on Wheels	*	1	1
Laundry	*	1	2
Incontinence service	*	1	1
Base	4,989	3,165	746

216

Table 4.25 continued

Col%s	Tenure				
	Owner-occupier	Council rented	Housing association rented	Private rented	Living with friends/relatives
District Nurse	1	2	1	21	4
Health Visitors	1	2	3	2	2
Physiotherapist	1	1	3	2	4
Occupational therapist	*	1	1	1	2
Doctor	2	3	3	2	4
Private nursing help	*	*	0	1	1
Social worker	1	2	1	2	5
Mobility officer for the blind	1	1	*	2	2
Chiropodist	5	8	7	6	10
Home help/home care aide	2	4	4	3	3
Private domestic help	1	*	0	1	1
Voluntary worker	1	1	1	2	2
Meals on Wheels	1	1	3	1	0
Laundry	1	1	1	1	1
Incontinence service	*	1	*	1	0
Base	4,952	2,620	377	423	270

Table 4.25 continued

Col%s	Household type				
	Single adult 65-74	Single adult 75+	2 adults: at least one aged 65-74 none aged 75+	2 adults: at least one aged 75+	3 adults: at least one aged 65+
District Nurse	1	2	1	2	4
Health Visitors	1	2	3	2	2
Physiotherapist	1	1	3	2	4
Occupational therapist	*	1	1	1	2
Doctor	2	3	3	2	4
Private nursing help	*	*	0	1	1
Social worker	1	3	1	2	2
Mobility officer for the blind	*	1	*	1	1
Chiropodist	5	8	4	9	6
Home help/home care aide	3	5	1	3	3
Private domestic help	*	1	*	1	*
Voluntary worker	1	1	*	1	1
Meals on Wheels	1	2	0	1	*
Laundry	1	2	*	1	*
Incontinence servide	*	1	*	*	*
Base	1,806	2,255	2,366	1,686	773

Table 5.2 Household type of elderly residents of specialised housing: by age, tenure, category of accommodation and level of dependency

Row%s	1 adult up to 65	2+ adults up to 65[1]	1 adult 65-74	1 adult 75+	2 adults: at least 1 aged 65-74 none 75+	2+ adults: at least 1 aged 75+	Base
All households	2	1	20	60	6	11	3,569
Age of respondent							
Up to 65	62	18	–	–	15	5	141
65-74	–	–	73	–	19	9	994
75-84	–	–	–	85	–	15	1,724
85+	–	–	–	94	–	6	705
Tenure of scheme							
Local authority	3	1	21	60	5	11	2,602
Housing assoc.	2	1	20	57	7	12	887
Abbeyfield/ Almshouse	1	0	6	87	2	2	80
Category of accommodation							
1/Other	3	2	23	50	10	12	368
1.5/2	2	1	20	60	6	11	2,747
2.5	3	0	18	68	1	10	454
Level of dependency (Clackmannan groupings)							
A/B	3	1	29	43	11	13	1,274
C	2	*	16	72	2	9	606
D	1	*	15	71	2	10	1,169
E/F	22	0	36	36	6	0	30
G	3	2	16	62	5	13	359

[1] This household type and single adults aged up to 65 no longer feature in any further tables.

Table 5.4 Registration as disabled or long-term illnesses and disabilities: by age of respondent, level of dependency, tenure and category of accommodation

Row%s	Registered as disabled	Long-term illnesses	Bedfast/ chairfast	Base
All residents	20	30	3[1]	3,569
Age of respondent				
Up to 65	38	18		141
65-74	20	26		994
75-84	20	32		1,724
85+	18	35		705
Tenure of scheme				
Local authority	21	31		2,602
Housing assoc.	16	28		887
Abbeyfield/ Almshouse	12	30		80
Category of accommodation				
1/Other	15	27		368
1.5/2	20	30		2,747
2.5	26	36		454
Level of dependency (Clackmannan groupings)				
A/B	4	15		1,274
C	18	37		606
D	32	44		1,169
E/F	20	10		30
G	46	37		359

[1] This figure has not been broken down by age of respondent, level of dependency, tenure of scheme and category of accommodation because of the small cell sizes involved. It was only asked of those who said they were registered as disabled or had long-term illnesses.

Table 5.7 Household type of recent entrants before and after entry to schemes

Col%s	Before entry to schemes	Base	After entry to schemes	Base
Single person	56	1,080	76	1,481
Elderly couples	34	656	18	371

Table 5.9 Length of residence of elderly residents of specialised housing: by age of respondent, category of accommodation and household type

Row%s	<5yrs	5-20 yrs	20+ yrs	Base
All residents	54	44	2	3,569
Age of respondent				
Up to 65	79	21	0	141
65-74	62	37	1	994
75-84	52	46	2	1,724
85+	44	52	4	705
Category of accommodation				
1/Other	48	50	2	368
1.5/2	53	45	2	2,747
2.5	69	30	1	454
Household type				
Single type 65-74	60	39	1	722
Single adult 75+	49	49	2	2,134
2 adults: at least 1 aged 65-74 none 75+	71	28	1	207
2+ adults: at least 1 aged 75+	57	40	2	388

Table 5.10 Type of housing in schemes: by recent entrants and category of accommodation

Row%s	House	Bungalow	Flat/Maisonette	Bedsit	Base
All residents	*	18	63	18	3,569
Recent entrants	*	15	66	18	1,943
Category of accommodation					
1/Other	2	42	36	18	368
1.5/2	*	17	64	18	2,747
2.5	*	3	78	18	454

221

Table 5.11 Lack of or shared facilities: by tenure

Col%s	All residents	Local authority	Housing association	Abbeyfield/ almshouse
Kitchen				
Sole use	99	100	100	53
Shared	*	0	0	10
Lack	1	0	0	36
Fixed bathroom/shower				
Sole use	92	93	94	31
Shared	8	7	6	69
Lack	*	0	0	0
Wash hand basin				
Sole use	99	100	99	73
Shared	1	0	1	27
Lack	*	0	*	0
Toilet				
Sole use	98	100	99	37
Shared	2	0	1	62
Lack	*	0	0	*
Base	3,569	2,602	887	80

Table 5.12 Satisfaction with home: by recent entrants, age of respondent, tenure, category of accommodation and level of dependency

Row%s	Very satisfied	Fairly satisfied	Fairly dissatisfied	Very dissatisfied	Base
All residents	72	22	2	1	3,569
All recent entrants	72	21	2	1	1,943
Age of respondent					
Up to 65	65	21	3	4	141
65-74	71	22	4	1	994
75-84	71	23	2	1	1,724
85+	77	20	1	*	705
Tenure of scheme					
Local authority	73	21	3	1	2,602
Housing assoc.	68	26	2	1	887
Abbeyfield/ Almshouses	78	18	1	0	80
Category of accommodation					
1/Other	67	26	4	1	368
1.5/2	72	22	2	1	2,747
2.5	75	20	1	1	454
Level of dependency					
A/B	73	22	3	1	1,247
C	73	22	2	1	606
D	74	22	2	1	1,169
E/F	61	24	0	8	30
G	65	24	4	2	359

Table 5.14 Desire to move amongst elderly residents of specialised housing: by age of respondent, category of accommodation and region

Row%s	Very/fairly likely to move within 12 months	Base
All residents	5	3,569
Age of respondent		
Up to 65	12	141
65-74	7	994
75-84	5	1,724
85+	2	705
Category of accommodation		
1/Other	9	368
1.5/2	5	2,747
2.5	2	454
DoE Region		
South East	4	484
South West	4	334
London	9	342
Eastern	4	390
West Midlands	3	354
East Midlands	5	377
North West	6	529
Yorks & Humberside	6	440
Northern	3	318

Table 6.2 Registration as disabled or long-term illness and disabilities: by age and type of carer

Col%s	Resident carer	Non-resident carer	18-44	45-64	65-74	75+
Disabled and registered	6	3	3	4	4	7
Disabled and not registered	18	9	3	8	18	26
No long-term illnesses	75	88	92	87	78	67
Base	411	421	100	372	210	150

Table 6.3 Length of time as a carer: by type of carer, number of hours per week provided in all care support and age of carer

Col%s	All carers	Resident	Non-resident	18-44	45-64	65-74	75+	Under 5 hrs	6-19 hrs	20+ hrs
Up to 5yrs	40	41	39	43	36	44	42	44	43	35
5-10 yrs	29	25	32	37	32	23	22	30	26	30
10+ yrs	31	33	29	20	32	33	36	26	31	35
Base	832	411	421	100	372	210	150	205	289	327

Table 6.5 Domestic care tasks: by type of carer, number of hours per week provided in all care support, gender of carer and level of dependency of dependant

Col%s	All carers	Resident	Non-resident	0	1-7	8-12	Male	Female	Under 5 hrs	6-19 hrs	20+ hrs
Light housework	65	84	46	68	57	69	65	64	30	59	92
Heavy housework	58	73	44	59	55	61	60	58	26	55	82
Ironing	52	65	40	56	40	61	31	60	21	47	75
Washing clothes	62	72	52	64	53	70	46	68	35	56	85
Making beds	53	72	33	52	43	62	53	52	20	44	82
Cooking meals	54	70	38	49	44	65	50	55	17	48	82
Light shopping	76	83	69	76	71	81	82	74	56	76	91
Heavy shopping	74	76	73	74	73	75	82	71	61	75	83
None of these	3	3	2	1	4	2	1	3	7	1	*
Base	832	411	421	180	308	344	227	605	205	289	327

Table 6.6 Number of hours spent performing domestic care tasks each week: by type of carer, level of dependency of dependant and gender of carer

Col%s	All carers	Resident	Non-resident	0	1-7	8-12	Male	Female
Up to 4	31	9	52	32	37	26	28	32
5-9	18	13	23	22	19	14	18	18
10-19	18	24	12	14	19	19	19	18
20-29	12	18	6	11	9	15	15	11
30+	19	34	4	20	13	24	20	19
Base	810	398	412	178	295	337	224	587

Table 6.17 Carers contributing towards housing costs: by type of carer and numbers of hours per week provided in all care support

Col%s	All carers	Resident	Non-resident	Under 5 hrs	6-19 hrs	20+ hrs
Yes	4	14	2	3	5	6
No	92	72	98	96	93	85
Base	528	107	421	189	205	129

Table 7.3 Household weekly income of non-elderly disabled adults: by age of respondent, household type and tenure

Row%s	Up to £50	£50-99	£100-150	£150+	Base
All households	11	22	26	42	850
Age of respondent:					
16-29	2	39	21	39	107
30-49	2	12	27	60	268
50-64	18	23	27	33	475
Household type:					
Single adult	11	55	19	15	148
2+ adults/no children	15	15	26	44	476
Children in households	1	14	30	55	226
Tenure:					
Owner-occupier	11	11	26	51	417
LA/HA rented	10	29	28	32	310
Other	9	39	18	34	123

Table 7.4 Savings and investments of non-elderly disabled people: by age, household type, tenure and household weekly income

Row%s	Savings	Base	Up to £5,000 in savings	£5,000-£15,999 in savings	£16,000+ in savings	Base[1]
All house-holds	50	850	48	16	16	423
Age of respondent:						
16-29	39	107	79	8	0	41
30-49	41	268	59	11	12	109
50-64	57	475	39	19	20	272
Tenure:						
Owner-occupier	67	417	38	20	21	280
LA/HA rented	29	310	61	12	6	89
Other	44	123	82	4	9	54
Household type:						
Single adult	47	148	59	11	11	69
2+ adults, no children	57	476	39	19	21	273
Children in household	35	226	71	10	6	80
Weekly household income:						
Up to £50	61	91	40	16	23	56
£50-£99	38	183	65	7	3	69
£100-£150	41	220	46	11	6	91
£150+	58	356	46	21	23	207

[1] This base figure includes all those who refused to state how much their savings or investments amounted to. This accounts for the percentages in the fourth, fifth and sixth columns of this table not adding up to 100%.

Table 7.5 Receipt of invalidity pension by non-elderly disabled adults: by gender, age tenure, household weekly income and level of dependency (combined respondent and spouse/partner)

Col%s	Receipt of invalidity pension	Base
All households	37	850
Gender		
Male	52	390
Female	25	460
Age of respondent		
16-29	17	107
30-49	31	268
50-64	45	475
Tenure		
Owner-occupier	32	417
Council/HA rented	48	310
Other	28	123
Household weekly income		
Up to £50	52	91
£50-£99	45	183
£100-£150	43	220
£150+	26	356
Level of dependency		
A/B	28	359
C	33	54
D	43	264
F/G	52	162

Table 7.6 State benefits or allowances received by non-elderly disabled people: by age, household type and level of dependency

Row%s	None of these[1]	Attendance allow.	Mobility allow.	Severe dis. allow.	Child benefit	Invalid care allow.	Housing Benefit[2]	Income Support	Base
All households	47	9	23	9	21	3	69	21	850
Level of dependency (Clackmannan grouping):									
A/B	80	4	7	4	24	1	63	18	359
C	70	4	17	13	19	0	81	22	54
D	70	10	39	11	19	2	69	20	264
F/G	65	25	37	16	18	9	71	28	162

1 This percentage figure does not include those who said they did not know if they received these benefits. Thus, 52% of all households claimed to receive at least one of these benefits and 1% were not sure or did not know.

2 The base for the percentage figures in this column is all renting/shared ownership.

Table 7.7 Long-term illnesses or health problems suffered by non-elderly disabled people: by age of respondent and level of dependency

Col%s	All households	A/B	C	D	F/G	16-29	30-49	50-64
Walking on level ground	31	13	24	43	52	13	27	37
Steps and stairs	55	33	69	70	80	27	51	63
Bending or straightening	44	25	43	57	75	27	44	48
Falling or keeping balance	29	13	24	35	61	17	29	32
Gripping or turning things	28	16	31	33	47	24	24	31
Reading newspaper print even with glasses	13	8	17	15	19	12	11	14
Hearing someone talking/deafness	18	20	9	17	17	11	16	21
Breathlessness/wheezing/coughing	41	42	39	38	43	43	35	43
Severe pain or irritation	42	25	54	54	60	26	42	46
Poor bladder control	13	3	0	21	31	6	12	16
Fits/convulsions (in past 2 years)	5	5	6	3	8	15	7	2
Getting confused/disorientated	11	6	7	11	23	19	8	11
None of these	2	4	0	1	0	2	2	2
Base	850	359	54	264	162	107	268	475

Table 7.10 Age of dwellings occupied by non-elderly disabled people: by tenure

Row%s	Pre-1919	Inter War	Post war	Post 1964	Base
All households	12	22	30	29	850
Tenure:					
Owner-occupier	15	23	27	32	417
LA/HA rented	4	22	35	27	310
Other	25	16	24	20	14

Table 7.11 Length of residence of non-elderly disabled people: by age of respondent and household type

Row%s	Less than 5 yrs	5-10 yrs	10-20 yrs	20+ yrs	Base
All households	31	18	24	28	850
Age of respondent:					
16-29	49	20	21	10	107
30-49	43	22	24	11	268
50-64	20	15	24	41	475
Household type:					
Single adult	41	16	19	24	148
2+ adults no children	22	14	26	38	476
Children in household	41	27	22	10	226

Table 7.13 Payment for repairs and improvements by non-elderly disabled adults: by household weekly income, tenure and household type

Row%s	Carried out repairs in the last 12 months	Base	Spent £1,000+ for repairs	Base
All households	64	850	27	500
Household type				
Single adult	44	147	17	64
2+ adults no children	67	433	27	289
Children in household	71	205	33	146
Tenure				
Owner-	75	417	39	313
Council/HA rented	52	310	7	162
Other	43	58	5	25
Household weekly income				
Up to £50	64	83	26	53
£50-£99	46	152	18	70
£100-£150	58	211	24	122
£150+	75	339	32	254

Table 7.14a Need for repairs and improvements in housing occupied by non-elderly disabled people: by tenure

Col%s	All households	Owner-occupier	Council/housing assoc. tenant	Other
External walls	9	10	9	5
External windows	21	18	25	20
Chimney stack	4	5	4	1
Roof	10	13	5	11
Drain pipes	6	7	7	5
Damp proofing	7	6	8	5
Damp/cond-ensation	12	9	15	14
Electrics/wiring	9	9	9	9
Lighting	2	2	2	4
Plumbing	4	3	5	7
Bath/shower	11	10	12	10
Internal toilet	3	2	4	2
Wash basin	2	2	2	1
Hot water supply	4	3	4	7
Heating system	13	8	18	14
None of these	47	54	37	47
Base	850	417	310	123

Table 7.14b Help and support needed with carrying out repairs

Row%s	Help and support with:						
	Org. of work	Raising finance	Technical/ legal advice	Support and reassurance	Financial advice	None of these	Base
All households	8	17	10	9	11	60	850

Table 7.19 Preferred tenure, size, self-containment and wheelchair access of property: by tenure, household type, age of respondent, household weekly income and level of dependency

Col%s	All house holds	Household type			Household weekly income				Tenure			Age of respondent			Level of dependency			
		Single adult 16-64	2+ adult no children	Children in house-hold	Up to £50	£50-£99	£100-£149	£150+	Owner-occupier	LA/HA rented	Other	16-29	30-49	50-64	A/B	C	D	F/G
A Preferred tenure																		
Own	52	37	49	66	49	32	42	67	81	20	38	49	64	43				
Rent	38	47	43	25	42	52	44	28	8	74	47	32	32	45				
B. No. of Bedrooms																		
1	16	53	11	1	18	35	12	9	9	21	22	6	15	20				
2	45	45	61	21	80	46	49	37	40	55	39	29	32	62				
3	27	2	20	50	2	12	22	40	37	17	18	52	29	14				
4+	12	0	7	26	0	7	14	15	13	6	20	12	23	3				
C. Wheelchair access																		
Yes	35	33	41	27	31	35	37	34	35	38	29	25	35	39	23	18	38	56
No	44	52	42	44	51	50	46	40	44	44	46	44	45	44				
Base A, B, C	243	45	121	78	18	50	63	113	114	89	40	45	88	110	104	11	65	52
D. Willing to share																		
Toilet	21	35	15	14	0	28	44	0	17	32	16	22	12	26				
Bathroom	21	35	15	14	0	28	44	0	17	32	16	22	12	26				
Kitchen	17	21	15	14	0	28	28	0	0	32	16	22	12	16				
Base	28	9	13	6	3	9	8	8	7	9	12	9	7	12				

Table 8.3 Regional estimates of need by elderly people for subsidised housing and housing with care provision

Col%s	DoE Region										
	South-East	South-West	London	Eastern	West Mids	East Mids	North West	Yorks & Humberside	Northern
No change in current circumstances	70.8	71.7	62.9	67.7	60.5	64.9	67.0	61.0	64.6
Staying at home 1	3.7	2.2	3.6	3.2	3.3	2.8	2.2	2.2	2.1
Staying at home 2	2.3	3.4	3.2	3.0	5.2	1.9	3.4	2.8	2.7
Staying at home 3	11.2	11.7	15.4	14.5	15.6	14.7	13.4	17.5	14.3
A move to ordinary mainstream accomm.	1.8	1.9	3.5	1.8	2.2	2.3	2.4	3.5	5.0
Living with friends/relatives	1.2	0.4	0.4	0.7	1.1	0.9	0.8	0.6	0.6
Category 1 accommodation	0.1	0.3	0.7	0.5	0.9	0.4	0.5	0.5	0.8
Category 1.5 accommodation	0.1	0.2	0.3	0.3	0.1	0.3	0.1	0	0
Category 2 accommodation	3.0	1.0	1.7	2.3	2.0	2.7	3.1	2.6	3.1
Category 2.5 accommodation	0.8	1.2	1.5	0.5	1.5	2.0	0.7	2.6	1.3
A move to residential/ nursing care	0.2	0.2	0.4	0.7	1.3	1.0	0.8	1.2	0.7
Base	1,417	955	1,058	1,017	1,008	753	1,236	958	499

Table 8.4-8.11 Selected characteristics of the sub-group compared with the full sample

Row%s	Tenure					Age of respondent			Household type					Household level of dependency						Base
	Owner-occupier	LA rented	HA rented	Private rented	Living with rels/friends	65-74	75-84	85+	Single adult aged 75+	Single adult aged 65-74	2 adults at least 1 aged 65-74 none 75+	2 adults at least 1 aged 75+	3 adults at least 1 aged 65+	A	B	C	D	F	G	
Sub-group	51	31	4	4	7	48	41	11	26	11	26	25	13	0	0	29	57	12	3	1,111
Full sample	56	29	4	4	4	56	36	8	25	20	27	19	9	46	7	10	25	6	2	8,901

Row %s	Housing type					Receipt of informal care (Col%s)					Cost of social and health care services received						Cost of aids and adaptations currently installed (£ per person per annum)						Base
	Detached house	Semi-detached house	Terraced house	Bunga-low	Flat/mais-onette	C	D	F	G	All house-holds	A	B	C	D	F	G	A	B	C	D	F	G	
Sub-group	7	24	19	29	17	8	21	36	29	19	0	0	126	181	315	552	0	320	393	629	629	363	1,111
Full sample	9	26	19	25	18	8	24	52	29	23	56	106	185	470	559	875	130	216	346	519	732	700	8,901
Base sub-group						322	629	131	29														
Base sample						867	2,247	569	201														

Table 8.12 Help and support needed with carrying out repairs, improvements and adaptations

Col%s	All households	Sub-group
None	73	82
Help with organisation	6	3
Help with raising finance	9	4
Technical and legal advice	7	4
Financial advice	6	2
Support and reassurance	9	5
Base	8,901	1,111

Appendix 4 Selected Allocation Model Rules and Syntax

Combination of variables used in the model definition	CODING OF VARIABLE PERMUTATIONS																								
	1	2	3	4	5	6	7	8	9	10	11	12	13	14	15	16	17	18	19	20	21	22	23	24	25
1 Is the client's cognitive level sufficient to make reasoned judgements?	No	Yes	Yes	Yes	Yes	Yes	Yes	Yes	Yes	Yes	Yes	Yes	Yes	Yes	Yes	Yes	Yes	Yes	Yes	Yes	Yes		Yes	Yes	Yes
2 If the client does not pass the cognitive filter, is help sufficient?		Yes																				No			
3 Does the client want to move?			No	No	No	Yes	Yes	Yes	Yes	No	No	No	No	No	No	No	No	No	No	No	Yes		No	No	Yes
4 Does the client want to move to relatives or friends?						No	No	No	No												Yes			No	No
5 Is the client or H/H member physically independent?			Yes	No	No	Yes	Yes	Yes	No	No	No	No	No	No	No	Yes	No	No	No	No				Yes	No
6 Are aids and adaptations sufficient for the clients needs?				Yes	No												Yes	Yes	No	No					
7 Does the client have a strong desire to move?										Yes	Yes	No	No	No	No	No	No	No	No	No					
8 Is current help sufficient?						Yes	Yes	No	Yes	Yes	Yes	Yes	Yes	No											
9 Can the client realise over £40,000 on sale of his/her home?							Yes	No															No	No	Yes
10 Is a member of the household eligible to receive grant contribution costs?										No	Yes	Yes	Yes	Yes	Yes	Yes	No	No	Yes	Yes					
11 Do household savings exceed £8,000?																			Yes	Yes					
12 Is the cost of required A&A & repairs less than max. set to client depy?				Yes					Yes	No	No	No	No	No	Yes										
13 Does the client receive informal care?												No	Yes	No	Yes	No	Yes	No	Yes	No	Yes	No	Yes	No	Yes

Coding of variable permutations	Outcome
1	No change
2	No change
3	No change
4	No change
5	No change
6	No change
7	No change
8	No change

Coding of variable permutations	Outcome
9	SAH 1 (some aids)
10	SAH 1 (all aids)
11	SAH 2 (care + some aids)
12	SAH 2 (care + some aids)
13	SAH 2 (care + all aids)
14	SAH 2 (care + all aids)
15	SAH 3 (care only)
16	SAH 3 (care only)
17	SAH 3 (care only)

Coding of variable Permutations	Outcome
18	SAH 3 (care only)
19	SAH 3 (care only)
20	SAH 3 (care only)
21	Move to friends/relatives
22	Residential Nursing Home
23	Test for Specialised Housing
24	Test for Specialised Housing
25	Retest for SAH options
	Unallocated

N.B. Options 23 and 24 were potentially eligible for specialised housing, and so went through the second filter to determine the type of specialised provision.
Options 25, 26 and 27 did not meet the above conditions for immediate allocation to SAH or specialised provision, because they wanted to move but failed the mean test criteria. These were retested in filter three for other SAH options.

Combination of variables used in the model definition

Code	Variable	28	29	30	31	32	33	34	35	36	37	38	39	40	41	42	43	44	45	46
		NEW CODING																		
	Input number	15	15	15	15	15	15	15	15	15	15	15	15	15	15	15	15	15	15	15
14	Smaller or same sized accommodation	yes	yes	yes	yes	yes	yes	yes	yes	yes	yes	yes	yes	yes	yes	yes				
15	Larger accommodation																yes	yes	yes	
16	Currently ground floor	yes	yes			yes	yes			yes	yes			yes	yes					
17	Needs more than 1 repairs	yes	no	yes	no	yes	no	yes	no	yes	no	yes	no	yes	no					
18	Household clackmannan	1or2	1or2	1or2	3	3	3	3	3	3	3	3	3	3	3	3	3	4or5	6	6or7
	Need warden alarm system or warden help									yes	yes	yes	yes							
20	People living in house													1	1	1	1			
21	No. relatives													0	0	0	0			
22	Any friends nearby?													no	no	no	no			
23	Help with chores, care, physical activites, difficulty inside, chairfast																	yes		
24	Anyone in household bed or chairfast																		yes	yes
25	Cognitive																		yes	no

New Coding	Outcome
28	Ordinary mainstream accommodation
29	Ordinary mainstream accommodation
30	No specialised – retest for SAH options
31	No specialised – retest for SAH options
32	Category 1
33	Category 1
34	No specialised – retest for SAH options
35	No specialised – retest for SAH options
36	Category 1.5
37	Category 1.5
38	No specialised – retest for SAH options
39	No specialised – retest for SAH options
40	Category 2
41	Category 2
42	No specialised – retest for SAH options

New Coding	Outcome
43	No specialised – retest for SAH options
44	Category 2.5
45	Wheelchair
46	Residential Nursing Home

N.B. Those allocated to 'No specialised – retest for SAH options', failed to meet the detailed criteria for specialised provision. They were then retested in the third filter.

Combination of variables used in the model definition		NEW CODING														
		47	48	49	50	51	52	53	54	55	56	57	58	59	60	61
	Input number	16or17	16or17	16or17	16or17	16or17	16or17	16or17	16or17	16or17	16or17	16or17	16or17	16or17	16or17	16or17
6	Are aids and adaptations sufficient for the clients needs?	yes	yes	yes	no	no	no	no	no	no	no	no	no	no	no	no
8	Is current help sufficient?	yes	no	no	yes	yes	yes	yes	no	no	no	no	no	no	no	no
10	Is a member of the household eligible to receive grant contribution costs?				yes	yes	yes	no	yes	yes	yes	yes	yes	yes	no	no
11a	Do household savings exceed £8,000?				yes	no	no		yes	yes	no	no	no	no		
12a	Is the cost of required A&A & repairs less than max. set for client dep'y?					no	yes				no	no	yes	yes		
13	Does the client receive informal care?		no	yes					no	yes	no	yes	no	yes	no	yes

New Coding	Outcome
47	No charge
48	SAH 3 (care only)
49	SAH 3 (care only)
50	No change
51	SAH 1 (some aids)
52	SAH 1 (all aids)
53	No change
54	SAH 3 (care only)
55	SAH 3 (care only)
56	SAH 2 (care and some aids)
57	SAH 2 (care and some aids)
58	SAH 2 (care and all aids)
59	SAH 2 (care and all aids)
60	SAH 3 (care only)
61	SAH 3 (care only)

Appendix 4 (cont.)
Sample of the syntax from the allocation model.

*Qu1: Is client's cognitive level sufficient to make reasoned judgements ?.

COMPUTE ALLOC1=1. IF (QM11A GE 0 AND QM11A LT 9) ALLOC1=0. IF (QM11A GE 9 OR QM11A=-99.99) ALLOC1=1.

*Qu2: If client did not pass cognitive filter is help sufficient ?.

COMPUTE ALLOC2=-99. IF (Q1=1 OR @Q6@022=1) ALLOC2=0. IF (Q1 GT 1 AND @Q6@022=0) ALLOC2=1.

*Qu3 :Does the client want to move ?.

COMPUTE ALLOC3=-99. IF (Q57=1 OR Q57=2 OR Q66 = 3 OR Q66 = 4 OR Q66 = 5) ALLOC3=0. IF (Q57=3 OR Q57=4 OR Q57=5 OR Q57 = 6 OR Q66 = 1 OR Q66 = 2) ALLOC3=1.

*Qu4 : Does the client want to move to friends or relatives ?.

COMPUTE ALLOC4=-99. IF (Q57 NE 6) ALLOC4=0. IF (Q57=6) ALLOC4=1.

*Qu5 : Is the client or other household member physically independent?.

COMPUTE ALLOC5A=-99. IF (HOUSCLAC=3 OR HOUSCLAC=4 OR HOUSCLAC=5 OR HOUSCLAC=6 OR HOUSCLAC=7) ALLOC5A=0. IF (HOUSCLAC=1 OR HOUSCLAC=2) ALLOC5A=1.

*Qu6: Is the current level of aids and adaptations in their present home sufficient for their needs?

COMPUTE ALLOC6=-99. IF (@Q551 = 1 OR @Q552 = 1 OR @Q553 = 1 OR @Q554 = 1 OR @Q555 = 1 OR @Q556 = 1 OR @Q557 = 1 OR @Q558 = 1 OR @Q559 = 1 OR @Q5510 = 1 OR @Q5511 =1 OR @Q5512 = 1 OR @Q5513 = 1 OR @Q5514 = 1 OR @Q5515 = 1 OR @Q5516 =1 OR @Q5517 = 1 OR @Q5518 = 1 OR @Q5519 = 1) ALLOC6=0. IF (@Q551 = 0 AND @Q552 = 0 AND @Q553 = 0 AND @Q554 = 0 AND @Q555 = 0 AND@Q556 = 0 AND @Q557 = 0 AND @Q558 = 0 AND @Q559 = 0 AND @Q5510 = 0 AND @Q5511 = 0 AND @Q5512 = 0 AND @Q5513 = 0 AND @Q5514 = 0 AND @Q5515 = 0 AND @Q5516 = 0 AND @Q5517 = 0 AND @Q5518 = 0 AND @Q5519 = 0) ALLOC6=1.

*Qu7 : Is current help sufficient ?.

COMPUTE ALLOC8=-99. IF (@Q581 = 1 OR @Q582 = 1 OR @Q583 = 1 OR @Q584 = 1 OR @Q585 = 1 OR @Q1041 = 1 OR @Q1042 = 1 OR @Q1043 = 1 OR @Q1044 = 1 OR @Q1045 = 1 OR @Q1046 = 1 OR @Q1081 = 1 OR @Q1082 = 1 OR @Q1083 = 1 OR @Q1084 = 1 OR @Q1085 = 1 OR @Q1086 = 1 OR @Q1131 = 1 OR @Q1132 = 1 OR @Q1133 = 1 OR @Q1134 = 1) ALLOC8=0. IF ((@Q581 = 0 AND @Q582 = 0 AND @Q583 = 0 AND @Q584 = 0 AND @Q585 = 0 AND @Q1041 = 0 AND @Q1042 = 0 AND @Q1043 = 0 AND @Q1044 = 0 AND @Q1045 = 0 AND @Q1046 = 0 AND @Q1081 = 0 AND @Q1082 = 0 AND @Q1083 = 0 AND @Q1084 = 0 AND @Q1085 = 0 AND @Q1086 = 0 AND @Q1131 = 0 AND @Q1132 = 0 AND @Q1133 = 0 AND @Q1134 = 0) OR (@Q586=1 AND@Q1047=1 AND @Q1087=1 AND @Q1135=1)) ALLOC8=1.

*Qu8 : Can the client realise over 40,000 in capital on sale of

*COMPUTE ALLOC9=-99. *IF ((Q12 = 4 OR Q12 = 5 OR Q12 = 6 OR Q12 = 7 OR Q12 = 8 OR Q12 = 9 OR Q12 = 10 OR Q12 = 11 OR Q12 = 12 OR Q12 = 13 OR Q12 = 14 OR Q12 = 15 OR Q12 = 16 OR Q12 = 17) OR (DRC1 LT 40000)) ALLOC9=0. *IF ((Q12 = 1 OR Q12 = 2 OR Q12 = 3) AND (DRC1 GE 40000)) ALLOC9=1. compute alloc9=0.

*Qu9 : Is a member of the household eligible to receive renovation grants etc ?.

*SYNTAX FOR GRANT91 AND GRANT93 FOR JOINT ELDERLY AND NON ELDERLY DISABLED.

*DEFINING CHILDREN OF HEAD OF HOUSEHOLD OR SPOUSE. *1YEAR. COMPUTE KID1YR=0. IF (Q1 NE 1 AND (Q7=1 OR Q7=2) AND ((Q2@02=3 AND Q4B=1) OR (Q2@03=3 ANDQ4C=1) OR (Q2@04=3 AND Q4D=1) OR (Q2@05=3 AND Q4E=1) OR (Q2@06=3 ANDQ4F=1) OR (Q2@07=3 AND Q4G=1))) KID1YR=1. COMPUTE KID2YR=0. IF (Q1 NE 1 AND (Q7=1 OR Q7=2) AND ((Q2@02=3 AND Q4B=1) OR (Q2@03=3 ANDQ4C=1) OR (Q2@04=3 AND Q4D=1) OR (Q2@05=3 AND Q4E=1) OR (Q2@06=3 ANDQ4F=1) OR (Q2@07=3 AND Q4G=1))) KID2YR=1. COMPUTE KID3YR=0. IF (Q1 NE 1 AND (Q7=1 OR Q7=2) AND ((Q2@02=3 AND Q4B=1) OR (Q2@03=3 ANDQ4C=1) OR (Q2@04=3 AND Q4D=1) OR (Q2@05=3 AND Q4E=1) OR (Q2@06=3 AND Q4F=1) OR (Q2@07=3 AND Q4G=1))) KID3YR=1. COMPUTE KID4YR=0. IF (Q1 NE 1 AND (Q7=1 OR Q7=2) AND ((Q2@02=3 AND Q4B=1) OR (Q2@03=3 AND Q4C=1) OR (Q2@04=3 AND Q4D=1) OR (Q2@05=3 AND Q4E=1) OR (Q2@06=3 AND Q4F=1) OR (Q2@07=3 AND Q4G=1))) KID4YR=1. COMPUTE KID5YR=0. IF (Q1 NE 1 AND (Q7=1 OR Q7=2) AND ((Q2@02=3 AND Q4B=1) OR (Q2@03=3 ANDQ4C=1) OR (Q2@04=3 AND Q4D=1) OR (Q2@05=3 AND Q4E=1) OR (Q2@06=3 AND Q4F=1) OR (Q2@07=3 AND Q4G=1))) KID5YR=1. COMPUTE KID6YR=0. IF (Q1 NE 1 AND (Q7=1 OR Q7=2) AND ((Q2@02=3 AND Q4B=1) OR (Q2@03=3 AND Q4C=1) OR (Q2@04=3 AND Q4D=1) OR (Q2@05=3 AND Q4E=1) OR (Q2@06=3 AND Q4F=1) OR (Q2@07=3 AND Q4G=1))) KID6YR=1. COMPUTE KID7YR=0. IF (Q1 NE 1 AND (Q7=1 OR Q7=2) AND ((Q2@02=3 AND Q4B=1) OR (Q2@03=3 ANDQ4C=1) OR (Q2@04=3 AND Q4D=1) OR (Q2@05=3 AND Q4E=1) OR (Q2@06=3 AND   Q4F=1) OR (Q2@07=3 AND Q4G=1))) KID7YR=1. COMPUTE KID8YR=0. IF (Q1 NE 1 AND (Q7=1 OR Q7=2) AND ((Q2@02=3 AND Q4B=1) OR (Q2@03=3 AND   Q4C=1) OR (Q2@04=3 AND Q4D=1) OR (Q2@05=3 AND Q4E=1) OR (Q2@06=3 AND   Q4F=1) OR (Q2@07=3 AND Q4G=1))) KID8YR=1. COMPUTE KID9YR=0. IF (Q1 NE 1 AND (Q7=1 OR Q7=2) AND ((Q2@02=3 AND Q4B=1) OR (Q2@03=3 AND   Q4C=1) OR (Q2@04=3 AND Q4D=1) OR (Q2@05=3 AND Q4E=1) OR (Q2@06=3 AND   Q4F=1) OR (Q2@07=3 AND Q4G=1))) KID9YR=1. COMPUTE KID10YR=0. IF (Q1 NE 1 AND (Q7=1 OR Q7=2) AND ((Q2@02=3 AND Q4B=1) OR (Q2@03=3 AND   Q4C=1) OR (Q2@04=3 AND Q4D=1) OR (Q2@05=3 AND Q4E=1) OR (Q2@06=3 AND   Q4F=1) OR (Q2@07=3 AND Q4G=1))) KID10YR=1. COMPUTE KID11YR=0. IF (Q1 NE 1 AND (Q7=1 OR Q7=2) AND ((Q2@02=3 AND Q4B=1) OR (Q2@03=3 AND   Q4C=1) OR (Q2@04=3 AND Q4D=1) OR (Q2@05=3 AND Q4E=1) OR (Q2@06=3 AND   Q4F=1) OR (Q2@07=3 AND Q4G=1))) KID11YR=1. COMPUTE KID12YR=0. IF (Q1 NE 1 AND (Q7=1 OR Q7=2) AND ((Q2@02=3 AND Q4B=1) OR (Q2@03=3 AND   Q4C=1) OR (Q2@04=3 AND Q4D=1) OR (Q2@05=3 AND Q4E=1) OR (Q2@06=3 AND   Q4F=1) OR (Q2@07=3 AND Q4G=1))) KID12YR=1. COMPUTE KID13YR=0. IF (Q1 NE 1 AND (Q7=1 OR Q7=2) AND ((Q2@02=3 AND Q4B=1) OR (Q2@03=3 AND   Q4C=1) OR (Q2@04=3 AND Q4D=1) OR (Q2@05=3 AND Q4E=1) OR (Q2@06=3 AND   Q4F=1) OR (Q2@07=3 AND Q4G=1))) KID13YR=1.

COMPUTE KID14YR=0. IF (Q1 NE 1 AND (Q7=1 OR Q7=2) AND ((Q2@02=3 AND
Q4B=1) OR (Q2@03=3 AND Q4C=1) OR (Q2@04=3 AND Q4D=1) OR (Q2@05=3 AND
Q4E=1) OR (Q2@06=3 AND Q4F=1) OR (Q2@07=3 AND Q4G=1))) KID14YR=1.
COMPUTE KID15YR=0. IF (Q1 NE 1 AND (Q7=1 OR Q7=2) AND ((Q2@02=3 AND
Q4B=1) OR (Q2@03=3 AND Q4C=1) OR (Q2@04=3 AND Q4D=1) OR (Q2@05=3 AND
Q4E=1) OR (Q2@06=3 AND Q4F=1) OR (Q2@07=3 AND Q4G=1))) KID15YR=1.
COMPUTE KID16YR=0. IF (Q1 NE 1 AND (Q7=1 OR Q7=2) AND ((Q2@02=3 AND
Q4B=1) OR (Q2@03=3 AND Q4C=1) OR (Q2@04=3 AND Q4D=1) OR (Q2@05=3 AND
Q4E=1) OR (Q2@06=3 AND Q4F=1) OR (Q2@07=3 AND Q4G=1))) KID16YR=1.
COMPUTE KID17YR=0. IF (Q1 NE 1 AND (Q7=1 OR Q7=2) AND ((Q2@02=3 AND
Q4B=1) OR (Q2@03=3 AND Q4C=1) OR (Q2@04=3 AND Q4D=1) OR (Q2@05=3 AND
Q4E=1) OR (Q2@06=3 AND Q4F=1) OR (Q2@07=3 AND Q4G=1))) KID17YR=1.
COMPUTE KID18YR=0. IF (Q1 NE 1 AND (Q7=1 OR Q7=2) AND ((Q2@02=3 AND
Q4B=1) OR (Q2@03=3 AND Q4C=1) OR (Q2@04=3 AND Q4D=1) OR (Q2@05=3 AND
Q4E=1) OR (Q2@06=3 AND Q4F=1) OR (Q2@07=3 AND Q4G=1))) KID18YR=1.

*COMPUTING NUMBER OF CHILDREN IN EACH AGE BAND. COMPUTE KIDU11=0.
IF (KID1YR=1 OR KID2YR=1 OR KID3YR=1 OR KID4YR=1 OR KID5YR=1 OR
KID6YR=1 OR   KID7YR=1 OR KID8YR=1 OR KID9YR=1 OR KID10YR=1)
KIDU11=KID1YR + KID2YR + KID3YR + KID4YR + KID5YR + KID6YR + KID7YR +
KID8YR + KID9YR + KID10YR. COMPUTE KID1115=0. IF (KID11YR=1 OR KID12YR=1
OR KID13YR=1 OR KID14YR=1 OR KID15YR=1) KID1115=KID11YR + KID12YR +
KID13YR + KID14YR + KID15YR. COMPUTE KID1617=0. IF (KID16YR=1 OR
KID17YR=1) KID1617=KID16YR=1 + KID17YR. COMPUTE KID18=0. IF (KID18YR=1)
KID18=KID18YR.

*COMPUTING TOTAL NUMBER OF CHILDREN. COMPUTE NKIDS=0. IF (KIDU11=1
OR KID1115=1 OR KID1617=1 OR KID18=1) NKIDS=KIDU11 + KID1115 + KID1617 +
KID18.

*CALCULATING THE GRANT INCOME ALLOWANCE FOR 1991 FIGURES. COMPUTE
GRANT91=40.0.

*CALCULATE BASIC ALLOWANCES.

*singles 24 or under and 25 years or over. IF (Q1=1 AND Q4A LE 24) GRANT91=GRANT91
+ 31.15. IF (Q1=1 AND Q4A GE 25) GRANT91=GRANT91 + 39.65. *couples under 18 and
18 years or over. IF (Q1 GT 1 AND Q4A LT 18 AND Q4B LT 18) GRANT91=GRANT91 +
47.30. IF (Q1 GT 1 AND (Q4A GE 18 OR Q4B GE 18)) GRANT91=GRANT91 + 62.25.

*ALLOWANCES FOR CHILDREN. *children under 11 years old. IF (KIDU11 GE 1)
GRANT91=GRANT91 + (KIDU11*13.35). *children 11 to 15 years old. IF (KID1115 GE 1)
GRANT91=GRANT91 + (KID1115*19.75). *children 16 and 17 years old. IF (KID1617 GE 1)
GRANT91=GRANT91 + (KID1617*23.65). *children 18 years old. IF (KID18 GE 1)
GRANT91=GRANT91 + (KID18*31.15).

*PREMIA FOR FAMILY/LONE PARENTS. *lone parents. IF (Q1=1 AND NKIDS GE 1)
GRANT91=GRANT91 + 10.05 + 7.95. *other families. IF (Q1 NE 1 AND NKIDS GE 1)
GRANT91=GRANT91 + 7.95.

*PREMIA FOR AGE AND DISABILITY. *single people: those aged 80+ and those disabled aged 60+. IF (Q1=1 AND (Q4A GE 80 OR (Q4A GE 60 AND (Q75@01=1 OR @Q791=1 OR @Q792=1 OR @Q793=1 OR @Q794=1 OR @Q794=1 OR @Q795=1 OR @Q796=1 OR @Q797=1 OR @Q798=1 OR @Q799=1 or @Q7910=1 OR @Q7911=1 OR @Q7912)))) GRANT91=GRANT91 + 18.45. *single people aged 75 to 79. IF (Q1=1 AND (Q4A GE 75 AND Q4A LE 79)) GRANT91=GRANT91 + 15.55. *single people aged 60 to 74. IF (Q1=1 AND (Q4A GE 60 AND Q4A LE 74)) GRANT91=GRANT91 + 13.75. *couples: those aged 80+ (respondent or partner) and those disabled aged 60+. IF (Q1 ne 1 AND (Q4A GE 80 OR (Q4A GE 60 AND (Q75@01=1 OR @Q791=1 OR @Q792=1 OR @Q793=1 OR @Q794=1 OR @Q794=1 OR @Q795=1 OR @Q796=1 OR @Q797=1 OR @Q798=1 OR @Q799=1 or @Q7910=1 OR @Q7911=1 OR @Q7912) OR (Q4B GE 80 OR (Q4B GE 60 AND Q75@01=1))))) GRANT91=GRANT91 + 26.20. *couples aged 75 to 79. IF (Q1 ne 1 AND ((Q4A GE 75 AND Q4A LE 79) OR (Q4B GE 75 AND Q4B LE 79))) GRANT91=GRANT91 + 23.35. *couples aged 60 to 74. IF (Q1=1 AND ((Q4A GE 60 AND Q4A LE 74) OR (Q4A GE 60 AND Q4A LE 74)))   GRANT91=GRANT91 + 20.90.

*INCOME DISREGARDS. *lone parents working full time/part time/on training scheme (YTS/ET). IF (Q1=1 AND NKIDS GE 1 AND (@Q6@015=1 OR @Q6@016=1)) GRANT91=GRANT91 + 25. *lone parents NOT working full time/part time/on training scheme (YTS/ET). IF (Q1=1 AND NKIDS GE 1 AND (@Q6@015 NE 1 OR @Q6@016 NE 1)) GRANT91=GRANT91 + 15. *single disabled people working full time/part time/on training scheme (YTS/ET). IF (Q1=1 AND (Q75@01=1 OR @Q791=1 OR @Q792=1 OR @Q793=1 OR @Q794=1 OR @Q794=1 OR @Q795=1 OR @Q796=1 OR @Q797=1 OR @Q798=1 OR @Q799=1 or @Q7910=1 OR @Q7911=1 OR @Q7912) AND (@Q6@015=1 OR @Q6@016=1)) GRANT91=GRANT91 + 15. *single disabled people NOT working full time/part time/on training scheme (YTS/ET). IF (Q1=1 AND (Q75@01=1 OR @Q791=1 OR @Q792=1 OR @Q793=1 OR @Q794=1 OR @Q794=1 OR @Q795=1 OR @Q796=1 OR @Q797=1 OR @Q798=1 OR @Q799=1 or @Q7910=1 OR @Q7911=1 OR @Q7912) AND (@Q6@015 NE 1 OR @Q6@016 NE 1))   GRANT91=GRANT91 + 5. *couple with kids working full time/part time/on training scheme. IF (Q1 ne 1 AND NKIDS GE 1 AND (@Q6@015=1 OR @Q6@016=1) OR (@Q6@025=1 OR @Q6@026=1)) GRANT91=GRANT91 + 15. *couple with at least one disabled working full time/part time/on training   scheme (YTS/ET). IF (Q1 NE 1 AND ((Q75@01=1 OR @Q791=1 OR @Q792=1 OR @Q793=1 OR @Q794=1 OR @Q794=1 OR @Q795=1 OR @Q796=1 OR @Q797=1 OR @Q798=1 OR @Q799=1 or @Q7910=1 OR @Q7911=1 OR @Q7912) OR (Q75@02=1)) AND (@Q6@015=1 OR @Q6@016=1) OR (@Q6@025=1 OR @Q6@026=1)) GRANT91=GRANT91 + 15.

*couple where at least one is disabled NOT working full time/part time/on   training scheme (YTS/ET). IF (Q1 NE 1 AND ((Q75@01=1 OR @Q791=1 OR @Q792=1 OR @Q793=1 OR @Q794=1 OR @Q794=1 OR @Q795=1 OR @Q796=1 OR @Q797=1 OR @Q798=1 OR @Q799=1 or @Q7910=1 OR @Q7911=1 OR @Q7912) OR (Q75@02=1)) AND (@Q6@015 NE 1 OR   @Q6@016 NE 1) OR (@Q6@025 NE 1 OR @Q6@026 NE 1)) GRANT91=GRANT91 + 15.

*CALCULATING THE GRANT INCOME ALLOWANCE FOR 1993 FIGURES. COMPUTE GRANT93=40.0.

*CALCULATE BASIC ALLOWANCES. *singles 24 or under and 25 years or over. IF (Q1=1 AND Q4A LE 24) GRANT93=GRANT93 + 34.8. IF (Q1=1 AND Q4A GE 25) GRANT93=GRANT93 + 44.0. *couples under 18 and 18 years or over. IF (Q1 GT 1 AND Q4A LT 18 AND Q4B LT 18) GRANT93=GRANT93 + 52.40. IF (Q1 GT 1 AND (Q4A GE 18 OR Q4B GE 18)) GRANT93=GRANT93 + 69.00.

*ALLOWANCES FOR CHILDREN. *children under 11 years old. IF (KIDU11 GE 1) GRANT93=GRANT93 + (KIDU11*15.05). *children 11 to 15 years old. IF (KID1115 GE 1) GRANT93=GRANT93 + (KID1115*22.15). *children 16 and 17 years old. IF (KID1617 GE 1) GRANT93=GRANT93 + (KID1617*26.45). *children 18 years old. IF (KID18 GE 1) GRANT93=GRANT93 + (KID18*34.80).

*PREMIA FOR FAMILY/LONE PARENTS. *lone parents. IF (Q1=1 AND NKIDS GE 1) GRANT93=GRANT93 + 10.95 + 9.65. *other families. IF (Q1 NE 1 AND NKIDS GE 1) GRANT93=GRANT93 + 9.65.

*PREMIA FOR AGE AND DISABILITY. *single people: those aged 80+ and those disabled aged 60+. IF (Q1=1 AND (Q4A GE 80 OR (Q4A GE 60 AND (Q75@01=1 OR @Q791=1 OR @Q792=1 OR @Q793=1 OR @Q794=1 OR @Q794=1 OR @Q795=1 OR @Q796=1 OR @Q797=1 OR   @Q798=1 OR @Q799=1 or @Q7910=1 OR @Q7911=1 OR @Q7912)))) GRANT93=GRANT93 + 23.55. *single people aged 75 to 79. IF (Q1=1 AND (Q4A GE 75 AND Q4A LE 79)) GRANT93=GRANT93 + 19.30. *single people aged 60 to 74. IF (Q1=1 AND (Q4A GE 60 AND Q4A LE 74)) GRANT93=GRANT93 + 17.30. *couples: those aged 80+ (respondent or partner) and those disabled aged 60+. IF (Q1 ne 1 AND (Q4A GE 80 OR (Q4A GE 60 AND (Q75@01=1 OR @Q791=1 OR @Q792=1 OR @Q793=1 OR @Q794=1 OR @Q794=1 OR @Q795=1 OR @Q796=1 OR @Q797=1 OR @Q798=1 OR @Q799=1 or @Q7910=1 OR @Q7911=1 OR @Q7912) OR (Q4B GE 80 OR (Q4B GE 60 AND Q75@01=1))))) GRANT93=GRANT93 + 33.70. *couples aged 75 to 79. IF (Q1 ne 1 AND ((Q4A GE 75 AND Q4A LE 79) OR (Q4B GE 75 AND Q4B LE 79))) GRANT93=GRANT93 + 29.00. *couples aged 60 to 74. IF (Q1=1 AND ((Q4A GE 60 AND Q4A LE 74) OR (Q4A GE 60 AND Q4A LE 74)))   GRANT93=GRANT93 + 26.25.

*INCOME DISREGARDS. *lone parents working full time/part time/on training scheme (YTS/ET). IF (Q1=1 AND NKIDS GE 1 AND (@Q6@015=1 OR @Q6@016=1)) GRANT93=GRANT93 + 25. *lone parents NOT working full time/part time/on training scheme (YTS/ET). IF (Q1=1 AND NKIDS GE 1 AND (@Q6@015 NE 1 OR @Q6@016 NE 1)) GRANT93=GRANT93 + 15. *single disabled people working full time/part time/on training scheme   (YTS/ET). IF (Q1=1 AND (Q75@01=1 OR @Q791=1 OR @Q792=1 OR @Q793=1 OR @Q794=1 OR   @Q794=1 OR @Q795=1 OR @Q796=1 OR @Q797=1 OR @Q798=1 OR @Q799=1 or   @Q7910=1 OR @Q7911=1 OR @Q7912) AND (@Q6@015=1 OR @Q6@016=1)) GRANT93=GRANT93 + 15. *single disabled people NOT working full time/part time/on training scheme (YTS/ET). IF (Q1=1 AND (Q75@01=1 OR @Q791=1 OR @Q792=1 OR @Q793=1 OR @Q794=1 OR @Q794=1 OR @Q795=1 OR @Q796=1 OR @Q797=1 OR @Q798=1 OR @Q799=1 or @Q7910=1 OR @Q7911=1 OR @Q7912) AND (@Q6@015 NE 1 OR @Q6@016 NE 1)) GRANT93=GRANT93 + 5.

*couple with kids working full time/part time/on training scheme. IF (Q1 ne 1 AND NKIDS GE 1 AND (@Q6@015=1 OR @Q6@016=1) OR (@Q6@025=1 OR @Q6@026=1)) GRANT93=GRANT93 + 15. *couple with at least one disabled working full time/part time/on training scheme (YTS/ET). IF (Q1 NE 1 AND ((Q75@01=1 OR @Q791=1 OR @Q792=1 OR @Q793=1 OR @Q794=1 OR @Q794=1 OR @Q795=1 OR @Q796=1 OR @Q797=1 OR @Q798=1 OR @Q799=1 or @Q7910=1 OR @Q7911=1 OR @Q7912) OR (Q75@02=1)) AND (@Q6@015=1 OR @Q6@016=1) OR (@Q6@025=1 OR @Q6@026=1)) GRANT93=GRANT93 + 15. *couple where at least one is disabled NOT working full time/part time/on   training scheme (YTS/ET). IF (Q1 NE 1 AND ((Q75@01=1 OR @Q791=1 OR @Q792=1 OR @Q793=1 OR @Q794=1 OR @Q794=1 OR @Q795=1 OR @Q796=1 OR @Q797=1 OR @Q798=1 OR @Q799=1 or @Q7910=1 OR @Q7911=1 OR @Q7912) OR (Q75@02=1)) AND (@Q6@015 NE 1 OR @Q6@016 NE 1)OR (@Q6@025 NE 1 OR @Q6@026 NE 1)) GRANT93=GRANT93 + 15.

COMPUTE ALLOC10=-99. IF (INCOME LE GRANT91) ALLOC10=1. IF (INCOME GT GRANT91) ALLOC10=0.

*NEW VARIABLE 11.

*Question 10 : Do household savings exceed 8,000.

COMPUTE ALLOC11A=-99. IF (Q137=1 AND (Q139 = 1 OR Q139 = 2 OR Q139 = 3 OR Q139 = 4 OR Q139 = 5)) ALLOC11A=0. IF ((Q139 = 6 OR Q139 = 7) OR Q137=2) ALLOC11A=1.

*Question 11 : Does the cost of required aids and adaptations and repairs

IF ((HOUSCLAC = 1 OR HOUSCLAC = 2) AND (Q10 = 1 OR Q10 = 2 OR Q10 = 3 OR Q10 = 4 OR Q10 = 5 OR Q10 = 6)) CAP = 3660. IF ((HOUSCLAC = 3) AND (Q10 = 1 OR Q10 = 2 OR Q10 = 3 OR Q10 = 4 OR Q10 = 5 OR Q10 = 6)) CAP = 3800. IF ((HOUSCLAC = 4)AND (Q10 = 1 OR Q10 = 2 OR Q10 = 3 OR Q10 = 4 OR Q10 = 5 OR Q10 = 6)) CAP = 3800. IF ((HOUSCLAC = 5) AND (Q10 = 1 OR Q10 = 2 OR Q10 = 3 OR Q10 = 4 OR Q10 = 5 OR Q10 = 6)) CAP = 3690. IF ((HOUSCLAC = 6 OR HOUSCLAC=7) AND (Q10 = 1 OR Q10 = 2 OR Q10 = 3 OR Q10   = 4 OR Q10 = 5 OR Q10 = 6)) CAP = 4400. IF ((HOUSCLAC = 1 OR HOUSCLAC = 2) AND (Q10 = 7 OR Q10 = 8 OR Q10 = 9 OR   Q10 = 10 OR Q10 = 11 OR Q10 = 12)) CAP = 710. IF ((HOUSCLAC = 3) AND (Q10 = 7 OR Q10 = 8 OR Q10 = 9 OR Q10 = 10 OR Q10 = 11 OR Q10 = 12)) CAP = 2220. IF ((HOUSCLAC = 4) AND(Q10 = 7 OR Q10 = 8 OR Q10 = 9 OR Q10 = 10 OR Q10 = 11 OR Q10 = 12)) CAP = 2380. IF ((HOUSCLAC = 5) AND(Q10 = 7 OR Q10 = 8 OR Q10 = 9 OR Q10 =10 OR Q10 = 11 OR Q10 = 12)) CAP = 2380. IF ((HOUSCLAC = 6 OR HOUSCLAC=7) AND (Q10 = 7 OR Q10 = 8 OR Q10 = 9 OR Q10 = 10 OR Q10 = 11 OR Q10 = 12)) CAP = 2430.

COMPUTE TOTAL1=-99. IF (@Q531=1) TOTAL1=1. COMPUTE TOTAL2=-99. IF (@Q532=1) TOTAL2=1. COMPUTE TOTAL3=-99. IF (@Q533=1) TOTAL3=1. COMPUTE TOTAL4=-99. IF (@Q534=1) TOTAL4=1. COMPUTE TOTAL5=-99. IF (@Q535=1) TOTAL5=1. COMPUTE TOTAL6=-99. IF (@Q536=1) TOTAL6=1. COMPUTE TOTAL7=-99. IF (@Q537=1) TOTAL7=1. COMPUTE TOTAL8=-99. IF (@Q538=1) TOTAL8=1. COMPUTE TOTAL9=-99. IF (@Q539=1) TOTAL9=1. COMPUTE TOTAL10=-99. IF (@Q5310=1) TOTAL10=1. COMPUTE TOTAL11=-99. IF (@Q5311=1) TOTAL11=1. COMPUTE TOTAL12=-99. IF (@Q5312=1) TOTAL12=1. COMPUTE TOTAL13=-99. IF (@Q5313=1) TOTAL13=1. COMPUTE TOTAL14=-99. IF (@Q5314=1) TOTAL14=1. COMPUTE TOTAL15=-99. IF (@Q5315=1) TOTAL15=1. COMPUTE TOTAL16=-99. IF (@Q5316=1) TOTAL16=1. COMPUTE TOTAL17=-99. IF (@Q5317=1) TOTAL17=1. COMPUTE TOTAL18=-99. IF (@Q5318=1) TOTAL18=1. COMPUTE TOTAL19=-99. IF (@Q5319=1) TOTAL19=1.

COMPUTE TOTAL1A=-99. IF (@Q551=1) TOTAL1A=1. COMPUTE TOTAL2A=-99. IF (@Q552=1) TOTAL2A=1. COMPUTE TOTAL3A=-99. IF (@Q553=1) TOTAL3A=1. COMPUTE TOTAL4A=-99. IF (@Q554=1) TOTAL4A=1. COMPUTE TOTAL5A=-99. IF (@Q555=1) TOTAL5A=1. COMPUTE TOTAL6A=-99. IF (@Q556=1) TOTAL6A=1. COMPUTE TOTAL7A=-99. IF (@Q557=1) TOTAL7A=1. COMPUTE TOTAL8A=-99. IF (@Q558=1) TOTAL8A=1. COMPUTE TOTAL9A=-99. IF (@Q559=1) TOTAL9A=1. COMPUTE TOTAL10A=-99. IF (@Q5510=1) TOTAL10A=1. COMPUTE TOTAL11A=-99.

IF (@Q5511=1) TOTAL11A=1. COMPUTE TOTAL12A=-99. IF (@Q5512=1)
TOTAL12A=1. COMPUTE TOTAL13A=-99. IF (@Q5513=1) TOTAL13A=1. COMPUTE
TOTAL14A=-99. IF (@Q5514=1) TOTAL14A=1. COMPUTE TOTAL15A=-99. IF
(@Q5515=1) TOTAL15A=1. COMPUTE TOTAL16A=-99. IF (@Q5516=1) TOTAL16A=1.
COMPUTE TOTAL17A=-99. IF (@Q5517=1) TOTAL17A=1. COMPUTE TOTAL18A=-99.
IF (@Q5518=1) TOTAL18A=1. COMPUTE TOTAL19A=-99. IF (@Q5519=1)
TOTAL19A=1.

COMPUTE TOTALA=(TOTAL1*338.55) + (TOTAL1A*338.55). COMPUTE
TOTALB=(TOTAL2*48.59) + (TOTAL2A*48.59). COMPUTE TOTALC=(TOTAL3*338.55)
+ (TOTAL3A*338.55). COMPUTE TOTALD=(TOTAL4*48.59) + (TOTAL4A*48.59).
COMPUTE TOTALE=(TOTAL5*266.11) + (TOTAL5A*266.11). COMPUTE
TOTALF=(TOTAL6*266.11) + (TOTAL6A*266.11). COMPUTE
TOTALG=(TOTAL7*1369.6) + (TOTAL7A*1369.6). COMPUTE
TOTALH=(TOTAL8*1506.43) + (TOTAL8A*1506.43). COMPUTE
TOTALI=(TOTAL9*746.08) + (TOTAL9A*746.08). COMPUTE
TOTALJ=(TOTAL10*554.59) + (TOTAL10A*554.59). COMPUTE
TOTALK=(TOTAL11*554.59) + (TOTAL11A*554.59). COMPUTE
TOTALL=(TOTAL12*452.46) + (TOTAL12A*452.46). COMPUTE
TOTALM=(TOTAL13*452.46) + (TOTAL13A*452.46). COMPUTE
TOTALN=(TOTAL14*490.12) + (TOTAL14A*490.12). COMPUTE
TOTALO=(TOTAL15*230.00) + (TOTAL15A*230.00). COMPUTE
TOTALP=(TOTAL16*187.41) + (TOTAL16A*187.41). COMPUTE
TOTALQ=(TOTAL17*187.41) + (TOTAL17A*187.41). COMPUTE
TOTALR=(TOTAL18*199.03) + (TOTAL18A*199.03). COMPUTE
TOTALS=(TOTAL19*224.80) + (TOTAL19A*224.80).

COMPUTE TOTAL= TOTALA + TOTALB + TOTALC + TOTALD + TOTALE + TOTALF
+ TOTALG + TOTALH + TOTALI + TOTALJ + TOTALK + TOTALL + TOTALM +
TOTALN + TOTALO + TOTALP + TOTALQ + TOTALR + TOTALS.

COMPUTE ALLOC12A=-99. IF (CAP GE TOTAL) ALLOC12A =1. IF (CAP LT TOTAL)
ALLOC12A =0.

COMPUTE ALLOC13=0. IF (QB1F=2 OR QB1F=3 OR QB1F=4 OR QB1F=5 OR QB1B=2
OR QB1B=3 OR QB1B=4 OR QB1B=5 OR @QB8D1=1 OR @QB8D2=1 OR @QB8D3=1
OR @QB8D4=1 OR @QB8E1=1 OR @QB8E2=1 OR @QB8E3=1 OR @QB8E4=1 OR
@QB12A1=1 OR @QB12A2=1 OR @QB12A3=1 OR @QB12A4=1 OR @QB12D1=1 OR
@QB12D2=1 OR @QB12D3=1 OR @QB12D4=1) ALLOC13 =1.

*STAGE 3: CALCULATING THE COST OF AIDS AND ADAPTATIONS FOR THOSE IN
SAH1 OR   SAH2.

*DOES THE COST OF REQUIRED AIDS AND ADAPTATIONS AND REPAIRS.

*CALCALATING THE CAP LEVEL.

IF ((HOUSCLAC = 1 OR HOUSCLAC = 2) AND (Q10 = 1 OR Q10 = 2 OR Q10 = 3 OR
Q10 = 4 OR Q10 = 5 OR Q10 = 6)) CAP = 3660. IF ((HOUSCLAC = 3) AND (Q10 = 1 OR
Q10 = 2 OR Q10 = 3 OR Q10 = 4 OR Q10 = 5   OR Q10 = 6)) CAP = 3800. IF ((HOUSCLAC
= 4)AND (Q10 = 1 OR Q10 = 2 OR Q10 = 3 OR Q10 = 4 OR Q10 = 5   OR Q10 = 6)) CAP =
3800. IF ((HOUSCLAC = 5) AND (Q10 = 1 OR Q10 = 2 OR Q10 = 3 OR Q10 = 4 OR Q10 = 5
OR Q10 = 6)) CAP = 3690. IF ((HOUSCLAC = 6 OR HOUSCLAC=7) AND (Q10 = 1 OR
Q10 = 2 OR Q10 = 3 OR Q10   = 4 OR Q10 = 5 OR Q10 = 6)) CAP = 4400. IF ((HOUSCLAC
= 1 OR HOUSCLAC = 2) AND (Q10 = 7 OR Q10 = 8 OR Q10 = 9 OR   Q10 = 10 OR Q10 =
11 OR Q10 = 12)) CAP = 710. IF ((HOUSCLAC = 3) AND (Q10 = 7 OR Q10 = 8 OR Q10 = 9
OR Q10 = 10 OR Q10 = 11 OR Q10 = 12)) CAP = 2220. IF ((HOUSCLAC = 4) AND(Q10 =
7 OR Q10 = 8 OR Q10 = 9 OR Q10 = 10 OR Q10 = 11 OR Q10 = 12)) CAP = 2380. IF
((HOUSCLAC = 5) AND(Q10 = 7 OR Q10 = 8 OR Q10 = 9 OR Q10 = 10 OR Q10 =   11 OR
Q10 = 12)) CAP = 2380. IF ((HOUSCLAC = 6 OR HOUSCLAC=7) AND (Q10 = 7 OR Q10 =
8 OR Q10 = 9 OR Q10 = 10 OR Q10 = 11 OR Q10 = 12)) CAP = 2430.

COMPUTE TOTAL1=0. IF (@Q531=1) TOTAL1=1. COMPUTE TOTAL2=0. IF (@Q532=1)
TOTAL2=1. COMPUTE TOTAL3=0. IF (@Q533=1) TOTAL3=1. COMPUTE TOTAL4=0. IF

(@Q534=1) TOTAL4=1. COMPUTE TOTAL5=0. IF (@Q535=1) TOTAL5=1. COMPUTE
TOTAL6=0. IF (@Q536=1) TOTAL6=1. COMPUTE TOTAL7=0. IF (@Q537=1)
TOTAL7=1. COMPUTE TOTAL8=0. IF (@Q538=1) TOTAL8=1. COMPUTE TOTAL9=0. IF
(@Q539=1) TOTAL9=1. COMPUTE TOTAL10=0. IF (@Q5310=1) TOTAL10=1.
COMPUTE TOTAL11=0. IF (@Q5311=1) TOTAL11=1. COMPUTE TOTAL12=0. IF
(@Q5312=1) TOTAL12=1. COMPUTE TOTAL13=0. IF (@Q5313=1) TOTAL13=1.
COMPUTE TOTAL14=0. IF (@Q5314=1) TOTAL14=1. COMPUTE TOTAL15=0. IF
(@Q5315=1) TOTAL15=1. COMPUTE TOTAL16=0. IF (@Q5316=1) TOTAL16=1.
COMPUTE TOTAL17=0. IF (@Q5317=1) TOTAL17=1. COMPUTE TOTAL18=0. IF
(@Q5318=1) TOTAL18=1. COMPUTE TOTAL19=0. IF (@Q5319=1) TOTAL19=1.

COMPUTE TOTAL1A=0. IF (@Q551=1) TOTAL1A=1. COMPUTE TOTAL2A=0. IF
(@Q552=1) TOTAL2A=1. COMPUTE TOTAL3A=0. IF (@Q553=1) TOTAL3A=1.
COMPUTE TOTAL4A=0. IF (@Q554=1) TOTAL4A=1. COMPUTE TOTAL5A=0. IF
(@Q555=1) TOTAL5A=1. COMPUTE TOTAL6A=0. IF (@Q556=1) TOTAL6A=1.
COMPUTE TOTAL7A=0. IF (@Q557=1) TOTAL7A=1. COMPUTE TOTAL8A=0. IF
(@Q558=1) TOTAL8A=1. COMPUTE TOTAL9A=0. IF (@Q559=1) TOTAL9A=1.
COMPUTE TOTAL10A=0. IF (@Q5510=1) TOTAL10A=1. COMPUTE TOTAL11A=0. IF
(@Q5511=1) TOTAL11A=1. COMPUTE TOTAL12A=0. IF (@Q5512=1) TOTAL12A=1.
COMPUTE TOTAL13A=0. IF (@Q5513=1) TOTAL13A=1. COMPUTE TOTAL14A=0. IF
(@Q5514=1) TOTAL14A=1. COMPUTE TOTAL15A=0. IF (@Q5515=1) TOTAL15A=1.
COMPUTE TOTAL16A=0. IF (@Q5516=1) TOTAL16A=1. COMPUTE TOTAL17A=0. IF
(@Q5517=1) TOTAL17A=1. COMPUTE TOTAL18A=0. IF (@Q5518=1) TOTAL18A=1.
COMPUTE TOTAL19A=0. IF (@Q5519=1) TOTAL19A=1.

*CALCULATING WANTS AND NEEDS (Q53 AND Q55).

COMPUTE TOTALA=((TOTAL1 + TOTAL1A + TOTAL3 + TOTAL3A)*201.15).
COMPUTE TOTALB=((TOTAL2 + TOTAL2A + TOTAL4 + TOTAL4A)*27.33). COMPUTE
TOTALC=((TOTAL5 + TOTAL5A + TOTAL6 + TOTAL6A)*315.66). COMPUTE
TOTALD=((TOTAL7 + TOTAL7A)*1726.07). COMPUTE TOTALE=((TOTAL8 +
TOTAL8A)*2070.37). COMPUTE TOTALF=((TOTAL9 + TOTAL9A)*7809.02). COMPUTE
TOTALG=((TOTAL10 + TOTAL10A + TOTAL11 + TOTAL11A)*1061.48). COMPUTE
TOTALH=((TOTAL12 + TOTAL12A + TOTAL13 + TOTAL13A)*904.22). COMPUTE
TOTALI=((TOTAL14 + TOTAL14A)*1367.47). COMPUTE TOTALJ=((TOTAL15 +
TOTAL15A)*269). COMPUTE TOTALK=((TOTAL16 + TOTAL16A + TOTAL17 +
TOTAL17A)*254.84). COMPUTE TOTALL=((TOTAL18 + TOTAL18A)*233.58).
COMPUTE TOTALM=((TOTAL19 + TOTAL19A)*208.37).

COMPUTE TOTALWN= TOTALA + TOTALB + TOTALC + TOTALD + TOTALE +
TOTALF +   TOTALG + TOTALH + TOTALI + TOTALJ + TOTALK + TOTALL +
TOTALM.

COMPUTE COSTSWN=-99. IF (CAP GE TOTALWN) COSTSWN =1. IF (CAP LT
TOTALWN) COSTSWN =0.

*CALCULATING NEEDS ONLY (Q55).

COMPUTE TOTALA1=((TOTAL1A + TOTAL3A)*201.15). COMPUTE
TOTALB1=((TOTAL2A + TOTAL4A)*27.33). COMPUTE TOTALC1=((TOTAL5A +
TOTAL6A)*315.66). COMPUTE TOTALD1=(TOTAL7A*1726.07). COMPUTE
TOTALE1=(TOTAL8A*2070.37). COMPUTE TOTALF1=(TOTAL9A*7809.02). COMPUTE
TOTALG1=((TOTAL10A + TOTAL11A)*1061.48). COMPUTE TOTALH1=((TOTAL12A +
TOTAL13A)*904.22). COMPUTE TOTALI1=(TOTAL14A*1367.47). COMPUTE
TOTALJ1=(TOTAL15A*269). COMPUTE TOTALK1=((TOTAL16A +
TOTAL17A)*254.84). COMPUTE TOTALL1=(TOTAL18A*233.58). COMPUTE
TOTALM1=(TOTAL19A*208.37).

COMPUTE TOTALND= TOTALA1 + TOTALB1 + TOTALC1 + TOTALD1 + TOTALE1 +
TOTALF1 + TOTALG1 + TOTALH1 + TOTALI1 + TOTALJ1 + TOTALK1 + TOTALL1 +
TOTALM1.

COMPUTE COSTSND=-99. IF (CAP GE TOTALND) COSTSND =1. IF (CAP LT
TOTALND) COSTSND =0.

*DEFINING THE CATEGORIES FOR COSTS OF AIDS AND ADAPTATIONS - WANTS AND NEEDS.

COMPUTE TOTALWN1=-99. IF (TOTALWN GE 0 AND TOTALND LE 2499.99) TOTALWN1=1. IF (TOTALWN GE 2500 AND TOTALWN LE 4999.99) TOTALWN1=2. IF (TOTALWN GE 5000 AND TOTALWN LE 7499.99) TOTALWN1=3. IF (TOTALWN GE 7500 AND TOTALWN LE 9999.99) TOTALWN1=4. IF (TOTALWN GE 10000 AND TOTALWN LE 12499.99) TOTALWN1=5. IF (TOTALWN GE 12500 AND TOTALWN LE 14999.99) TOTALWN1=6. IF (TOTALWN GE 15000 AND TOTALWN LE 17499.99) TOTALWN1=7. IF (TOTALWN GE 17500 AND TOTALWN LE 19999.99) TOTALWN1=8. IF (TOTALWN GE 20000) TOTALWN1=9. VALUE LABELS TOTALWN1 1 'Under 2500' 2 '2500 to under 5000' 3 '5000 to under 7500' 4 '7500 to under 10000' 5 '10000 to under 12500' 6 '12500 to under 15000' 7 '15000 to under 17500' 8 '17500 to under 20000' 9 '20000 and over'. VARIABLE LABELS TOTALWN1 'Costs of aids and adaptations (pounds)'.

*DEFINING THE COSTS OF AIDS AND ADAPTATIONS - NEEDS ONLY.

COMPUTE TOTALND1=-99. IF (TOTALND GE 0 AND TOTALND LE 2499.99) TOTALND1=1. IF (TOTALND GE 2500 AND TOTALND LE 4999.99) TOTALND1=2. IF (TOTALND GE 5000 AND TOTALND LE 7499.99) TOTALND1=3. IF (TOTALND GE 7500 AND TOTALND LE 9999.99) TOTALND1=4. IF (TOTALND GE 10000 AND TOTALND LE 12499.99) TOTALND1=5. IF (TOTALND GE 12500 AND TOTALND LE 14999.99) TOTALND1=6. IF (TOTALND GE 15000 AND TOTALND LE 17499.99) TOTALND1=7. IF (TOTALND GE 17500 AND TOTALND LE 19999.99) TOTALND1=8. IF (TOTALND GE 20000) TOTALND1=9. VALUE LABELS TOTALND1 1 'Under 2500' 2 '2500 to under 5000' 3 '5000 to under 7500' 4 '7500 to under 10000' 5 '10000 to under 12500' 6 '12500 to under 15000' 7 '15000 to under 17500' 8 '17500 to under 20000' 9 '20000 and over'. VARIABLE LABELS TOTALWN1 'Costs of aids and adaptations (pounds)'.

Appendix 5 The bedroom standard

1.   The Bedroom Standard is defined in the General Household Survey as follows:

'This concept is used to estimate occupation density by allocating a standard number of bedrooms to each household in accordance with its age/sex/marital status composition and the relationship of the members to one another. A separate bedroom is allocated to each married couple, any other person aged 21 or over, each pair of adolescents aged 10-20 of the same sex, and each pair of children under 10. Any unpaired person aged 10-20 is paired if possible with a child under 10 of the same sex, or, if that is not possible, is given a separate bedroom, as is any unpaired child under 10. This standard is then compared with the actual number of bedrooms (including bedsitters) available for the sole use of the household....'. **1991 General Household Survey, Appendix A, Definitions and terms, p237**

Appendix 6 References and bibliography

Chapter 1

Access Committee for England, *Building Homes for Successive Generations*, 1992.

Barelli J, *Under-occupation in Local Authority and Housing Association Housing*, HMSO 1992.

Bond J and Carstairs V, *Services for the Elderly*, Scottish Home and Health Department 1982.

Butler A, Oldman C and Greve J, *Sheltered Housing for the Elderly: Policy Practice and the Consumer*, Allen and Unwin, 1983.

Challis D and Davies B, *Case Management in Community Care*, Gower, 1986.

Clapham D and Munro M, *A Comparison of Sheltered and Amenity Housing for Older People*, Scottish Office Central Research Unit Papers, 1988.

Department of the Environment, *Adaptations of Housing for people who are physically handicapped*, DOE Circular, 59/78, HMSO 1978.

Department of Health and Social Services Inspectorate, *Care Management and Assessment - Practioners' Guide*, 1991.

Department of the Environment, *Housing for People who are Physically handicapped*, DOE Circular 74/74, HMSO, 1974.

Department of the Environment and Department of Health, *Housing and Community Care*, DOE/DH Circular 10/92, HMSO, 1992.

Department of Health, Caring for People: *Community care in the next decade and beyond* Cmnd 849, HMSO, London 1989.

English House Condition Survey 1991, HMSO 1993.

Goldsmith S, *Wheelchair Housing*, DOE, Housing Development Directorate, Occasional Paper 2/75, 1975 (HMSO 1980).

Goldsmith S, *Mobility Housing,* DOE, Housing Development Directorate, Occasional Paper 2/74, 1974 (HMSO 1980).

MHLG, *The Housing of Old People*, MHLG Circular 32/56, HMSO 1956.

MHLG, *Housing Standards and Costs: accommodation specially designed for old people*, MHLG Circular 82/69, WO Circular 82/69, HMSO, 1969.

Micallef M, *Difficult-to-let Sheltered Housing*, Anchor Housing Trust 1994

National Federation of Housing Associations, *Rented Housing for Older People - Consultation Green Paper*, 1993.

Office of Population Censuses and Surveys, *Surveys of disability in Great Britain - Reports 1-4*, HMSO 1989.

Sainsbury S, *Measuring Disability*, London: Bell and Sons, 1973.

The Approved Document Part M of the Building Regulations, 1992 Edition.

Tinker A, *An Evaluation of Very Sheltered Housing*, HMSO 1989.

Tinker A, *Staying at Home: Helping Elderly People,* HMSO, 1984.

Wirz H, *Sheltered Housing in Scotland - A Report*, Department of Social Administration, University of Edinburgh, 1981.

Chapter 2 Barelli J, *Under-occupation in Local Authority and Housing Association Housing*, HMSO 1992.

Goldsmith S, *Wheelchair Housing*, DOE, Housing Development Directorate, Occasional Paper 2/75, 1975 (HMSO 1980).

Goldsmith S, *Mobility Housing*, DOE, Housing Development Directorate, Occasional Paper 2/74, 1974 (HMSO 1980).

Micallef M, *Difficult-to-let Sheltered Housing*, Anchor Housing Trust 1994

Tinker A, *An Evaluation of Very Sheltered Housing*, HMSO 1989.

Chapter 3 MHLG, *Housing Standards and Costs: accommodation specially designed for old people*, MHLG Circular 82/69, WO Circular 82/69, HMSO, 1969.

Perkins G, Berthoud R and Marsh A, *Elderly People and their Adult Children* (forthcoming), Policy Studies Institute.

Price Waterhouse, *Empirical Study of the Costs of Local Authority Housing Management*, HMSO 1992.

Tinker A, *An Evaluation of Very Sheltered Housing*, HMSO 1989.

Tinker A, *Staying at Home: Helping Elderly People*, HMSO, 1984.

Chapter 4	Bridgwood A and Savage D, *1991 General Household Survey*, OPCS/HMSO, 1993.
	English House Condition Survey 1991, HMSO 1993.
Chapter 5	Butler A, Oldman C and Greve J, *Sheltered Housing for the Elderly: Policy Practice and the Consumer*, Allen and Unwin, 1983.
	Clapham D and Munro M, *A Comparison of Sheltered and Amenity Housing for Older People*, Scottish Office Central Research Unit Papers, 1988.
	Middleton L, *So much for so few*, Institute of Human Ageing, Occasional Paper 3, University of Liverpool, 1987.
	Temple C, *Allocation and its relevance to the role of sheltered housing and in meeting the needs of the elderly.* M Soc Sc Dissertation, Centre for Urban and Regional Studies, University of Birmingham, 1980.
	Tinker A, *An Evaluation of Very Sheltered Housing*, HMSO 1989.
Chapter 6	Green H, *Informal Carers,* OPCS/HMSO, 1988.
	Office of Population Censuses and Surveys, *1985 General Household Survey,* HMSO, 1986.
Chapter 7	Bridgwood A and Savage D, *1991 General Household Survey*, OPCS/HMSO, 1993.
	English House Condition Survey 1991, HMSO 1993.
	Office of Population Censuses and Surveys, *Surveys of disability in Great Britain* - Reports 1-4, HMSO 1989.
Chapter 8	*English House Condition Survey* 1991, HMSO 1993.
Chapter 9	Age Concern Institute of Gerontology, *Study of Difficult-to-let Sheltered Housing* (currently being carried out).
	Barelli J, *Under-occupation in Local Authority and Housing Association Housing*, HMSO 1992.
	Bradshaw J and Gibbs I, *Needs and Changes*: *A Study of Public Support for Residential Care*, Gower 1988.
	Butler A, Oldman C and Greve J, *Sheltered Housing for the Elderly: Policy Practice and the Consumer*, Allen and Unwin, 1983.
	Challis D and Davies B, *Case Management in Community Care*, Gower, 1986.

Clapham D and Munro M, *A Comparison of Sheltered and Amenity Housing for Older People*, Scottish Office Central Research Unit Papers, 1988.

Goldsmith's College, *"Who cares now" The Impact of Community Care on Independent Sector Providers of Residential Services for Alcohol and Drug Misusers in England,* 1993.

Griffiths R, *Community Care: Agenda for action Report to the Secretary of State for Social Services,* HMSO 1988.

Hart D and Chalmers K, *Housing Needs of Elderly People in Scotland*, Scottish Office, Central Research Unit Papers, 1990.

Leather P and Mackintosh S, *Monitoring Assisted Agency Services: Part 1 Home Improvement Agencies - An Evaluation of Performance*, HMSO, 1990a.

Mackintosh S and Leather P, *Monitoring Assisted Agency Services: Part IV Monitoring Performance,* HMSO 1990b.

Mackintosh S, Leather P and McCafferty P, *The Role of Housing Agency Services in Helping Disabled People*, HMSO, 1993b.

Mackintosh S and Leather P, *The Performance of Home Improvement Agencies in 1990*, HMSO, 1993a.

Micallef M, *Difficult-to-let Sheltered Housing*, Anchor Housing Trust 1994

Middleton L, *So much for so few*, Institute of Human Ageing, Occasional Paper 3, University of Liverpool, 1987.

Neill J E, Sinclar I A C, Gorbach P and Williams J, *A Need for Care: A study of Elderly Applicants for Local Authority Residential Care*, Gower 1988.

NFHA/Anchor Housing Trust, *The Future of Sheltered Housing - Who Cares?*, 1991.

NFHA, *Maximising the use of sheltered housing: discussion document*, 1994.

Oldman C, *Moving in Old Age: New Directions in Housing Policies*, HMSO 1990.

Plank D, Caring for the Elderly: *Report of a Study of Caring for Dependent Elderly People in Eight London Boroughs*, GLC 1977.

Salvage A, *Attitudes of the over 75s to Health and Social Services*, Final Report, Research Team for the care of the elderly, University of Cardiff, 1986.

Smith K, *'I'm not complaining'* Kensington and Chelsea Staying Put for the Elderly Ltd in association with Shelter Housing Advisory Centre, 1986.

Temple C, *Allocation and its relevance to the role of sheltered housing and in meeting the needs of the elderly.* M Soc Sc Dissertation, Centre for Urban and Regional Studies, University of Birmingham, 1980.

256

Tinker A, *An Evaluation of Very Sheltered Housing*, HMSO 1989.

Tinker A, *Staying at Home: Helping Elderly People*, HMSO, 1984.

Townsend, P. and Wedderburn, D., *The Aged in the Welfare State*, G. Bell and Sons, 1965.

Wagner G, *Residential Care - A Positive Choice*, HMSO 1988.

Wheeler R, *Don't move: we've got you covered*, Institute of Housing, 1985.

Printed in the UK for HMSO Dd 0300044 C19 12/94 59226